Includes a 30-day fully functional version of Photoshop Elements

Photoshop® Elements Solutions

The Art of Digital Photography

Mikkel Aaland

SYBEX®   San Francisco • Paris • Dusseldorf • Soest • London

Associate Publisher: CHERYL APPLEWOOD

Acquisitions and Developmental Editor: BONNIE BILLS

Editor: SHARON WILKEY

Production Editor: DENNIS FITZGERALD

Technical Editor: GARY COHEN

Book Designer: LORI BARRA

Electronic Publishing Specialist: JAN MARTI

Production Assistant: LAURA M. LEVY

Graphic Illustrator: ERIC HOUTS, EPIC

Proofreaders: DAVE NASH, LAURIE O'CONNELL, YARIV RABINOVITCH

Indexer: LYNNZEE ELZE

CD Coordinator: CHRISTINE HARRIS

CD Technician: KEVIN LY

Cover Designer: LORI BARRA

Front Cover Photographers: MIKKEL AALAND, MONICA LEE, MICHELLE VIGNES

Back Cover Photographers: Statue: MIKKEL AALAND; Child composite: Photos by
MAGGIE HALLAHAN, compositing by BRETTON NEWSOM, PJA AGENCY;
Smile: MIKKEL AALAND

Library of Congress Card Number: 2001093082

ISBN: 0-7821-2973-0

Photoshop
Elements
Solutions

To my daughters

Ana Mikaela and Miranda Kristina

Acknowledgments

There are many people who have made this book possible. I'll start with Richard Koman, who encouraged me all the way. Sybex's Bonnie Bills and Cheryl Applewood shared my vision and added their own to make the book even better. Studio B's Neil J. Salkind and David Rogelberg stood solidly behind me.

I'd especially like thank my good friend Tom Mogensen, who contributed his wisdom, images, and techniques to the book. Other special friends who were there when I needed them are Rudy Burger, Michael Rogers, Scott Highton, Maggie Hallahan, Monica Suder, Michelle Vignes, Laena Wilder, Monica Lee, Luis Delgado, Mark Ulriksen, Marcia Briggs, Julie Christensen, Sebastian DeWitt, Jacques Gauchey, and, as always, Sean Parker and Valerie Robbins.

I'd also like to thank the other contributors: William Rutledge, Michael Angelo, Laura Laverdiere, David Mlodzik, Bretton Newsom, Maurice Martell, and Sally Rogers. You'll find more on each of them in the back section of the book.

Thank you to Barbara Smyth, Dennis Fitzgerald, Tara McGoldrick, Cathryn Domrose, Martha Emmanouilides, Esmeralda Marquez, Craig Sandoski, Anne Compton, Audrey Tomaselli, Diana Howard, Andrew Tarnowka, Tony Barnard, Micha X. Peled, Karen Thomas, Lisa Friedman; Olympus and Joe Runde; Eastman Kodak, Tracy and Chris Cantello, David Robertson, Cindy Adams, and Jeanne Zimmermann.

It's been an absolute thrill working with several people at Adobe: Kevin Connor, who wrote the foreword to the book, promised me his full support, and proved he is a man good to his word. Susan Doering was so helpful; she's an author's dream. Mark Dahm, John Peterson, Marc Pawliger, Karen Gauthier, Christie Evans, and Gregg Wilensky all gave me valuable advice. Gary Cohen tech edited the book and patiently answered my many questions.

As you can see by several of the photos in the book, this has been a family affair. Thanks to the Aalands (Kris, Beth, Erik, and Hans), Schneiders (Steve and Francisca), Michael Taggart, Sr., and Michael Taggart, Jr. And to my wife, Rebecca, who kept a four year old and a six month old out of my office while I wrote: I love you.

Finally I'd like to thank Lori Barra and Jan Martí for making a beautiful book, Sharon Wilkey for editing it, and Laura M. Levy for helping me get it in on time.

—MIKKEL AALAND, SAN FRANCISCO, 2001

Foreword

You are holding in your hands the first book ever conceived for Adobe Photoshop Elements. In fact, Mikkel began thinking about this book before he even knew Photoshop Elements would exist. I know this because he called me at the time to talk about his idea. His timing couldn't have been better.

Mikkel believed there was a market for a book that would teach the everyday user how to get professional-quality results out of their digital photography. The growing audience of digital camera and scanner enthusiasts would need a book that showed them how to make effective use of digital imaging software. The problem—at least as Mikkel saw it—was figuring out what digital imaging software to feature in the book. Adobe Photoshop had long been the standard-bearer for digital imaging, but with a vast set of features, and a professional-level price, it wasn't for everyone. A variety of low-cost consumer-oriented applications focused on projects such as greeting cards and calendars. In the middle, a handful of applications offered Photoshop-like features at a consumer-friendly price, but none entirely achieved the right mix of tools for these users. What Mikkel didn't know was that the Photoshop team at Adobe had already laid plans for a product to serve the audience he was writing for. A marriage of ideas was inevitable.

Once I filled him in on the details of Adobe's plans, it wasn't hard to convince Mikkel to build his book around our new software. In turn, Mikkel became a great resource, helping us to refine our product plans. There are at least a few features that made it in based on Mikkel's urging. In the end, I believe Adobe created a product that has all the key features the typical scanner or digital camera user needs, wrapped up in an interface that makes it easy to get started. Once you get to know Photoshop Elements, however, you'll soon discover that getting the best results is less a matter of knowing all the features than it is a matter of knowing the proper techniques.

That's where this book comes in. Mikkel starts out with the kinds of ho-hum digital snapshots and scans you deal with in the real world and shows, step by step, how to use Photoshop Elements to turn them into great images. With Photoshop Elements and this book, you'll make the sky in your favorite photograph look as blue as it really was that day. You'll restore the tattered portrait of your great-grandparents. You'll produce awe-inspiring company brochures with corporate headquarters looking as impressive as it did the day you were hired. The engaging work of the author and his many talented colleagues will inspire you to bring out the best in your digital images. With Mikkel as your guide, you will also have fun doing so.

KEVIN CONNOR
Group Product Manager, Adobe

Contents

 "No longer will you look at an image simply for what it is. From now on you'll see what it can become."

Introduction

The full potential of digital images can't be realized without editing and processing software. Until now, the imaging software that could help you create professional looking images was either too limited in features or very expensive. That's all changed with the release of Adobe's Photoshop Elements. Photoshop Elements is an extremely useful, and much less expensive, version of the world's most powerful image editing program, Photoshop. For most people, Photoshop Elements offers all the features they will ever need.

With Photoshop Elements—and information presented in this book—it is possible to easily:

- Sharpen out-of-focus pictures
- Compensate for wrong exposures
- Straighten a crooked scan
- Get rid of red eye
- Change a product's color and background
- Remove unwanted objects from outdoor shots
- Optimize photos for the Web and e-mail transmission
- Create panoramics
- Add type to your image
  And much much more.

In short, Photoshop Elements and this book are for anyone familiar with the computer who wants to create great looking images. No longer will you look at an image simply for what it is. From now on you'll see what it can become.

Differences between Photoshop Elements and Photoshop

For a program that is a fraction of the cost of the world's leading image editing program you'd expect it to have a lot fewer features. Right? Wrong. Not only does Photoshop Elements include many powerful Photoshop tools and features, it actually contains some very useful features that are not even included in the latest version of Photoshop. These features include:

- **A File Browser** that conveniently displays many thumbnails at once and opens a digital file with a single click.
- **A Photomerge command** that seamlessly blends multiple images together to create stunning panoramics and composites.
- **Online help** that quickly tells you just about everything you need to know about tools and commands.
- **Visual cues** of the effects of different filters, layer styles, and effects so you can see what you'll get before applying the effect.
- **Round-trip animated GIF capabilities** so you can open an animated GIF and have access to all the frames as layers.

Of course, Photoshop Elements is lacking some of the high-end features found in Photoshop. For example, Photoshop Elements doesn't give you the ability to work on separate color channels, and you can't work in the prepress CMYK mode. But you'll see throughout the book that when a Photoshop feature is missing from Photoshop Elements, I've included a simple workaround.

At some point, if you find that Photoshop Elements can't get you where you need to go, it is really easy to upgrade to the full version of Photoshop. The programs are so similar, you'll be instantly ramped up to speed and able to apply just about everything you learned to do with Photoshop Elements to Photoshop. Nothing you've learned here will be wasted.

What You Need to Know

I've written this book with the assumption that the reader has basic computer skills, such as using the mouse and saving and storing digital files. However, if this is the first time you've worked with a graphics or image editing program, you may find Photoshop Elements a bit challenging. After all, this is powerful, feature-rich program. It's simply unrealistic to think that you can jump right in and get exactly what you want without some trial and error. Having said this, I think you'll agree that the Photoshop Elements interface is extremely intuitive and will enable you to quickly get up to speed. To make things even easier, the Adobe online help is the best I've ever seen. At the click of the mouse, you have instant access to tutorials and hyperlinked help. Just waving your cursor over a tool brings up the tool's name, and in a separate Hints palette, you'll find a concise explanation of what the tool does. I've been using the full version of Photoshop for many years and I still find Photoshop Elements online help extremely useful.

Platform Differences

Very little differs between the PC and Mac versions of Photoshop Elements, and most of it is cosmetic. I use a Mac, so if you're running Photoshop Elements on Windows, your basic interface may look a little different from the screen shots in the book. For example, you may notice that the Quick Start screen looks different on the Windows version as compared to the Mac version; there are also minor differences between platforms in the display of thumbnails in the File Browser.

There are some non-cosmetic differences but they are slight. The way memory and image caching is handled are different. Windows automatically determines the percentage of available memory to allocate to Photoshop Elements, whereas the Mac uses the default memory allocation of the application, which is configurable in the Finder. I've addressed such differences the few times they've cropped up in the text.

Some of the keyboard commands differ but only slightly. For shortcuts that differ on the PC and Mac, I've put the PC command first, followed by the Mac command. For example, when I write *Enter/Return* to apply a command, you press Enter on the PC or Return on the Mac. When I write *Ctrl/Command+D* to deselect, you press Ctrl+D on the PC or Command+D on the Mac.

The Future Is Now

Nearly ten years ago I wrote a book titled *Digital Photography* (Random House, 1992). The book was dedicated in part to the great photographer, Ansel Adams, who introduced me to digital photography in 1980. In the book I wrote that the future of digital photography is now. I wrote "the new technology would enable people to make photographic expressions for their own amusement, for the enjoyment of others, or for professional gain." Well, I was a little ahead of myself. Adobe had just introduced Photoshop 1.0 and the first consumer digital cameras and scanners were on the market. I thought it would be just a matter of months or at the most, a few years, and the digital photography revolution would be in full swing. We all had to grow a little. Photoshop had to evolve and so did digital cameras and scanners. Now, with the introduction of Photoshop Elements and affordable digital cameras and scanners, that time I anticipated ten years ago is here. I've really enjoyed writing this book, especially since I can truly say: "The future is now."

—Mikkel Aaland, San Francisco, 2001

It's tempting *to jump right in, opening an image and immediately starting to work on it. But to get the most out of Photoshop Elements, it's best to take a moment to set up your preferences, familiarize yourself with the work area, and learn about the various options for getting images into the program. This "aim before you shoot" approach may not give you immediate satisfaction, but in the long run it will pay off in terms of less frustration and better images. In addition to getting you ready to work in Photoshop Elements, this chapter discusses organizing your digital images and other tasks that make using the program easier.*

Up and Running with Photoshop Elements

Up and Running with Photoshop Elements

Setting Preferences

Adobe ships Photoshop Elements with preferences set in a way that may or may not suit your particular needs. Through these settings, you can change how Photoshop Elements handles a whole range of tasks, from color management to memory allocation to saving files. Let's look at some of the more important choices you can make and see what you can do to customize the program so that it works better for you.

Note: If at any point you want to reset Photoshop Elements preferences to their original settings, here's how to do so: Throw away the Photoshop Elements preferences file. Window users will find the **Adobe Photoshop Elements Prefs** file in **C:\Windows\Application Data\Adobe\Photoshop\Elements\Adobe Photoshop Elements Prefs**. On Windows NT/2000, the preferences are located in **C:\Documents and Settings\User\Application Data\Adobe\Photoshop\Elements**. Macintosh users will find this file in the **System\Preferences\Adobe Photoshop Elements Prefs** folder. The next time you launch Photoshop Elements, all your settings will be reset to their defaults. You can also hold down Ctrl/Command+Alt/Option+Shift while the program launches to trash the preferences file.

Color Settings

Every scanner, every computer system, and every printer handles color differently. In order to maintain some control over the way your digital images look in this chaotic world, you need to know how Photoshop Elements handles color.

Under the Edit menu at the top of your screen you'll see an option for Color Settings (see Figure 1.1). When you choose this, you are faced with three options: No Color Management, Limited Color Management, and Full Color Management (see Figure 1.2). The default setting is No Color Management, and even if you are tempted otherwise, I suggest you keep it this way. You might be in for some surprises if you select either of the other two options.

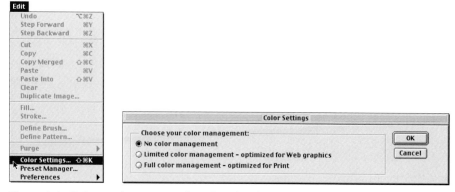

Figure 1.1: Color preferences are found under the Edit menu. Figure 1.2: For simplicity, choose No Color Management.

Here are the basic differences between the options:

No Color Management

If you keep the default setting at No Color Management, you'll work in the RGB mode. *RGB* stands for red, green, and blue. These are the colors that when combined make up the entire spectrum of color displayed on your monitor. In RGB mode, there is a very slight possibility that some color banding will occur when your work is viewed on some monitors. (*Banding* is what happens when you create a graphic in a color space and then view the same graphic on a device that displays a narrower range of colors; a range of colors is referred to as *gamut*. With less gamut, colors are squished, or banded together.) I believe that the potential loss of quality on some monitors is worth it, because you don't have to deal with the issues associated with Limited or Full Color Management.

Limited Color Management

If you choose Limited Color Management, you will find yourself working in a color space called sRGB, instead of just plain RGB. The *sRGB* color space is a limited color space that Adobe and others claim is good for Web work. It has a narrower gamut than the RGB color space and more faithfully represents the color capabilities of most commonly used display systems. However, the difference between the sRGB and RGB color space is slight, and many other applications that you use may not support the sRGB color space. Sure, you'll be able to open your files in those programs but you may find some maddening color shifts.

Full Color Management

If you choose Full Color Management, you'll work in the sRGB color space, but Photoshop Elements will also assign an ICC color profile to your image file. A *color profile* is a universally accepted point of reference developed by the International Color Consortium (ICC). In theory, this means that when you open the file with another computer and monitor, the image will be displayed exactly as it was on your monitor.

Also, in theory, if you have an ICC-compliant printer, you'll get a print that closely matches the image on your monitor. This is fine in theory, but in reality it doesn't always work. All the devices need to understand your color profile, and if they don't you'll have an even greater mess on your hands. Later in the book I'll tell you about ways to make your print look good regardless of whether your file has a color profile attached to it (☞ "Using Desktop Printers" in Chapter 12).

Whether you choose color management or not, it is absolutely critical that you take a moment to calibrate your monitor. Your monitor is your canvas, and you need to make sure that when it comes to color and brightness, you are at least in the ball-park. How else will you know how much contrast or brightness to add to your carefully optimized image, or how will you know when your colors are right? Adobe makes it easy to calibrate your monitor by providing the Adobe Gamma utility. In both Windows and the Mac, the Adobe Gamma utility is located in the **Control Panels** folder.

The utility walks you step by step through the process of calibrating your monitor. Just make sure that your monitor has been on for at least half an hour before you start. It needs time to warm up and reach a stable operating brightness. Also make sure that your monitor is set to display at least thousands (16 bits) of colors, or the calibration software won't work.

Preset Manager

When you use a brush, gradient, pattern, or swatch, you are presented with a default set of corresponding brushes, gradients, patterns, or colors. Except for the swatches, these options appear in the options bar under the shortcuts bar. The swatches are found in the Swatches palette itself. For most people, the default sets provide enough options, but you can also add sets or create custom sets by using the Preset Manager, which, like Color Settings, is found under the Edit menu (see Figure 1.3). To load a set of *custom libraries*, as the custom sets are called, simply click Load and select a library from the list or click the triangle icon at the top of the dialog box. A pop-up menu will appear with a list of choices, including the choice to reset back to the default setting. You can also create your own set by Shift+clicking various brushes and choosing Save Set.

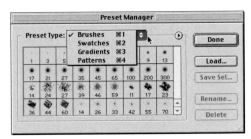

Figure 1.3: The Preset Manager, found under the Edit menu, controls various tool and swatch options.

History States

Most of the time, when you work on the pixels of a digital image, Photoshop Elements records each step of the process in the History palette. You can go back to a previous step at any point, but only as long as that step remains in the History palette. Photoshop Elements records 20 steps by default, but if you have enough RAM you can boost that number to as many as 100. To change the default, choose Edit ➢ Preferences ➢ General and then simply type in a new number, as shown in Figure 1.4.

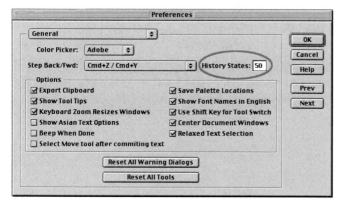

Figure 1.4: Increase the number of history states in the General Preferences window.

Saving Files

When you save a file, Photoshop Elements by default creates an image preview (Windows) or an icon and thumbnail (Mac). Although this makes it easy to identify an image on the desktop or in a dialog box, and the saved thumbnail is used by the File Browser, it adds size to your image. If restricting file size is important to you, consider turning this option off and using only a descriptive name to identify your file. Do this by choosing Edit ➢ Preferences ➢ Saving Files (see Figure 1.5).

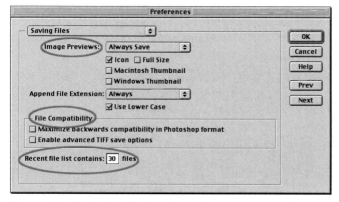

Figure 1.5: Optimize file size by paying attention to the options in the Saving Files Preferences dialog box.

If you are creating a lot of JPEG images for the Web or for e-mail transmission, you should probably turn off the image preview options (Windows) or icon and thumbnail options (Mac). Not only will this save file size, but it will lessen the chances that your JPEG will become corrupted and unreadable.

In the Saving Files Preferences dialog box, you also have the choice of whether to Maximize Backwards Compatibility in Photoshop Format. If you want to save up to a third of your file size, I suggest you turn this option off. If you leave this option checked, Photoshop Elements creates a second file, one with the layers (if you have any) flattened. You need this only if you are planning to use Photoshop version 2.5 or earlier, which is unlikely. Keep in mind that turning off backward compatibility affects only PSD files, not GIFs or JPEGs.

You can also choose to Enable Advanced TIFF Save Options. With this option selected, you can save layered TIFFs or apply JPEG compression to a TIFF. For most people this won't be necessary, so leave it unchecked. (If you are wondering what the point is of a layered TIFF, it so happens that some web browsers can read a layered TIFF file. This could be useful for anyone who wants to share layered image files over the Web.)

By default, the recent file list (found under File ➤ Open Recent) includes 10 recent files. In the Saving Files Preferences dialog box, you can change it so Photoshop Elements displays up to 30 recent files.

Units and Rulers

Photoshop Elements displays dimensions in inches by default. In the Units & Rulers dialog box, found under the Preferences menu, you can change that to centimeters or pixels (see Figure 1.6). (Picas, points, and percent will be useful for only a select few). You can also change these preferences in the Info palette. When I am working on images destined for the Web, I always use pixels; otherwise, I leave my setting at inches.

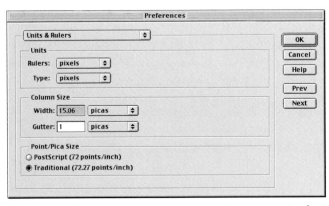

Figure 1.6: Choose an appropriate measuring system in the Units & Rulers dialog box.

Plug-ins

When Photoshop Elements is launched, it automatically searches for a folder called Plug-Ins in the application folder. These plug-ins are mini software programs developed both by Adobe and third-party vendors. They add various functionalities to Photoshop Elements. You also may be using another program that uses compatible Photoshop plug-ins. You can tell Photoshop Elements where to find that folder and to open these plug-ins as well by going to Edit ➢ Preferences ➢ Plug-Ins & Scratch Disks (see Figure 1.7).

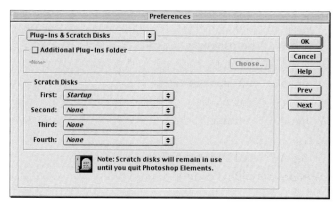

Figure 1.7: Manage plug-ins and scratch disks through the Plug-Ins & Scratch Disks dialog box.

Memory

If you don't have enough RAM, Photoshop automatically creates and uses a portion of your startup hard drive as a scratch disk. It's never as fast or as optimal as having enough RAM, but if you have a large hard disk you'll avoid the dreaded "out-of-memory" warning. If you have more hard drives, you can assign scratch disks to them by going to Edit ➢ Preferences ➢ Plug-Ins & Scratch Disks (see Figure 1.7). Choose the drive that is the fastest and has the most contiguous free space to use as your primary scratch disk. You can create up to 200GB of scratch disk space.

Note: Sometimes cameras and other devices that mount themselves on the desktop as hard drives will show up as valid options in the Memory Preferences dialog box. It is important that you do not choose them. They are usually small in size and are slow. You should only choose devices that are real hard drives and not removables such as Zips.

Customizing and Organizing the Work Area

Look at anyone's desk and you'll see variations in the way people like to work. It's the same with the Photoshop Elements work area. One person might prefer a desktop tiled with palettes, whereas someone else might find this cluttered look distracting. With Photoshop Elements, palettes can be stacked and tiled. You can even customize the opening screen to include a family picture or an inspirational picture that puts you in the mood for work.

The Work Area Revealed

Look at Figure 1.8. It shows the entire work area of Photoshop Elements, including the opening splash screen. This is how your screen should look when you first open the program (taking into consideration the differences between the PC and Mac platforms).

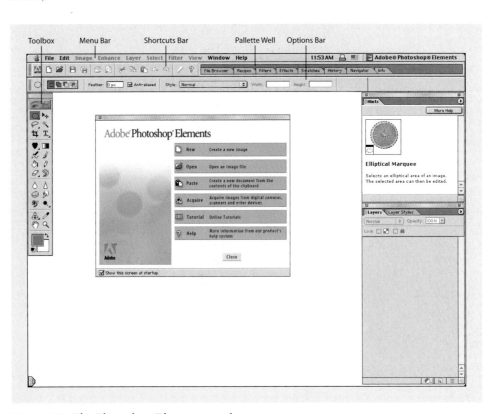

Figure 1.8: The Photoshop Elements work area.

At the top is the *menu bar*, which contains drop-down menus for performing tasks. Under Enhance, for example, you'll find ways to modify the contrast and color of your digital image. Unlike most of the other components of the work area, the menu bar can't be moved or altered in any way.

Below the menu bar, and to the left, is the *shortcuts bar*. Here you'll find buttons for common commands such as Print, Cut, Paste, Save, and Undo. (Position the pointer over any icon in the shortcuts bar and its name will appear.) You can move this bar and dock it at the top or bottom of the screen by dragging the gripper bar at the left edge. You can also hide the shortcuts bar by selecting Window ➢ Hide Shortcuts from the menu bar.

Just to the right of the shortcuts bar is the *palette well*. Palettes help you modify and monitor images. You open a palette by clicking its tab. A palette will remain open until you click outside it or click the palette's tab again. When a palette is fully open, it takes up valuable monitor space, and that's why the palette well is a handy place to keep palettes when you aren't using them. You can also drag a palette's tab to move the palette from the well to any place you want on the screen (➥ "Docking, Stacking, and Resizing Tool Palettes," next).

Below the shortcuts bar and palette well is the *options bar*, which contains various options for using a selected tool. The options bar can also be moved by using the gripper bar at the left edge. As you select a tool from the toolbox, different options will appear in the options bar. Some settings are common to several tools, and others are specific to one tool.

To the left of the work area is the *toolbox*. The icons refer to various tools for creating and editing images. Remember that several tools are "hidden," and to access them you'll need to click and hold on the box before they appear. When you position the pointer over a specific tool, the name of the tool appears. When a tool is selected, more information about the tool appears in the Hints palette. (To see this information, you must have the Hints palette open.)

Docking, Stacking, and Resizing Tool Palettes

When you first open Photoshop Elements, the Hints and Layers palettes are undocked and open on the desktop. You can tuck them neatly away in the palette well by simply clicking the Close icon on the palette title bar. You can place other palettes from the palette well onto the work area by dragging the palette's tab. You can also dock palettes together on the work area by dragging the palette's tab onto the body of the target palette (see Figure 1.9).

Figure 1.9: For easy access, dock palettes together on the work area.

Personally, since I use them so much, I group the Layers palette and the History palette together and keep them undocked and readily accessible on my work area. When I want them out of the way, I collapse the palette window by double-clicking the palette's tab (for Windows, click the Minimize/Maximize box).

Personalizing the Quick Start Screen

When you open Photoshop Elements, you are greeted with a Quick Start screen. Through this screen, you can quickly open an existing image file or create a new one. You can acquire an image from a scanner or digital camera or have instant access to Adobe's online tutorials. The window disappears when you start to work on an image, but you can get it back at any time by selecting Window ➢ Show Quick Start.

It's also easy to personalize this startup screen. In Figure 1.10 you can see a picture of my older daughter that greets me every time I open the program.

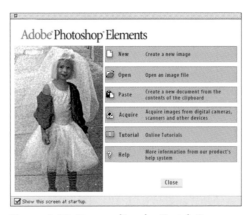

Figure 1.10: Personalize the Quick Start screen.

Here's what I did to customize my screen:

1. I resized the digital camera shot of my daughter to 174×282 pixels at 72dpi.
2. I saved the image in the GIF file format and named it **index_02.gif**.
3. I opened the folder on my hard disk that contained the Photoshop Elements application and folders. I then opened the folder titled **HTMLPalettes**. Within that folder I opened the one called **Welcome**. Then, inside that folder I opened the folder titled **Images**. This is where all the graphics for the opening screen are stored.
4. I deleted the graphic titled **index_02.gif** from the folder and replaced it with the new image that I had made, also titled **index_02.gif**.
5. The next time I launched Photoshop Elements, my photo appeared in place of the Adobe graphic.

Changing the Canvas Color

In Figure 1.11 you see the default color for the Photoshop Elements canvas areas. Gray is a good choice because it is neutral and doesn't interfere with the colors of your digital image. At times, however, you might want another canvas color. For example, you can choose a color that approximates the color of a web page background (see Figure 1.12). That way you can see what your image will look like once it is on the Web.

Figure 1.11: The default canvas color is gray. Figure 1.12: Change the canvas color to a color of your choice.

To change the color of the canvas, do the following:

1. Choose a foreground color. In this case, I've chosen gold, the background color for many of the pages in my website, **www.cyberbohemia.com**.
2. Select the Paint Bucket tool ( ) from the Tools menu. (Make sure that Fill to Foreground is selected in the options bar and not Fill to Pattern.)
3. While holding the Shift key, click inside the canvas.

Shooting Digital: Must-Have Accessories

Digital camera salespeople will eagerly try to sell you dozens of camera accessories. I recommend that you take the following four accessories seriously:

· Extra rechargeable batteries
· As much extra digital memory as you can afford
· A lightweight tripod
· A polarizing filter, to increase color saturation of most daytime shots

Little else will be as consistently useful, except maybe a sturdy camera bag to hold everything in.

Getting Digital Images into Photoshop Elements

There are several ways to get your images into Photoshop Elements:

- **File** ➢ **Open** opens all compatible file formats. This brings up an Open dialog box with controls for locating and previewing files.

- **File** ➢ **Open** ➢ **Open Recent** opens up to 30 of the most recently viewed files.

- **File** ➢ **Import** gives you access to any plug-in module compatible with Photoshop Elements. Use Import to bring scans or digital camera images directly into Photoshop Elements. You may need to install the specific plug-in yourself. See the documentation for your scanner or digital camera for more instructions.

- **The File Browser,** located in the palette well, is one of the most useful ways of opening digital images in Photoshop Elements. Just click its tab to open it. Thumbnails of image files are displayed (see Figure 1.13). Use the drop-down menu to show the directories and files on the hard disk or on your desktop. Double-click a file folder to view its contents. When you find the image you want to open, double-click it, drag and drop the file onto the work area, or select the file and press Enter/Return. (Enter/Return works only if the File Browser is docked in the palette well.)

Figure 1.13: View before you open.

Changing the Image Orientation

If your digital image opens with a wrong orientation, the first thing you'll want to do is change it (see Figures 1.14 and 1.15).

Figure 1.14: Some digital images open sideways.  *Figure 1.15: Rotate the canvas before you start work.*

To re-orient your image, do the following:

1. Choose Edit ➤ Rotate from the menu bar. Then, depending on which way your image lies, choose either Canvas 90 Left or Canvas 90 Right.
2. Don't worry if you get it wrong. I always mix my left from my right! Just undo your mistake by using one of the various Undo controls and try again (☞ "What Do You Do When You Mess Up?" later in this chapter).

Knowing Your File Size

Just as you wouldn't lift something without knowing its weight for fear of injuring your back, you shouldn't begin working on a digital image without knowing its pixel size. Why? The larger the image, the more the pixels, and the more "processing" power it takes to do even the simplest tasks.

How do you determine file size?

Go to the bottom of the application window (Windows) or document window (Mac) and look at the middle section (see Figure 1.16). Document Dimensions displays the size in pixels. If you click the triangle in the status bar and choose Document Sizes, you can get information on the amount of data in an image. The number to the left is the approximate size of the saved, flattened file in the Photoshop format. The number next to it is the file's approximate size, including layers. If an image contains only one layer, the numbers will be the same. These numbers are useful to know when working on an image within Photoshop Elements. However, the numbers aren't representative of the file size of the image if it is saved in other file formats such as JPEG or GIF. For that, you'll either have to leave the program and check the file size on your desktop, or open Photoshop Elements' Save for Web plug-in and check the file size in the lower-left corner.

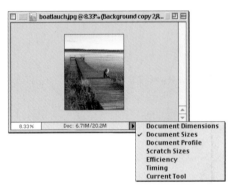

Figure 1.16: You can readily view image size data by choosing Document Sizes.

Using Contact Sheet II to Organize Images

Once you start saving digital images, you'll quickly need to find a way to manage them. You'll be asking yourself, "Now in which folder, which hard drive, which Zip drive, did I put that darn thing?" Descriptive names help. So does Photoshop Elements' File Browser, which enables you to view all the contents of a folder.

Another thing that can help manage images is the Contact Sheet II tool in Photoshop Elements. Contact Sheet II creates a file like the one shown in Figure 1.17. Although it is not interactive—that is, you can't click on an image to bring up the original file as you can with the File Browser—you can catalog your images and then print out the results for easy reference.

Figure 1.17: Contact Sheet II helps organize digital images.

Here's how I made the contact sheet in Figure 1.17:

1. I chose File ➢ Automate ➢ Contact Sheet II (see Figure 1.18).

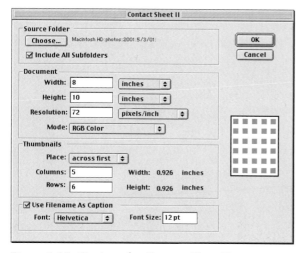

Figure 1.18: Options for Contact Sheet II.

2. I clicked Choose and selected a folder from my hard disk.

3. Under Document, I kept the default document dimensions. A resolution of 72dpi is adequate for a sheet I'm just using for reference, so I kept that setting too.

4. Under Thumbnails, I kept the default settings for how the thumbnails would be placed on the page. I also selected Use Filename As Caption; this labeled the thumbnails by using the source image filenames.

5. I clicked OK and printed out the result.

What Do You Do When You Mess Up?

It's comforting to know that when you are working within Photoshop Elements, it's difficult to permanently damage a digital image. There is hardly a mistake you can make that can't be fixed by using the History palette or the Undo command. Even if you accidentally save a copy of your work, as long as you haven't closed the file you can revert to a previous version.

Here are your choices if—and when—you mess up:

- The simplest way to undo an action you've just made is to click the Step Backward button ( ) in the shortcuts bar. This button is connected to the History palette, and each time you click it you move backward through the various recorded states in the History palette. You can continue stepping backward this way until you reach the end of the recorded states in the History palette. To redo the operation, click the neighboring Step Forward button ( ).

- You can also go directly to the History palette to correct mistakes (see Figure 1.19). By default, the History palette records 20 states, or changes, to your image. You can increase this number in the Preferences window ("Setting Preferences," earlier in this chapter). States are added from top down, with the most recent state at the bottom. The name of the tool or command you used is included. To undo a mistake, simply select a state above the one you want to redo, and the History palette will revert your image to that state.

Figure 1.19: Every action you take is recorded in the History palette as a state. *By selecting a state, you undo all the states underneath it.*

- You can also choose Edit ➢ Undo from the menu bar. Or you can use the keyboard command Alt+Ctrl+Z (Windows) or Command+Shift+Z (Mac). To redo, choose Edit ➢ Redo or use Alt+Crtl+Y (Windows) or Command+Shift+Y (Mac). You can customize the keyboard command by choosing Edit ➢ Preferences ➢ General.

- As a last recourse, you can always revert to the last saved version. To do this, choose File ➤ Revert. If you decide this isn't what you want, you can always undo Revert in the History palette.

Fixing a mistake is easy, but most people will find a way to mess up so badly that the methods just described won't help. I can't give you a good example, but trust me, it'll happen, and it will probably happen when you are working on a really important digital image. That's why throughout this book you'll see that I strongly advocate creating a copy of your digital image and working on that file. It won't matter as much if you mess up because you'll always have an original to go back to.

Where Do You Go for Help?

Within Photoshop Elements, there are several ways to get specific help on specific subjects without ever taking your eyes off the screen. Adobe has provided some of the best screen help I've ever encountered, and because Photoshop Elements is such a powerful program, with so many features, I encourage you to use the help whenever you have a question about a particular tool or feature.

- The Hints palette, located in the palette well and shown it Figure 1.20, automatically displays an illustration and description about any palette or tool your mouse pointer is on. If you click the More Help button located in the upper right of the Hints palette, you are taken to an even more comprehensive HTML-based system.

Figure 1.20: The Hints palette tells you about palettes and tools.

- Under the Help menu, you'll find Help and Photoshop Elements Tutorials, both of which are HTML-based help systems that are very useful. Help is a hyperlinked version of the printed manual, with a powerful index and search engine so you can quickly get the answer to just about any Photoshop Elements question. The tutorials walk you step by step through various tasks by using images that come on the program disc.
- If you position your mouse over a tool or palette and pause, words will appear that tell you the name of the tool and what keyboard shortcut (if any) to use.
- The Recipes palette, located in the palette well, is full of useful step-by-step instructions, including ways to enhance text and correct color. Adobe plans to make more recipes available online, so be sure to check their Web site, **www.adobe.com**, to download the latest recipes or just select Download New Recipes, which is the last option in the Recipe pop-up.

Remember, the screen help is useful but it's no substitute for solutions-oriented books like this one!

Every digital image *is different and therefore requires individual evaluation to determine what improvements are needed. This chapter focuses primarily on improvements that affect the entire image, including cropping, optimizing color and tonal range, removing unwanted dust and scratches, sharpening, and resizing. Subsequent chapters concentrate on more localized problems that require you to work on a specific area or part of an image.*

Your Images: Global Solutions and Considerations

Deciding Which Tasks Come First

The first thing I do when I open a digital image is visually examine it and make mental notes about how to improve it. Depending on the inherent size of the image, I do this at 100 percent, 50 percent, or 25 percent. Using other view options, such as 66.7 percent or 33.3 percent, distorts the image on the monitor. I ask myself: Does the image look flat or dull and lack vibrancy and crispness? Is it "soft" or out of focus? Is it too dark? Too light? Sometimes I find it helpful to look at the image's histogram. The histogram graphically indicates the tonal range of an image and can show you whether that range is satisfactory.

Next I check for unwanted dust, scratches, or electronic noise. I do this by using the magnification and navigation tools in Photoshop Elements (☞ "Viewing & Navigation Tools" in Zooming In). I magnify my image to about 300 to 400 percent and scroll around the image, paying special attention to the important areas in the foreground (such as a human face) or expanses of flat color (such as a blue sky), where artifacts will be most noticeable and distracting.

After making my evaluation, I typically do the following tasks in Photoshop Elements:

1. Use the Crop tool to crop an image to its essential elements. There is no good reason to work on an unnecessarily large image (☞ "Knowing Your File Size" in Chapter 1).

2. Use the Enhance commands and adjustment layers to optimize the color and tonal range of the image.

3. Use a variety of tools and filters to remove unwanted dust and scratches.

4. Use the Unsharp Mask filter to sharpen images that were shot out of focus or that look particularly soft for some reason.

5. Save a copy of my work in the Photoshop file format (File ➤ Save As). I do this now, before resizing, because resizing always degrades an image to some degree.

6. Resize the image to meet the specific needs of its final destination, be it the Web, a high-resolution ink-jet print, a printed document, or an e-mail attachment. I also apply the Unsharp Mask filter to the image to compensate for the loss of clarity that results from the resizing process.

7. Use File ➤ Save As to save my image. I rename my file to differentiate it from the copy I saved before resizing and then I select an appropriate file format (JPEG, GIF, TIFF, etc.).

I admit that I vary the preceding order slightly from time to time. For example, there is no logical reason why you'd need to optimize colors and tonal values before removing unwanted dust, scratches, and electronic noise. However, whatever order you follow, always keep resizing for last. Throughout this chapter, I'll give you exact details about how to perform these tasks.

Cropping to the Essential Parts

Cropping is one of the most important ways to improve your digital image. Not only does cropping strengthen the composition of an image, it also reduces the overall size with no degradation in quality. In Photoshop Elements, using the Crop tool or Crop command is also one of the easiest things you can do.

This is a good time to emphasize the value of working on a copy of your original digital image. I can't tell you how may times I've cropped an image to what I thought was an optimal composition but then later decided I needed more sky or more foreground. I would have been in trouble if I didn't have the original to go back to.

In Figure 2.1 you'll see a shot I took at the opening gala event of a local dance group. The people are generous and enthusiastic patrons of the group but a little camera shy, and I got only one shot. Obviously, it is not a perfect shot. The couple is off to one side and framed back farther than I would like. With a little cropping—and, I might add, tonal correction and sharpening—I made a perfectly acceptable image (see Figure 2.2).

Figure 2.1: Before cropping, the image is unnecessarily large and poorly composed. Figure 2.2: The shaded area outside the bounding box denotes the area that will be cropped.

This is what I did:

1. I selected the Crop tool (⊐) in the toolbox.
2. I clicked and dragged over the part of the image I wanted to keep, in this case the couple. When I released the mouse button, the crop marquee appeared as a bounding box with handles at the corners and sides.
3. The area to be cropped appears gray by default, which makes it easier to visualize how my image will look after it is cropped.

Note: The Crop tool's default shield color, gray—or more precisely, black at 75 percent opacity—is fine for most images. However, if you are working with images that contain large dark expanses, the gray shield may not be visible, In such cases, you can choose a lighter color and opacity by using the color selection box and the opacity pop-up slider in the options bar.

4. I then adjusted the size of the crop marquee by dragging the corner handle. (You can move the marquee to another position by clicking inside the bounding box and dragging. To rotate the marquee, just position the pointer outside the bounding box—the pointer turns into a curved arrow—and drag. You can constrain the proportions by holding down Shift as you drag a corner handle.)

5. After I finished, I clicked the Commit button (☑) in the options bar. I also could have double-clicked inside the crop marquee, selected a different tool in the toolbox, or pressed Enter/Return. If I had decided not to crop, I could have clicked the Cancel button (☒) in the options bar or pressed the Esc key.

I also could have cropped this image by using the Crop command. In that case, I would have done the following:

1. Selected the part of the image I wanted to keep by using any of the marquee selection tools (☞ "Selection Tools" in Zooming In).

2. Choose Image ➢ Crop from the menu bar.

At times you'll want to crop to a specific resolution and size. Figure 2.3 shows a series of thumbnail shots that I created for Newsweek.com. I started with literally hundreds of screen-sized images, all of which required a smaller, thumbnail version to be used as a navigation device. The job was so big that any extra steps added unwanted time to the process. Instead of cropping and then resizing each cropped image, I simply put the required size and resolution values of the thumbnail version into the Width, Height, or Resolution text boxes in the option bar. (Clicking the Clear button in the options bar resets the values to their defaults.) I then followed the steps outlined above. After I had finished making my cropping selection, I clicked OK and ended up with exactly the size and resolution I needed, in this case, 30×30 pixels at 72 dots per inch (dpi).

Figure 2.3: The Crop tool can be set to crop to a specific size and resolution. (Photos by Peter Turnley, with permission from Newsweek *magazine, Inc.)*

Although this procedure saved time, there was a trade-off in quality. By resizing so radically in one jump, I degraded the final image more than I would have if I had taken it down slowly in increments (☞ "Resizing," later in this chapter).

Straightening Crooked Scans

No matter how hard I try, I seem to always end up with a crooked scan. I lay the print or transparency carefully on my flatbed scanner, holding it in place by hand as long as I can. But then, when the lid descends and I pull away my hand, the image invariably shifts a degree or two. Photoshop Elements makes it easy to straighten these skewed scans.

Figure 2.4 shows a scan I made for a neighborhood oral history project. Darn. Crooked.

To straighten the image, choose Image ➢ Rotate ➢ Straighten and Crop Image. The results are shown in Figure 2.5.

Figure 2.4: A crooked scan is a typical mistake. (Photo by Telegraph Hill Dwellers Oral History Project.) Figure 2.5: Fixed with the Straighten and Crop Image command.

I have to admit that I don't always get such perfect results from the Straighten and Crop Image command. I've discovered that the results are not satisfactory if the edges of the rotated scan are too close to the image window boundaries *or* if they are too far away. To improve the odds that the Straighten and Crop Image command will work properly, you can manually pre-crop the scan or use the Canvas Size command (Image ➢ Resize ➢ Canvas Size) to enlarge the work canvas.

If you want to straighten the image but leave the canvas size the same, choose Image ➢ Rotate ➢ Straighten Image. Using this command results in an image with a transparent border at its edges.

Making Dull Images Shine

Look at the image in Figure 2.6. It's a nicely composed scene, but something is wrong. It looks "flat" and suffers from a poor distribution of tonal values and poor color saturation. The clouds blend into the sky without any distinction. In the case of this photo—taken with a digital camera at Lake Tahoe—it's a matter of a wrong exposure. I simply forgot to switch the camera from manual to auto mode. Sometimes the quality of light will make a digital image look flat. Think fog or haze. Regardless of the reason, most of the time Photoshop Elements can easily make a dull image pop.

Figure 2.6: *Before applying Auto Levels.*

I use one of three methods to improve images that suffer from this "dull" syndrome: the Auto Levels command, the Levels controls, or adjustment layers combined with the Levels controls and masking.

The Simplest Way: Auto Levels

I nearly always start with the Auto Levels command, and in many cases that's all it takes to make a dull image shine. Auto Levels finds the darkest and lightest pixels of an image and then remaps the intermediate pixels proportionately. Color casts may be removed or introduced because Auto Levels adjusts the red, green, and blue channels individually.

To apply Auto Levels, choose Enhance ➤ Auto Levels.

That's what I did to the Lake Tahoe shot, and you can see in Figure 2.7 that it worked. Figure 2.8 shows the histogram before Auto Levels; Figure 2.9 shows it after. Notice that the fixed shot has a much better distribution of tonal values.

Figure 2.7: After Auto Levels.

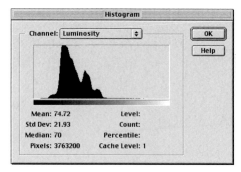
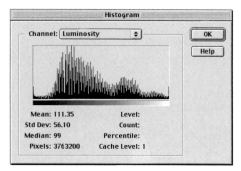

Figure 2.8: Before Auto Levels: a narrow distribution of tonal values. Figure 2.9: After Auto Levels: a wider distribution of tonal values.

Auto Contrast, by the way—found just under Auto Levels in the Enhance menu—isn't nearly as useful for color images. It adjusts the overall contrast and mixture of colors but it does not adjust each color channel (red, green, and blue) individually. I rarely use Auto Contrast, and when I do it's mostly for grayscale images.

More Control: Levels

The Auto Levels command doesn't always work satisfactorily. The bag in Figure 2.10, shot with a digital camera for a commercial website, lacks color intensity and contrast. But applying Auto Levels makes it look worse (see Figure 2.11). At times like this, I turn to the Levels controls found in the menu bar under Enhance ➤ Brightness/Contrast ➤ Levels. The truth is, I probably use Levels more than any other single Photoshop

Elements' control. It enables me to manually adjust the intensity of my shadow, mid-tone, or highlight areas. Not only does it give me sophisticated control over the look of my digital images, it is intuitive and relatively easy to use.

Figure 2.10: The original image lacks color intensity and contrast. ◎ *Figure 2.11: Auto Levels didn't help this image.*

Here is how I used Levels to make the bag look more attractive and saleable:

1. I chose Enhance ➢ Brightness/Contrast ➢ Levels. This brought up the dialog box shown in Figure 2.12.

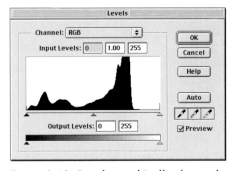

Figure 2.12: Levels graphically shows the distribution of tonal values and provides a means to individually adjust shadows, midtones, or highlights.

2. Looking at the Levels histogram, I saw the problem. Most of the values were to the left, toward the shadow areas. I needed to spread the values across the spectrum and increase the contrast. To do this, I dragged the Input Levels white triangle (lower right of the histogram) to the left, toward the edge of the black mound. As I did this, I saw the whites, or highlights, in my actual image lighten and the overall contrast increase. (Be sure you have checked the Preview option in the Levels dialog box. With this option checked, any changes you make in the Levels dialog box will be shown in the actual image.)

3. Next I adjusted the midtones by dragging the Input Levels gray triangle (found in the middle) to the right. This darkened and intensified the midtones. The numbers in the three boxes found above the histogram represent numerically, in order, shadows, midtones, and highlight areas. As you move the triangle sliders, you'll see these values change to reflect the new values. You can also enter numeric values into these boxes, but it's a lot easier to manually slide the sliders.

4. At various points in the process, I found it useful to carefully examine the effects of my changes on detailed parts of the image. For example, when I adjusted the midtones, I wanted to make sure I didn't lose any details in the gold embroidery. Even though the Levels dialog box was open, I could still use my navigation keyboard commands to magnify and scroll around the image.

5. The shadow areas (again, represented in the left side of the histogram) looked fine, but I went ahead and moved the black triangle anyway. In Figures 2.13 and 2.14, you can see how I adjusted the Levels so that the shadow areas became too dark. At this point I could have slid the black triangle back to its original position, but I decided to start over completely and reset the image to its original state. To do this, I held down the Alt/Option key and clicked on the Reset button in the Levels dialog box.

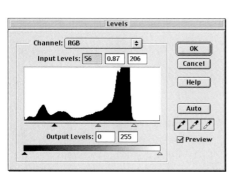

Figure 2.13: Moving the shadow triangle to the right resulted in the image shown in Figure 2.14. Figure 2.14: Changes made in the Levels dialog box are reflected in the image window. In this case, sliding the shadow triangle to the right made the dark areas too dark.

6.   I went back and adjusted my highlights and midtones and left the shadows alone. When I was finished, I clicked OK (see Figure 2.15).

Figure 2.15: Corrected image using Levels.

Note: If you click Auto in the Levels dialog box, you get the same results as using the Auto Levels command. This dialog box also enables you to change the brightness and contrast of the image by dragging the gray slider at the bottom. This affects all the pixels equally and does not affect the color values. You can also choose to work specifically on a red, green, or blue channel by selecting from the Channel drop-down menu found at the top of the dialog box. Unless I know one specific color is off, I work in the default composite RGB mode.

Complex But Powerful: Layer Adjustments with Masks

Sometimes the Levels controls aren't enough. Take, for example the photo of Mt. Shasta in Figure 2.16. When I use the Levels controls to adjust the image, I can either make the foreground trees look good (Figure 2.17) or the mountain and sky look good (Figure 2.18). But I can't make both look good at the same time. I need a way to apply a different set of Levels adjustments to each area of the image separately. There are a couple of ways of doing this, but I've found a combination of layer adjustments and masks to be the most effective and versatile.

Figure 2.16: The original photo.

Figure 2.17: The foreground is OK, but the background is washed out.
Figure 2.18: Now the background is OK, but the foreground is too dark.

Adjustment layers are layers that apply color and tonal adjustments to an image without permanently modifying the pixels in the image (☞ "All about Layers" in Zooming In). A *layer mask* can be added to an adjustment layer to protect sections of an adjustment layer and control the effect that the adjustment layer has on the layer beneath it.

This is what I did to improve the digital photo of Mt. Shasta:

1. I created a new adjustment layer by choosing Layer ➤ New Adjustment Layer ➤ Levels from the menu bar (see Figure 2.19). I also could have created a new adjustment layer by clicking the Create New Fill or Adjustment Layer button (◕) located at the bottom of the Layers palette and choosing Levels from the various options, as shown in Figure 2.20. I named this new layer **Trees**.

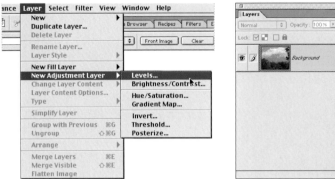

Figure 2.19: Choose an adjustment layer from the Layer menu. Figure 2.20: Or choose an adjustment layer directly from the Layers palette.

2. I used the Levels palette to adjust the midtones so my trees looked right. I didn't pay any attention to the sky and the mountain. When I was finished, I turned the layer visibility off by clicking on the Eye icon found in the leftmost column of the Layers palette. I did this so my new adjustment layer wouldn't interfere with the next adjustment in step 3.

3. I created another Levels adjustment layer and called it **Mt./Sky**. I used the Levels controls to adjust the tonal values so Mt. Shasta and the sky looked right and I didn't worry about my foreground.

4. Next came the tricky part. In the adjustment layer called **Mt./Sky** I created a mask that blocked the effect of the Levels adjustment on the trees. To do this, I clicked the Gradient tool (▭) found in the toolbox. In the options bar I selected the following options:
    - Gradient: Foreground to Transparent
    - Style: Linear Gradient
    - Blend mode: Normal
    - Opacity: 100 percent

    I made sure that the foreground and background colors in the color selection boxes in the toolbox were set to their default black-and-white. (To set them to black-and-white, simply click the Default Colors icon (▪) at the bottom of the toolbox.) With the **Mt/Sky** layer selected, I placed my cursor on the image window. While holding the Shift key, I started at the bottom of the image, then clicked and dragged about halfway up the image and let go of the mouse. Holding the Shift key constrained the Gradient tool to a 90 degree angle. Then I selected the adjustment layer called **Trees** and made another similar mask by using the Gradient tool with the same settings as in the preceding list. Selecting the **Trees** layer automatically turned on its visibility, which I had turned off in step 2. This time I created a mask by holding the Shift key and dragging downward from the top of the image. This blocked the effect of the Levels command on the mountain and sky areas of the image (see Figure 2.21).

Figure 2.21: Both adjustment layers are selectively masked with gradient fills.

Note: Because the layer mask is a grayscale image, what you paint or fill in black will be hidden, what you paint or fill in white will show, and what you paint or fill in gray shades will show in various levels of transparency. Masks can be edited like a grayscale image with any painting or editing tool. Hold down Alt/Option+Shift and click the adjustment layer thumbnail to view the mask in a rubylith masking color. Hold down Alt/Option+Shift and click the thumbnail again to turn off the rubylith display. Shift-click the adjustment layer thumbnail to turn off the masking effects temporarily; click the thumbnail again to turn on the mask.

5. For the most part, the mask created by the Gradient tool was enough. However, I did go back into the adjustment layer called **Mt./Sky** with the paintbrush and mask in a few other areas, including the tree on the right.

Note: You can edit an adjustment layer at any time: Double-click the adjustment layer's thumbnail in the Layers palette or choose Layer ➢ Layer Content Options.

6. As you can see in Figure 2.22, I've now managed to get both the foreground and background right. And as long as I keep my adjustment layers, I can go back and tweak the levels at any time.

Figure 2.22: With just a little work, both the foreground and background are right.

Correcting Color Casts

A digital image can contain an unwanted color cast, perhaps because of an improper white balance setting, or a mismatch between film and ambient light, or a poor scan. Whatever the reason, Photoshop Elements makes it easy to rid the digital image of the unwanted colors and make the colors more true.

You can manipulate colors in several ways by using Photoshop Elements. In this section, I present two of the easiest ways: one uses a simple Remove Cast command, and the other uses the Variations command. You'll find more on removing and replacing colors later in the book (☞ "Changing a Product's Color" in Chapter 5).

Removing Unwanted Cast with One Click

Figure 2.23 shows a photograph I took of a new MRI scanner at the University of California Medical Center in San Francisco. The balance between daylight film and ambient light was off, and the result was a greenish tint.

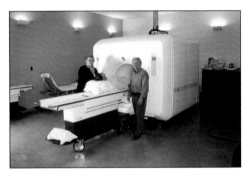

Figure 2.23: A mismatch between film sensitivity and ambient light caused the greenish tint.

It was easy to fix the image by using Photoshop Elements' Color Cast command, which analyzes color samples taken from selective parts of the image and attempts to shift the color cast to a neutral color.

Here's what I did:

1. I chose Enhance ➢ Color ➢ Color Cast to open the dialog box shown in Figure 2.24).

2. Using the Eyedropper tool (🖊), I clicked on different areas in the image. I was particularly looking for areas that I knew should be gray, white, or black but weren't because of the unwanted color cast. The image changed according to the color I selected. When I didn't like a result, I simply clicked the Reset button and the image reverted to its original state.

Note: The Color Cast eyedropper samples only one pixel at a time. To be precise about where you are sampling, you need to magnify your image.

3. I poked around until I got what I was looking for and then I clicked OK. The resulting image is shown in Figure 2.25.

Note: Normally I find the notes that Adobe includes in their dialog boxes to be excellent. However, I must confess that reading the note in the Color Cast Correction dialog box confused me at first. It reads: "To correct color cast, click around the area of the image that should be gray, white, or black." The first time I read this, I didn't pay particular attention to the word *should*. Instead I tried to find an area in my image that was gray, white, or black. I didn't get good results until I realized that I needed to look for areas that *should* be gray, white, or black. The tool works by taking a sample from these areas and then assuming that you want the sampled area to be neutral—in other words, to consist of equal amounts of red, green, and blue. It then shifts all the colors to create this neutral state.

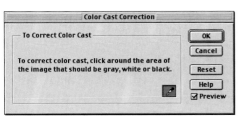 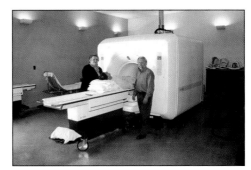

Figure 2.24: The Color Cast command helps remove unwanted color casts. Figure 2.25: Color cast removed

Shooting Digital: Use the Right Side of Your Brain

When shooting with a digital camera—or, for that matter, any camera—keep in mind that photography is a visual language dependent on light and form. It works best when it speaks to the nonverbal, intuitive side of the brain, complementing words but not necessarily competing with them. A billboard framed against a brilliant blue sky is interesting not only because of the words on the billboard but because of its shape and the way that light strikes it and the inherent tension between something man-made and something natural. I always tell my students that the best way to learn this language is to take classes and examine images in books and see what works and what doesn't. I tell them to go to exhibitions and art galleries, and by all means, just pay attention to the way the summer light strikes a gnarled old oak tree or glances off a sleeping child's face.

Using Variations to Get the Color Right

While on assignment for *Wired* magazine, I used daylight film to shoot the portrait of cold war warrior and futurist Andrew Marshall in the fluorescent-lit halls of the Pentagon. The mismatch between outdoor film and the indoor lighting caused Marshall to be bathed in an interesting combination of magenta and green light, as shown in Figure 2.26.

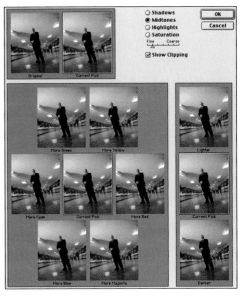

Figure 2.26: The colors in this photo needed to be adjusted. Figure 2.27: The Variations command is a good way to visually adjust color, contrast, and saturation.

To tone down the strong casts, I used Photoshop Elements' Variations command. The Variations command lets you adjust the color balance, contrast, and saturation of an image by showing you thumbnails of alternatives. Like the Color Cast command, Variations is most useful for images that don't require precise color adjustments.

I followed these steps:

1. I chose Enhance ≻ Variations to create the thumbnails (see Figure 2.27). The thumbnail on the top left of the dialog box shows the original image (Original). As I made adjustments, the Current Pick thumbnail changed to reflect my choices. When I went too far and wanted to revert to my original, I simply clicked the Original thumbnail.

2. I didn't need to adjust the brightness of this particular image but I could have by clicking on the thumbnails on the right side of the dialog box. Instead, I adjusted the color by clicking the More Yellow thumbnail. That took care of some of the green cast. Next I clicked the More Blue thumbnail, and that took care of some of the magenta cast. Neither adjustment removed all the magenta or green cast, but I still liked the result. Understanding basic color theory and how a color wheel works might be helpful to your own work. To decrease the amount of green in an image, you increase magenta, which is opposite green on the color wheel. To decrease the amount of red, you increase the amount of cyan, which is opposite red on the color wheel.

Note: In the Variations dialog box, dragging the Fine/Coarse slider determines the amount of each adjustment. Moving the slider one tick mark doubles the adjustment amount. Also, by choosing Shadows, Midtones, or Highlights, you can emphasize adjustment of the dark, middle, or light areas. (Midtones is the default setting.) To change the degree of hue in the image, select Saturation.

3. When I was finished, I clicked OK. Figure 2.28 shows the adjusted image.

Figure 2.28: The adjusted image.

Scanning Digital: Scanning Old Black-and-White Photos

When scanning old black-and-white photos, keep your scanning software set at RGB. Don't scan in grayscale even though that might seem like the logical way to go. Most old photos contain subtle colors or tints, caused by the aging process or the characteristics of the photographic paper. It's these colors that make the image look authentic.

Tinting an Image

I like grayscale images. I really do. But sometimes they benefit from a color tint. The tint need not be overwhelming. In fact, sometimes a subtle shade of yellow or red is all it takes to give a grayscale image an added pop so it jumps from a page.

Take, for example, the 1761 engraving from a Russian bath shown in Figure 2.29. The image was published in black-and-white in a book I wrote on bathing. It looked fine. However, when I went to place the image on my website, it was lacking. It needed to stand out more.

Figure 2.29: The original grayscale image.

This is what I did:

1. I opened the Hue/Saturation dialog box (Enhance ➤ Color ➤ Hue Saturation), shown in Figure 2.30.

 Note: This will work only if you are in RGB mode. If you aren't, choose Image ➤ Mode ➤ RGB to convert the image to RGB.

2. I selected Colorize. The image was converted to the hue of the current foreground color, in this case red.
3. I then slid the Hue and Saturation sliders to select variations of color.
4. When I got the tint I wanted, I clicked OK. The tinted image is shown in Figure 2.31.

Figure 2.30: To tint, make sure the Colorize option is selected in the Hue/Saturation dialog box. Figure 2.31: The tinted image.

Eliminating or Diminishing Dust, Scratches, and Electronic Noise

Most digital images suffer from dust, scratches or other marks, or electronic "noise." Even high JPEG compression can cause unwanted artifacts, which show up as "blocks" and are especially obvious in flat areas of an image. Any of these flaws can detract from the look of a digital image. Fortunately, Photoshop Elements offers several tools for getting rid of them.

I used a combination of the Dust & Scratches filter, a selection tool, and the Clone Stamp tool to fix the 50-year-old photo shown in Figure 2.32.

Figure 2.32: This 50-year old photo is full of scratches and other artifacts of age.

Here's what I did:

1. I cropped the edges of the scan by using the Crop Command (☞ "Crop to the Essential Parts" earlier in this chapter).

2. I applied Auto Levels to optimize the colors and tone (☞ "Making Dull Images Shine" earlier in this chapter).

3. At a magnification level of 300 percent, I noticed the sky was filled with dust and scratches and other artifacts of age (Figure 2.33). As I scrolled around, I saw there were also moiré patterns caused by the scanning process. Glass against glass often causes a swirling pattern, called a *moiré*, to form. The old transparency was sandwiched between two pieces of glass. I was tempted to use the Dust & Scratches filter to clean up the entire image but I knew this wasn't a good idea because it would blur all of the image. Instead I selected the sky by using the Lasso selection tool (℘) and applied the filter only to this selected area. I set the Radius at 4 and the Threshold at 0 (see Figure 2.34). In general, higher Radius values effectively remove more dust and scratches but blur other pixels in the image as well. Depending on the image, you can still remove dust and scratches but diminish the blur caused by higher Radius values by selecting higher Threshold values.

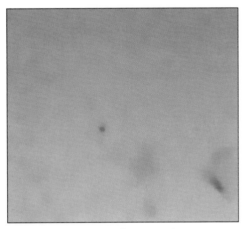

Figure 2.33: A magnification of 300 percent reveals the details of the problem.

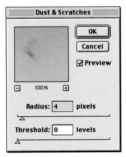

Figure 2.34: Applying the Dust & Scratches filter to the selected background removed many of the artifacts and left the foreground area sharp.

4.   Although the filter got rid of most of the smaller artifacts, the larger ones remained. To get rid of these, I selected the Clone Stamp tool (⚓) from the toolbox. In the options bar, I selected the following options for the Clone Stamp tool:

- Brush: Soft Round 100 pixels
- Mode: Normal
- Opacity: 100 percent
- Aligned: Checked on
- Use All Layers: Checked on

I positioned the cursor slightly to the side of a scratch or smudge, in an area of the sky devoid of spots. While holding the Alt/Option key, I clicked and sampled. Then I clicked and "stamped" over a flawed area, careful not to drag and smear the pixels and cause an unnatural looking blur.

5.   After deselecting the sky, I turned to the foreground and to the woman on the road (see Figure 2.35). This area wasn't as bad as the sky but it still needed some cleaning up. Again, I used the Clone Stamp tool to selectively rid the woman's arm and face of spots, this time using a smaller brush setting for the smaller areas.

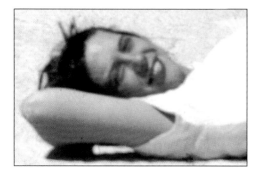

Figure 2.35: I used the Clone Stamp tool to selectively clean up the woman on the road.

This was a particularly difficult image, and, frankly, I had to draw the line at how much time I was going to put into it. I could have continued to use the Clone Stamp tool to make each and every detail perfect. Frankly, I was satisfied with cleaning up the sky and most of the woman. After all, it is a historical photo and I wanted to keep some of its authenticity. The final image is shown in Figure 2.36.

Figure 2.36: The image after applying the Dust & Scratches filter and using the Clone Stamp tool for extensive cloning.

Converting Color Images to Black-and-White

There are several reasons why you might convert a color image to black-and-white: black-and-white images stand out in a world saturated with color images, they are often more economical to print, and, if you save an image in Photoshop Elements' Grayscale mode, they take up less file space.

The image in Figure 2.37 was shot by North Beach, California resident Julie Christensen for a local newspaper. The newspaper prints only black-and-white photos, and Julie gave me a color print to scan and convert.

I scanned the print in color and converted it to black-and-white simply by choosing Enhance ➤ Color ➤ Remove Color (see Figure 2.38). This command converted the colors in the image to gray values, assigning equal red, green, and blue values to each pixel in the RGB image. The lightness value of each pixel did not change and, because the image remained in RGB mode, the file size didn't change either.

Figure 2.37: The original image. (Photo by Julie Christensen). Figure 2.38: Quickly convert to black-and-white by choosing Enhance ➤ Color ➤ Remove Color.

If you want to keep your file size down, I suggest you convert an image to black-and-white by simply changing modes from RGB to Grayscale (Image ➤ Mode ➤ Grayscale). If you use this method, you won't have access to many of Photoshop Elements' filters and effects, which work only in RGB mode. But because grayscale images are only 8 bits per pixel, versus 24 bits per pixel, your file size will be about 75 percent smaller.

Sharpening

If you've got a digital image that appears soft or blurry, Photoshop Elements gives you several options for sharpening it. The Sharpen filter globally increases the contrast of adjacent pixels, whereas the Sharpen Edges filter sharpens only the areas of a major brightness change and leaves smooth areas untouched. The toolbox also has a Sharpen tool, which sharpens specific areas of an image.

But the tool I consistently use is the Unsharp Mask filter. This filter is based on a traditional film compositing technique that creates a blurred negative version of the image. It then averages this copy with the original and through three controls—Amount (percentage), Threshold, and Radius—gives you precise control over the amount of sharpening and the way the sharpening is applied.

Here is how I used the Unsharp Mask filter to improve the photo (1700 × 1680 pixels, 72 pixels/inch) shown in Figure 2.39.

1. I chose Filter ➤ Sharpen ➤ Unsharp Mask and made sure the Preview option was selected (see Figure 2.40).

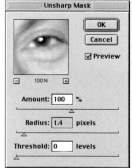

Figure 2.39: The original image is lacking sharpness. Figure 2.40: The Unsharp Mask dialog box. Your settings will vary depending on the size and content of the image.

2. I then dragged the Amount slider until it reached 100 percent.

3. I set the Threshold at 12. (Setting the Threshold slider at a higher value forces the Unsharp Mask filter to leave the flesh tones, or other areas containing contiguous pixels of similar tonal values, relatively alone. Leaving the Threshold set at 0 forces the filter to sharpen all the pixels in the image equally and may introduce unwanted artifacts in flat-colored areas such as the skin.)

4. I then slid the Radius slider until I was visually happy with the amount of sharpening. In the case of this image, a value of 4.2 was just about right.

Note: If the Preview option is checked, you can see the effects of the Unsharp Mask on the image in the document window. Selecting and deselecting the Preview option gives you a way to toggle back and forth between a sharpened and unsharpened version of your image. You can also view the effect of the Unsharp Mask in the dialog box's small preview window. If you click on the image in the preview window, you'll see how the image looks without the effect of the Unsharp Mask. In the preview window you can also drag to see different parts of the image and click the plus sign (+) or the minus sign (-) to zoom in or out.

5. I then clicked OK. Figure 2.41 shows the resulting image.

Figure 2.41: Image sharpened with the Unsharp Mask filter.

The values that you use for your image will vary depending on such factors as the image's content, size, and final destination. For an average-sized image that contains a lot of detail—say an architectural shot at 1600 × 1800 pixels—try setting your percentage at 150 percent and your Radius at 2. For these kinds of images, I generally leave the Threshold setting at 0, which forces the Unsharp Mask filter to sharpen all the pixels equally.

For an image of the same size that contains expanses of color and tone, such as a face, I recommend setting your percentage at 100 percent, your Radius between 0.5 and 1, and your Threshold between 2 and 15. Playing with your Threshold setting will help you avoid introducing noise in the flat areas of color.

Increase these numbers if you are working with larger images. Decrease them for smaller images.

Resizing

One of the secrets of success in digital imaging is matching the size of your digital image to the requirements of your output. This means that if your digital image is destined for print, you'll need more resolution than you would if it were destined for a monitor (👁 "From Hard Copy To Many Copies: Sharing and Processing Images" in Chapter 12). Most likely, the original image that you are working with is larger or smaller than needed, and you'll have to resize. Keep in mind that resizing, up or down, always involves some loss of image quality. It is also the last step that you want to perform.

Figure 2.42 shows a 720 × 480 at 72dpi video frame grab from film maker/producer Micha X. Peled's acclaimed PBS film, *Store Wars: When Wal-Mart Comes to Town*. Micha wanted to use the frame for a publicity shot, but it didn't have enough resolution for the higher demands of print.

Figure 2.42: A frame from a video grab contains obvious scan lines and is of low resolution.

Here is what I had him do to boost the resolution and make the image more acceptable:

1. I had him apply the De-Interlace filter (Filter ➤ Video ➤ De-Interlace), keeping the default settings: Odd Fields and Interpolation. This removed the odd interlaced lines and, by interpolation, replaced the lines with adjacent pixels, which made the video grab appear smoother. Just from this simple move, the picture quality greatly improved. See Figures 2.43 and 2.44.

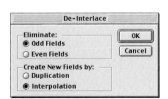

Figure 2.43: The De-Interlace filter dialog box. Figure 2.44: With its scan lines removed and its resolution increased, the video grab is now a perfectly acceptable still image.

2. I had him select Image ➤ Resize ➤ Image Size to open the Image Size dialog box (see Figure 2.45). I made sure that the Constrain Proportions option was checked and that the interpolation method was set at Bicubic—the default settings.

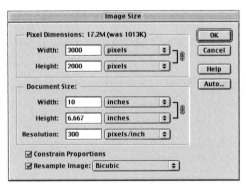

Figure 2.45: The Image Size dialog box.

3. I had Micha enter 300 pixels/inch in the Resolution box and, voila, he had a digital image that would look great in a magazine as long as it wasn't published much larger than a quarter page.

What about going the other way? Making a large image small? This is a common task when you are resizing digital images for the Web or for e-mail transmission to many people. You'd think all you have to do is enter the values into the Image Size dialog box and leave it at that. That's fine if you are reducing the image, say, only 50 percent—but a big mistake if you need to shrink it more than that.

Take the image in Figure 2.46. It is 2700 × 1932 pixels at 288 pixels/inch. Now look at Figure. 2.47. I've reduced it to 675 × 624 pixels at 72 pixels/inch in one swoop. The image looks mushy and soft. It's best to reduce your file size in increments of no more than 50 percent at a time and to apply the Unsharp Mask slightly after each step. It takes a little longer to resize this way, but the results make it worthwhile, as you can see in Figure 2.48.

Figure 2.46: The original image started at 2700 × 1932 pixels at 288 pixels/inch. (Photo by Monica Lee.)

Figure 2.47: Resizing in one step to 675 × 624 pixels at 72 pixels/inch creates this mushy looking image. Figure 2.48: Resizing incrementally, with an Unsharp Mask filter applied between each step, results in a sharper looking resized image.

Grabbing Digital: Which File Format Should You Choose?

Many popular video frame grabbers give you the option of saving your image in various file formats, such as JPEG, TIFF, PICT, or PSD. Which one should you select? For the best quality, choose TIFF or PSD, which is Photoshop Elements' native file format. If you do this, your file won't be as small as it would be if you saved it as a JPEG, but the TIFF and PSD file formats are lossless, which means no data is thrown away during the conversion. PICT is a Mac-only file format and is therefore inherently limited.

Framing Your Image

Frames, or border treatments, are a final touch that, if done properly, can enhance and bring out the best of your digital images. Photoshop Elements ships with more than a dozen styles of frames, ranging from a fancy brushed aluminum frame to an artsy rippled frame. These complex frames—like other image effects found in the Effects palette—are achieved through the automatic sequencing of filters, layer styles, and/or program functions. After you choose a frame effect and start the process, you have no control over details such as color, bevel size, or drop shadow depth. (The Foreground Color Frame effect uses the color you select in the upper color selection box in the toolbox.) However, it is possible with just a little more work to customize the effect.

This is what I did to create the frame shown in Figure 2.49:

1. I made sure the Effects palette was visible. (Choose Window ➢ Show Effects Browser, or click the Effects tab in the palette well.) I opened the Effects palette and made sure that Frame Effects was chosen from the drop-down menu (other choices are All, Textures, Text Effects, and Image Effects).

2. I chose the Wild Frame from the Effects palette and applied the frame effect by double-clicking on the effect. I also could have applied the effect by dragging the effect from the Effects palette to the image or by clicking the Apply button in the upper-right corner of the Effects palette.

3. The amount of time it takes for Photoshop Elements to generate an effect will vary depending on how complex the effect is and the processing speed of your computer. You can see the process in action by opening the History palette before you start. Figure 2.50 shows the steps it took for Photoshop Elements to create the Wild Frame effect.

Figure 2.49: This is what you get when you choose Wild Frame from the Effects palette.
Figure 2.50: The History palette shows the steps to creating a Wild Frame.

4. After my frame was complete, a dialog box appeared asking, "Do you wish to keep this Effect?" Although I wasn't completely satisfied with the result, I clicked Yes. Now began the work of tweaking the frame to my liking.

This is what I did to change the effect:

1. In the History palette, I clicked back one step, to the step named Deselect in Figure 2.50. This is the step before all the layers generated by the effect were flattened.

2. Now, in the Layers palette, the working layers are visible and can be changed (see Figure 2.51). Because I didn't particularly like the colors of the Wild Frame, I selected Layer 1. I enhanced the color saturation by a factor of + 50 with the Enhance ➢ Color ➢ Hue/Saturation controls.

3. To change the bevel, I double-clicked the *f* symbol in the right corner of Layer 1. This brought up the Style Settings palette shown in Figure 2.52. I enlarged the Bevel Size from 8 to 35 and changed the Lighting Angle from 30 degrees to 125 degrees. After I was finished, I simply flattened the image (Layer ➢ Flatten Image). The new frame is shown in Figure 2.53. (I also could have changed the amount and direction of the drop shadow by clicking the f symbol in Layer 2 and playing with the Shadow Distance setting and Lighting Angle.)

Figure 2.51: By stepping back in the History palette, the layers are revealed. Figure 2.52: I changed the Bevel Size from 8 to 35 and changed the Lighting Angle from 30 degrees to 125 degrees.

Figure 2.53: The customized Wild Frame.

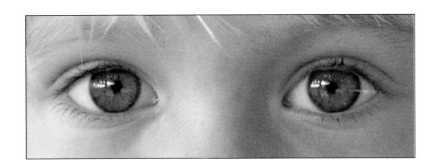

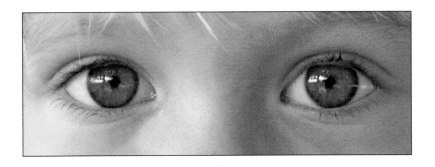

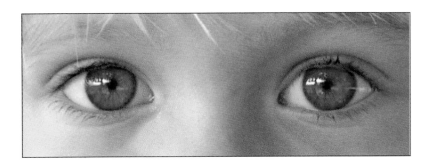

How many times *have you heard someone look at a picture and say, "That doesn't look like me!" You may even have said it as you stared at a picture of yourself. Sometimes the criticism is based entirely on vanity. But often the fault lies with the photograph. Blame it on the camera, the lens, the lighting, or even more likely, the photographer. With the help of Photoshop Elements, there are no more excuses. You can make better faces. This chapter shows you simple tips and techniques for using Photoshop Elements to intensify eyes, eliminate red eye, reduce wrinkles, and otherwise help improve digital images of the human face.*

Better Faces

Better Faces

What Comes First

Before starting work on a face or faces, I usually begin by cropping the image to its essential parts and optimizing the tonal values (☞ "Cropping to the Essential Parts" in Chapter 2). What I do next depends on the image, the person depicted in the image, and where it is ultimately going to be shown or published.

Many times a face needs only a little tweaking to get it just right. Typically this means whitening the white part of the eyes and teeth, slightly increasing the color saturation of the eyes and lips, and selectively diminishing wrinkles. Other relatively easy tasks include selective burning and dodging, removing red eye, and applying a digital fill flash.

Some faces are more challenging. For example, when a face is distorted because of natural or unnatural causes, I use various Transform commands or the Liquify filter to get it right. Although it is relatively easy to change the color of hair, or to lighten or darken hair, removing or adding hair requires a little more work, and for this I almost exclusively use the Clone Stamp tool.

The last thing you'll ever do to a digital image is resize it to the needs of your final destination (☞ "Resizing" in Chapter 2). Be sure to keep an original, full-sized version of your image for future purposes.

Note: How far do you want to go? The possibilities for improving or changing a face by using Photoshop Elements are almost unlimited. That's why I suggest you ask yourself how far you want to go and how much time you want to spend. There are no easy answers, no hard rules to follow. The answers to these questions invariably depend on the wishes of your subject and the final destination of the image. If the picture is just for fun and the person in the picture has a good sense of humor, well, anything goes. If you are preparing an image for a corporate brochure or other serious purpose, tread lightly and make subtle changes.

Whatever you do, please keep in mind that it's a special day when the subject of your work actually likes their own portrait. Unless you've really messed up their face, you can chalk that up to vanity and human nature!

Intensifying and Changing Eyes

The first thing we usually notice about someone is their eyes. Are they bright, dull, shiny? Bloodshot? Yellow? Sick? The eyes are the gateway to the soul, and that is where I usually start.

Whitening the Whites

Both of the methods I use to whiten the whites of the eyes use the Dodge tool. One method is slightly quicker than the other but less precise.

Here's method 1:

1. I select the Dodge tool (🔎) from the toolbox. The Dodge tool shares the same space as the Burn tool (✋). If the Dodge tool is not visible, just click and hold the Burn tool and the Dodge tool will appear. Now select it.

2. In the options bar, I select Midtones from the Range menu, and 50 percent from the Exposure menu. (Remember that no one has perfectly white whites, and at 100 percent exposure it's easy to overdo the amount of whitening. I choose 50 percent exposure because it gives me more control over the amount of dodging.)

3. I then select an appropriate brush size. To alter the image in Figure 3.1, I chose a Soft Round 35 pixels brush, which fit nicely in the space between the eyelids and the pupils. (The brush size that works in your image will vary depending on the size of your image and the white space itself.)

4. I start by clicking and dragging carefully over the parts of the eye that I want to whiten. If I need a better view of the area I am working on, I magnify my image by using one of the View tools. I dodge incrementally, dragging over a small area and then releasing the mouse button. By doing this, I can undo incrementally as well. If you do all your dodging in one click, the Undo command will undo all your work to the point of that first click.

5. When I get the look I want, I stop. Remember, it's tempting to go too far and make the white perfectly white. Don't. It won't look natural. Figure 3.2 shows my final shot.

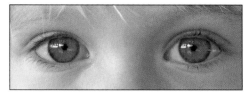 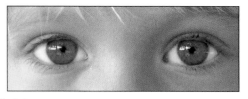

Figure 3.1: Before dodging. Figure 3.2: After dodging.

The second method I use is similar to the first one, but this time I create a selection that protects the nonwhite areas from the effects of the dodging. This way, the size of my brush isn't so important and I don't need to be nearly as precise when I dodge.

Here's method 2:

1. I select the Lasso section tool (🔾) from the toolbox. In the options bar, I make sure that the Anti-aliasing box is checked. I also set the Feather option to

3 pixels. Anti-aliasing softens the color transition between edge pixels and background pixels and smoothens the jagged edges of a selection. Feathering causes some loss of detail at the edge of my selection, but when I apply the Dodge tool it also creates a smooth transition between the white and adjacent areas.

2. I carefully select one white area, as shown in Figure 3.3. Then, while holding down the Shift key, I select the white area on the other side of the pupil. A plus sign appears next to the pointer. While holding down the Shift key again, I select the whites in the other eye.

 Note: You can also add selections by choosing the Add to Selection option in the options bar.

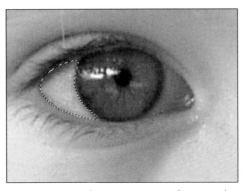

Figure 3.3: A selection protects the nonwhite areas from the effects of the Dodge tool.

3. Now I select the Dodge tool from the toolbar. This time I choose a fairly large brush because the selection will protect the rest of my image. Then I dodge incrementally, just as I did in the first example, until I get the effect I want.

4. To deselect my selection, I use the keyboard command Ctrl/Command+D. You can also deselect a selection by choosing Select ➤ Deselect from the menu bar or by clicking anywhere in the image outside the selected area.

Enhancing the Color

It's easy to enhance the color of the eyes. I use a method similar to the one I just described, but instead of using the Dodge tool on the white areas of the eye, I use the Sponge tool to saturate the colors of the iris (see Figure 3.4).

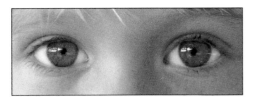

Figure 3.4: Use the Sponge tool to saturate the colors.

To create this effect, I did the following:

1. I selected the Sponge tool (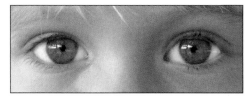) from the toolbox.

2. In the options bar, I selected Saturate from the Mode menu and 50 percent from the Pressure menu.

3. I then selected an appropriate brush size. For this image, I chose a Soft Round 65 pixels brush.

4. I started by clicking and dragging carefully over the parts of the eye that I wanted to enhance. I saturated incrementally, dragging over a small area and then releasing the mouse button.

5. When I got the saturation I wanted, I stopped. It's easy to go too far and make the eyes look unnatural.

If you want to be more precise, you can also make a selection as described in the preceding section and saturate the selection only.

Changing the Color

It's also easy to change the color of the eyes from, say, green to blue. Although there are other ways of doing this, I've discovered a simple, yet effective method using the Red Eye Brush tool. Sure, the Red Eye Brush tool is great for getting rid of red eye (and I'll describe how to use it that way shortly). However, the Red Eye Brush tool is really a color replacement tool in disguise, and it is great for changing the color of just about anything. Take a look at Figure 3.5.

Figure 3.5: Change color using the Red Eye Brush tool.

This is what I did to change the color of the eyes:

1. I selected the Red Eye Brush tool ( ) from the toolbar.

2. I chose a brush size from the pop-up palette in the options bar. I choose a Soft Round 65 pixels brush, but the brush you choose will depend on the specifics of your particular image.

3. I specified a target color (the color I wanted to replace) by choosing First Click from the Sampling pop-up menu in the options bar.

4. I specified a replacement color by clicking the Replacement color swatch and picking a light blue from the Color Picker. You can pick any color you want.

5. I set the Tolerance in the options bar to 30 percent. A higher percentage would have replaced adjacent pixels with a broader range of color values. A lower percentage would have replaced only a few adjacent pixels with similar color values.

6. I then clicked and dragged over the irises. The parts of the eye that matched the target color were colorized with the light blue. To sample new target colors, I

simply released the mouse and clicked again on another part of the iris. To be honest, for some images, I've found that no matter what Tolerance setting I choose, the color still spills onto unwanted areas of the eye, for example, the eyelashes. If this happens to you, I suggest that you make a selection around the iris and then apply the Red Eye Brush tool.

Eliminating Red Eye

Red eye occurs when light from an on-camera flash reflects off the back of the eye, giving someone a demonic look. Red eye is such a common problem in color images that Photoshop Elements includes an easy-to-use tool devoted to fixing the problem. (This tool really is a color replacement tool and has other uses as well, as I showed you in the preceding section.) Figure 3.6 shows an image with red eye, and Figure 3.7 shows the same image after I used the Red Eye Brush to fix it.

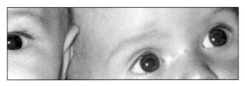 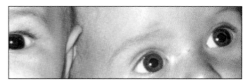

Figure 3.6: Before using the Red Eye Brush. *Figure 3.7: After using the Red Eye Brush.*

Here is what I did to get rid of the red eye:

1. I selected the Red Eye Brush tool ( ) from the toolbar.
2. I chose a Soft Round 65 pixels brush from the pop-up palette in the options bar. (The brush you choose will depend on the specifics of your particular image.) I clicked Default colors in the options bar to specify black as the replacement color. I selected First Click from the Sampling pop-up menu. I specified a Tolerance of 30 percent.
3. By clicking first on the red area of the pupil, I automatically specified that color for removal. I then dragged over the pupil until the red was replaced with black. (Sometimes the replacement to black is too light. You can fix this by using the Burn tool ( ) to darken the pupil. Also, if a person's face is pink, sometimes the Red Eye Brush doesn't work as well. To reduce this problem, use the Lasso tool ( ) to select the red-eye area and then apply the Red Eye Brush tool.)

Enlarging the Eyes

Portrait painters learned long ago that they could make their wealthy patrons happy by slightly enlarging the eyes of their female subjects. Enlarged eyes evoke youth, innocence, and receptiveness. When it's appropriate, you can easily do something similar by using Photoshop Elements Liquify filter. The Liquify filter enables you to warp, twirl, expand, contract, shift, and reflect areas of your image. It's as if your image were turned into easily manipulated molten pixels (, "Liquify Filter" in Zooming In). I used the Liquify filter to enlarge the eyes shown in Figure 3.8.

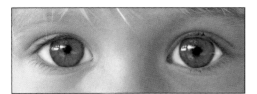

Figure 3.8: Use the Liquify filter to enlarge the eyes.

Here's what I did:

1. I chose the Liquify filter from the Filter menu. This opened the dialog box shown in Figure 3.9. (There are no magnification tools within the Liquify filter, so if you are working on a small part of your image, it is best to create a selection around that area before choosing the Liquify filter. Also, keep in mind that the Liquify filter works on the selected layer of an image. In my case, I had only one layer, so selecting a layer wasn't an option.)

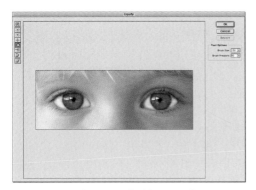

Figure 3.9: The Liquify filter work area.

2. I selected the Bloat tool ( ) and then adjusted the brush size so the brush fit over the entire eye. I then adjusted the brush pressure. I chose a low brush pressure so that changes occurred more slowly and it was easier to stop when I got what I wanted.

3. I placed the brush over one of the eyes, and then clicked and held the mouse without moving the cursor. The Bloat tool moved pixels away from the center of the brush, effectively making the eye bigger.

Note: If you go too far, you have a couple of choices: You can revert to the original version by clicking Revert. You can also Alt+click (Windows) or Option+click (Mac), and the Cancel button turns into Reset. Or you can use the Reconstruct tool ( ) and hold down the mouse button or drag over the distorted areas.

4. When the first eye looked the way that I wanted it to, I did the same to the other eye, making sure to apply the same amount of enlarging. Then I clicked OK.

Sometimes it's enough to slightly enlarge the pupil, or the dark part of the eye. To do this, simply choose a smaller brush size and apply the Bloat tool to just that area.

Working on Lips

After the eyes, the next area I work on is the lips. Again, a lot of what I do is very subtle and yet very effective. Mostly, I slightly enhance the color of the lips by using the Saturate tool. However, as with the eyes, it's also fun to change the color of the lips or to imitate a Julia Roberts look by using the Liquify filter. See Figures 3.10 and 3.11 for before and after images.

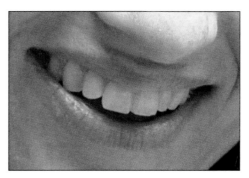 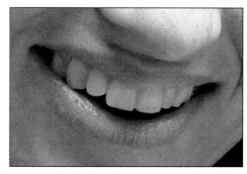

Figure 3.10: Before color enhancement. Figure 3.11: After using the Sponge tool to enhance color.

To saturate the color as shown in Figure 3.11:

1. Select the Sponge tool (🔘) in the toolbox.

2. Pick a brush size from the options bar and set the Mode option to Saturate and the Pressure option to 20–30 percent.

3. Gently stroke the lips, adding just enough saturation to make the lips more noticeable.

To colorize the lips as shown in Figure 3.12:

1. Choose the Red Eye Brush tool (🖌️) from the toolbar.

2. Pick an appropriate color from the Replacement color swatch.

3. Click and drag over the lips. The parts of the lip that match the target color will be colorized with the Replacement color. If your colors spill over, you can either use the selection method described earlier, or simply go back later and clean up the unwanted colors with the Clone Stamp tool (🔨).

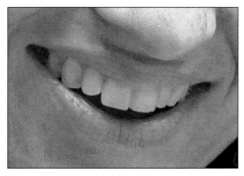

Figure 3.12: Use the Red Eye Brush to replace lip color.

To enlarge the lips as shown in Figure 3.13:

1. Select the mouth by using any of the selection tools.

2. Choose Filter ➢ Liquify.

3. Select the Bloat tool (⬦) and choose an appropriate sized brush and a relatively low brush pressure.

4. Place the brush over the lips. Click and selectively add fullness. If you don't overdo it, the effect can look realistic. Go too far, and it's pretty outrageous!

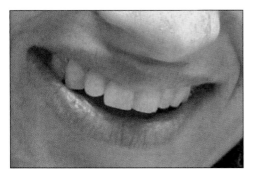

Figure 3.13: Use the Liquify filer to enlarge the lips.

Whitening and Fixing Teeth

People spend a lot of money making their teeth look good. After the eyes and the lips, teeth are probably the most noticed part of the face. You can do someone a big favor by removing years of coffee or tobacco stains with a few selective brush strokes. Whatever you do, don't go too far. Teeth that are perfectly white look unnatural.

To use the Dodge tool to whiten teeth:

1. Select the Dodge tool (◕) from the toolbox.

2. In the options bar, select Midtones from the Range menu, and 50 percent from the Exposure menu.

3. Select an appropriate brush size.

4. Click and drag carefully over the parts of the teeth that you want to whiten. Magnify your image if needed. Dodge incrementally, dragging over a small area and then releasing the mouse button.

5. Stop when you get the look you want. You've gone too far if the teeth look unnatural or if you lose the texture of the teeth. Figures 3.14 and 3.15 show before and after shots.

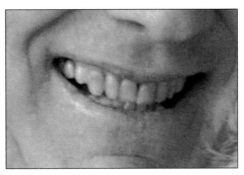 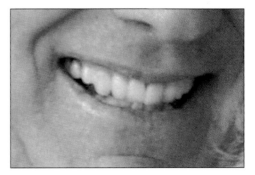

Figure 3.14: Before using the Dodge tool. Figure 3.15: After using the Dodge tool.

To use the Paint Brush to whiten teeth:

1. Choose a color to paint with by selecting the Eyedropper tool ( ) from the toolbar. Click on the lightest section of a tooth. Now click on the foreground color swatch ( ) in the toolbar. This opens the Color Picker. Now select a color that is brighter than the sampled color. The sampled color is shown in one circle. The new, lighter selection is shown in a larger circle that is above and to the left of the sampled color (see Figure 3.16).

2. Select the Paintbrush tool ( ) from the toolbar.

3. Select an appropriate sized, soft-edged brush from the options bar. Set the Mode to Lighten and Opacity to 15–20 percent.

4. Paint carefully over the teeth until you get the effect you want.

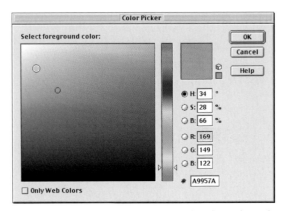 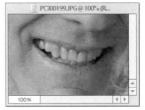

Figure 3.16: Select a color that is brighter than the tooth.

To fix a tooth with the Liquify filter:

1. Make a selection around the area you want to fix.

2. Open the Liquify filter (Filter ➤ Liquify).

3. Select the Bloat tool ( ) if you want to enlarge a tooth, the Pucker tool ( ) if you want to shrink one, or the Warp tool ( ) if you want to straighten one. Choose an appropriate brush size and a relatively low brush pressure.

4. Place the brush over the area you want to fix. It will take some experimentation, but you can shrink the gaps between teeth, fill in a missing piece of enamel, or straighten a crooked tooth.

BETTER FACES

In Figures 3.17 and 3.18, you can see how I've fixed two teeth by using the Liquify filter and the Bloat tool.

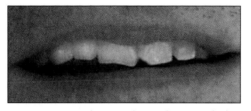 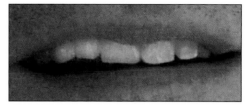

Figure 3.17: Before applying the Liquify filter. Figure 3.18: After applying the Liquify filter.

Selectively Reducing Wrinkles

Personally, I like wrinkles; they show character and maturity. However, I know that not all wrinkles are caused by age and character, Many times they are unwanted artifacts of a high-speed contrasty film or harsh lighting. Here are some techniques for either getting rid of them or playing down their prominence. Keep in mind that wrinkles are technically just shadows on a digital image. You can largely diminish their appearance by simply lightening them up.

To use the Dodge tool to reduce wrinkles:

1. Select the Dodge tool (◉) from the toolbar. Set it to Midtones and use an appropriate sized, soft-edged brush. If needed, magnify your image so the wrinkles fill the screen.

2. With a very low exposure—say 10–20 percent—gently stroke the wrinkle away with the brush. Don't go too far. Before you make a final judgement, you should zoom back to normal magnification. That way, you'll have a more objective view of your work.

I used this method to diminish the wrinkles shown in Figure 3.19. The after shot is shown in Figure 3.20.

Figure 3.19: Wrinkles before dodging. Figure 3.20: After dodging.

To use the Clone Stamp tool to eliminate wrinkles:

1. Select the Clone Stamp tool (⚒) from the toolbar. In the Clone Stamp options bar, set the Mode option to Normal. Select an appropriate sized, soft-edged brush. Set the Opacity to 50 percent or less, which will give you more control over the amount of cloning.

2. Pick an area adjacent to the wrinkle and sample it by holding down the Alt/Option key and clicking. Now click on the wrinkle. It's best if you just click on, and not click and "brush," the target area. If you click and drag the Clone Stamp tool, it'll smear the texture. Click incrementally, building up the cloned area with the sampled area until the wrinkle is gone. Again, don't go too far.

I used this method to remove the wrinkles shown in Figure 3.21. The result is shown in Figure 3.22.

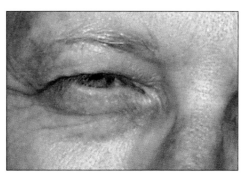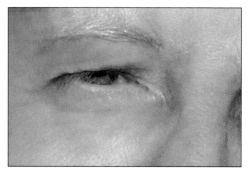

Figure 3.21: Before using the Clone Stamp tool. Figure 3.22: After using the Clone Stamp tool.

As shown in Figures 3.23 and 3.24, the Clone Stamp tool can also be used to remove blemishes and other unwanted artifacts from the face.

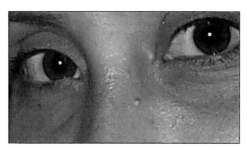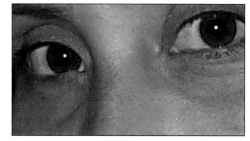

Figure 3.23: Before using the Clone Stamp tool. Figure 3.24: After using the Clone Stamp tool.

Diminishing and Straightening the Nose

Wide-angle lenses or oblique camera angles can make a nose seem much larger than it is. Again, the Liquify filter is a good way to diminish an unnaturally large nose—or to straighten a crooked one.

To use the Liquify filter to diminish or straighten a nose:

1. Select the nose by using any of the selection tools.
2. Choose Liquify from the Filter menu (Filter ➢ Liquify).
3. To diminish a nose, select the Pucker tool (⁖). Pick a brush size that fits over the entire nose. Select a brush pressure less than 50. Hold the cursor over the nose and click incrementally until you get the effect you want.
4. To straighten a nose, select the Warp tool (⬚). Click and drag to shift the nose into a straighter position.

I used a combination of these techniques to achieve the effects shown in Figures 3.25 and 3.26, and in Figures 3.27 and 3.28.

Figure 3.25: Before applying the Liquify filter. *Figure 3.26: After applying the Liquify filter.*

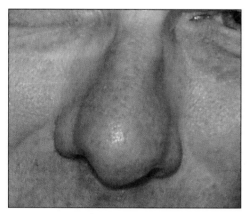
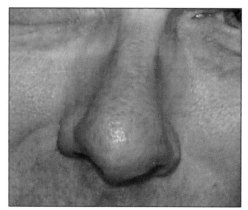

Figure 3.27: Before applying the Liquify filter. *Figure 3.28: After applying the Liquify filter.*

Shooting Digital: Making a Better Portrait

Getting a person to relax is essential to taking a good portrait. And before they can relax, you must relax too. If you are nervous or unsure of yourself, your subject will respond accordingly. Make an effort to smile, be confident, and at least act like you know what you're doing. It helps also to know ahead of time where you will be shooting the picture. Scout out a quiet spot with good light (window light works well) and a simple, uncluttered background. Many digital cameras enable you to instantly view a picture on an electronic display. Show your subject a few shots and engage them in the process. Before you know it, that fake smile will disappear and be replaced by a real one.

Making People Glow

In the "old days" I used to stretch a nylon stocking over my darkroom enlarger lens to give a portrait a glamorous, dreamy glow. It's easy to simulate this look with Photoshop Elements.

Look at the difference between Figures 3.29 and 3.30.

Figure 3.29: The original photo. Figure 3.30: It's easy to create a softer look.

Here's what I did to create the softer effect:

1. I selected and made a copy of the background layer and named it **Blur**. (Copy a selected layer by either choosing Layer ➢ Duplicate Layer from the menu bar, or choosing Duplicate Layer from the Layers palette menu. You can also duplicate a layer by selecting it and dragging it to the New Layer button (▣) at the bottom of the Layers palette. Windows users can right-click on the layer bar—but not the thumbnail—and choose Duplicate Layer from the pop-up menu. Mac users can do the same by Ctrl+clicking on the layer bar.)

2. With the **Blur** layer selected, I applied a strong Gaussian blur (Filters ➢ Blur ➢ Gaussian Blur). The exact amount of blurring will depend on the size of your image. In the case of this image, I chose a Radius of 30 pixels from the Gaussian Blur filter dialog box.

3. In the Layers palette, I selected Soft Light from the Blending Mode pop-up menu (see Figure 3.31). (You can also experiment with the Hard Light and Screen blending options.) I diminished the Opacity setting in the Layers palette to 90 percent, which gave me the effect I wanted. Again, the exact opacity will depend on your image.

4. I liked the effect of the blurring on the face. However, I wasn't pleased with the way the effect blurred the tie and shirt area. To selectively remove the effect from that area, I chose the Eraser tool (✐) from the toolbox and selected an appropriate sized, soft-edged brush. With the **Blur** layer selected, I used the eraser to remove the blur effect from the tie and shirt area (see Figure 3.32).

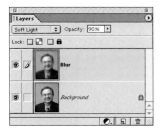 

Figure 3.31: The soft look is created with a combination of blurring and different Layer settings. Figure 3.32: The blur effect is selectively removed from the neck and chest area with the Eraser tool.

As you can see in Figure 3.33, the effect also works well in grayscale. To soften this image, I followed the same steps; however, before I began, I desaturated the image by choosing Enhance ➢ Color ➢ Remove Color from the main menu bar. I also chose Screen, instead of Soft Light, from the Blending Mode pop-up menu and dropped the Opacity setting to 25 percent. I also could have turned the color image into black-and-white by changing the mode from RGB to Grayscale (Image ➢ Mode ➢ Grayscale from the main menu).

Figure 3.33: The soft-focus effects work with black-and-white as well.

Creating a Grainy 35mm Black-and-White Look

What do you think of when you see an old, grainy, black-and-white print? To me it evokes the '60s and '70s and movies like *Blow-Up*. Whatever. The fact is, it's easy to simulate this grainy, gritty look with Photoshop Elements.

That's what I did to a contemporary color photo I took of my hip friend Leonard Koren (see Figures 3.34 and 3.35). Koren is a prolific author and creator of the '70s avant-garde magazine, *Wet*.

Figure 3.34: The original color image. Figure 3.35: The image after applying desaturation and the Noise filter.

Here's how I created the effect I wanted:
1. I desaturated the color image (Enhance ➢ Color ➢ Remove Color).
2. I used Levels to increase the contrast (Enhance ➢ Brightness/Contrast ➢ Levels).
3. I applied the Noise filter (Filter ➢ Noise ➢ Add Noise). In the Add Noise filter dialog box, I chose Gaussian rather than Uniform to authentically duplicate the erratic size and shape of silver halide crystals. To prevent the introduction of color, I checked Monochromatic (see Figure 3.36). I played with the Amount setting until I got the look I wanted. In this case, 30 percent was about right.

Figure 3.36: Add Noise filter dialog box and settings.

To duplicate a similar effect, you can also try the Mezzotint filter (Filter ➢ Pixelate ➢ Mezzotint). I prefer the Add Noise filter because I have more control over the way the image looks, but some people may prefer the Mezzotint look.

Using Digital Fill Flash

It's common to take a picture of a person against a bright background. However, if you don't use a fill flash or specifically expose for the skin tones, a face will turn into a silhouette (see Figure 3.37). Photoshop Elements includes a useful Fill Flash command that does a good job of creating a digital fill flash effect, balancing the foreground with the background (see Figure 3.38).

Figure 3.37: Before applying the Fill Flash, the faces are too dark. Figure 3.38: After applying the Fill Flash, both the faces and background are fine.

Here is what I did to fix this picture:

1. I selected Fill Flash from the Enhance menu (Enhance ➢ Fill Flash).
2. I dragged the Lighter slider settings until the faces looked right.
3. I clicked OK. That's all. It was that easy.

Making Distorted Faces Normal

Facial distortion is often caused by inferior optics or by the inherent effect of wide-angle lenses. It can also be caused by illness or certain prescription drugs. I've noticed that some faces are more puffy in the morning than later in the day, or at certain times of the month. Whatever the cause, if the distortion is unwanted, you can use Photoshop Elements' Transform tools to compress and reshape a face.

Selectively Fixing a Face

See the boy on the lower left of the image in Figure 3.39? This is not the normal face of my little friend Ryan; it's the result of an optical distortion caused by Ryan being situated near the edge of the picture frame. Interestingly, the other faces are unaffected. And yes, the fish was that big—that's no distortion. The trick here is to selectively fix the distorted face and leave the others alone. With a good suggestion from my artist friend Tom Mogensen, I fixed the image by using Photoshop Elements' Transform commands. (You can also use the Liquify filter, but it's more difficult to get good results.)

Here's what I did, using the Transform commands:

1. I loosely selected Ryan's body by using the Lasso tool (⌞) (see Figure 3.40).
2. I copied the selection and pasted it. (It's fastest to use the keyboard commands to do this: Ctrl/Command+C copies, and Ctrl/Command+V pastes. When you paste, a new layer is automatically created containing only your selection.) I named the layer **Ryan**.

66

BETTER FACES

Figure 3.39: Bad optics caused off-center distortion in this image.   *Figure 3.40: First I selected the distorted area with the Lasso tool.*

3. With the **Ryan** layer selected, I put the pointer on the layer bar—but not the thumbnail—and then clicked while holding the Ctrl/Command key. This simple keyboard command re-selects Ryan without having to use any selection tools.

4. With **Ryan** selected, I chose Image ➤ Transform ➤ Free Transform from the menu bar. Before fixing the distortion, I needed to make Ryan slightly larger. You'll see why shortly. I did this by holding the Shift key and grabbing the side handles and dragging until Ryan was just a little bigger. Holding the Shift key while I did this ensured that no distortion occurred. When I was done, I applied the Resize command by clicking the Commit Transform button (✔) at the top of the options bar.

5. Now I was ready to fix the distortion. To do this, I chose Image ➤ Transform ➤ Distort. I moved the side handles inward, alternating between the handle on the left and the one on the right. I "squeezed" Ryan until he was just right and then I clicked the Commit Transform button at the top of the options bar (see Figure 3.41).

*Figure 3.41: With the **Ryan** layer selected, I applied a Transform ➤ Distort command.*

6. When I was finished, I flattened the layers by using the Layers palette.

The reason I enlarged Ryan in step 4 should now be obvious. If I hadn't enlarged him before "squeezing" him, I would have had an obvious overlap with the original Ryan. As it is now, there is almost a perfect match, and I don't need to do anything else except clean up around the edges a little with the Clone Stamp tool (♣).

Globally Making a Face More Symmetrical

Figure 3.42 shows another example of distortion caused by poor optics. In this case, artist Tom Mogensen used a digital video camera at a San Francisco Giants baseball game to capture a still image frame of the legendary Bobby Thomson and Debby Magowan, the wife of one of the owners of the Giants. Instead of selectively fixing just one face as I did in the preceding example, Tom applied a global fix to the entire image.

Figure 3.42: This distortion is global and affects the entire image. (Photo by Tom Mogensen.)

Here is what he did:

1. He selected the entire image (Select ➢ All).
2. He selected Image ➢ Transform ➢ Distort.
3. He dragged the right side handle slightly toward the center, then the left side handle toward the center. He went back and forth until the faces looked just right. When he was finished, he clicked the Commit transform button (✔) at the top of the options bar. Figure 3.43 shows the results.

Figure 3.43: After applying the Transform ➢ Distort command, the image looks normal.

Fixing Hair

You can do a lot to hair with the help of Photoshop Elements. You can tint it, you can change the color entirely, you can shape it, and you can even add or delete it. As usual, the subtle approach is the most realistic.

Changing Color and Trimming a Beard

Tracy took the photo in Figure 3.44 of her husband, Chris, in their backyard in Chico, California. Tracy told me that she wanted to see her husband without the gray. "And, oh, by the way," she asked, "could you trim his beard as well?"

Figure 3.44: Chris in real life. Figure 3.45: Chris with his beard trimmed and darkened.

This is what I did:

1. I selected the Burn tool (🖐) from the toolbar.
2. I selected an appropriate sized, soft-edged brush and set the Range to Midtones and the Opacity to 50 percent.
3. I burned until the beard was the right shade.
4. I selected the Clone Stamp tool (🔖) and carefully trimmed the edges.
   The results are shown in Figure 3.45.

Adding Hair

Hair, or the lack of it, can be a sensitive subject. I want to thank my friend Jonathan for agreeing to let me use a before and after shot of him and his family to illustrate what Photoshop Elements can do to, well...add hair. Check out Figures 3.46 and 3.47.

Figure 3.46: Jonathan and his family before.   *Figure 3.47: Jonathan and his family after.*

Here is what I did to go from the before shot to the after shot:

1. I made a new layer and named this layer **Hair** (Layer ➢ New).
2. I selected the Clone Stamp tool (⚒) and chose an appropriate sized, soft-edged brush from the options bar. I set the Mode to Normal and the Opacity to 80 percent. I made sure that All Layers was checked in the options bar.
3. With the **Hair** layer selected, I sampled Jonathan's son's hair with the Clone Stamp tool. (To take a sample, click on the desired area while holding the Alt/Option key.) I then brushed Jonathan's head, filling it with the hair from his son. This new set of hair was painted on its own layer, keeping the real Jonathan intact for future reference (see Figure 3.48).

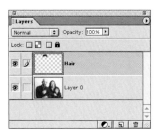

Figure 3.48: The new hair is on its own layer.

4. When I was finished, I selected the background layer containing Jonathan and his family and, using the Burn tool (✋), burned in his beard.

Changing the Color and Tinting Hair

My hairdresser, Robert, tells me that most of the colorizing he does is really lightening and darkening certain parts of the hair to model or mold it. The secret, he says, is to lighten the front part so it creates a glow around the face while darkening the back to bring out the highlights in the front. He also adds streaks of light and dark to give the hair a sense of depth. All of this is easy to do in Photoshop Elements. Look at the difference between Figures 3.49 and 3.50.

Figure 3.49: Before. Figure 3.50: After.

Here is what I did to add the highlights:

1. I chose New layer from the Layer menu (Layer ➢ New ➢ New Layer). This brought up the dialog box shown in Figure 3.51. Here I chose Color Dodge from the Mode pop-up menu and selected Fill with Color-Dodge-Neutral Color (Black). I named this layer **Highlights**. Then I clicked OK.

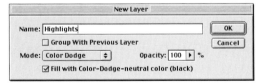

Figure 3.51: By selecting a new layer with these settings, you can literally paint highlights onto an image.

2. I selected the Airbrush tool (✎) from the toolbar. I selected an appropriate sized, soft-edged brush from the options bar and set the Mode to Normal and the Pressure to 4 percent. In the Color Picker at the bottom of the toolbox, I selected white for the foreground. On the layer called **Highlights**, I applied the airbrush to the hair in the front, airbrushing lightly until I got the right amount of "modeling."

3. To enhance the shadows, I created another new layer (Layer ➤ New ➤ New Layer). This time in the dialog box, I chose Color Burn from the Mode pop-up menu and selected Fill with Color-Dodge-Neutral Color (White). I named this layer **Shadow**. I applied the Airbrush tool to this layer, but this time I painted the back of the hair with a black foreground color instead of white. Figure 3.52 shows all my layers after painting with the airbrush.

Figure 3.52: Highlights and shadows are painted onto their own layers.

It's easy to add color to hair by using the Red Eye Brush tool. Compare Figures 3.53 and 3.54.

Figure 3.53: Hair before using the Red Eye Brush. *Figure 3.54: Hair after using the Red Eye Brush.*

Here's what I did to go from the first image to the second:

1. I chose the Red Eye Brush ( ) from the toolbar. In the options bar, I chose First Click from the Sampling pop-up menu and set the Tolerance to 33 percent. I sampled a color from the bird by using the Eyedropper tool ( ) in the tool-box and used that color as the replacement color.

2. Then I applied the color to the hair. That's all. It's that easy.

Getting Rid of Glasses Glare

Glare from glasses is always distracting. Look at Figure 3.55. The glare on the left is noticeable but slight and it is easy to fix. The glare on the right fills the lens and blocks a view of the eye. Although it takes a bit more work, it's also relatively easy to fix. Figure 3.56 shows the results.

Figure 3.55: The glare on the left lens is easy to fix; the glare on the right takes a little more work. Figure 3.56: Glare gone.

To fix the glare on the left:

1. I selected the Clone Stamp tool (🖳). In the options bar, I choose an appropriate sized, soft-edged brush and set the Mode to Normal and the Opacity to 75 percent.

2. I sampled an area outside the glare and then "cloned" this area to the glare.

To fix the glare on the right:

1. I used the Lasso tool (👁) to make a selection of the left eye. I then made a copy of this and pasted it onto its own layer (Ctrl/Command+C and then Ctrl/Command+V). I named this layer **Right Eye**.

2. I selected the eye in the layer called **Right Eye**. (An easy way to do this is to put the pointer on the layer bar—but not the thumbnail—and then click while holding the Ctrl/Command key.)

3. I chose Image ➢ Rotate ➢ Flip Horizontal from the main menu bar. This effectively made the left eye a right eye.

4. I moved the eye by using the Move tool (🛦) in the toolbox. I positioned it over the glare on the right side.

5. I used the Clone Stamp tool to touch up the edges and make the fit perfect.

Outside shots depend *a lot on the undependable. The weather may not cooperate. Power lines, telephone poles, or even people can get in the way. It may be the wrong time of year or the wrong time of day. It may even be day when you really want night. You lose a lot of control when a picture is taken outside, but with the help of Photoshop Elements you can get some of it back.*

4

Better Outside Shots

Intensifying the Sky
Changing the Time of Day
Working with the Midday Sun
Adding Lighting Effects
Working around a Difficult Angle
Making a Bluer Pond and
    Greener Grass
Removing Unwanted Objects
Adding Selective Focus
Using Statue Fill Flash

Better Outside Shots

Intensifying the Sky

Many outside shots benefit from a dramatic sky filled with intense colors, interesting cloud patterns, or even a rainbow. Techniques I described earlier will help many skies reach their full potential (↝ "Making Dull Images Shine" in Chapter 2). However, if your digital image inherently suffers from a boring sky, you can use some other simple Photoshop Elements' techniques to "clone" a dramatic sky from one digital image and place it instead on another.

Cloning Clouds

Figure 4.1 is a photograph I took on the Spanish island of Menorca. It's not a bad photograph, but a dramatic sky would make it a lot better.

By using Photoshop Elements, I was able to create the new image shown in Figure 4.2. You can apply these techniques to make your own dramatic sky.

Figure 4.1: By cloning a sky from another image, this photo will become a lot more interesting. ◎ *Figure 4.2: This is the same photo with a new sky.*

This is what I did to create the new image:

1. I opened the image shown in Figure 4.1 and another image containing a dramatic sky, shown in Figure 4.3. Both of these images came from a Kodak Photo CD and were opened at 1536 × 1024 pixels at 144 pixels/inch. (If your images have resolutions that are different from each other, resample the image containing the dramatic sky to match the resolution of your target image. To resample, select Image ➢ Resize ➢ Image Size and type in the matching pixel values.)

Figure 4.3: These clouds will liven up almost any sky.

2. In the image containing the man and the horse, I created a new layer and called it **Clouds** (Layer ➤ New ➤ Layer). I did this because I wanted to clone the new sky to its own layer and keep the old sky intact.

3. I selected the Clone Stamp tool (⎈) from the toolbar and selected the image containing the dramatic sky. In the options bar, I selected the following: Brush: Soft Round 300 pixels; Mode: Normal; Opacity: 100 percent; Aligned: checked on; Use All Layers: checked on. (The brush size you choose will depend on your image.)

4. I positioned the cursor to the top far left of the dramatic sky and, while holding the Alt/Option key, I clicked and sampled.

5. I placed the cursor on the top far left of the image of the man and the horse and "painted" the new sky. I started with a horizontal stroke, going from left to right, filling in the top 33 percent of the sky. Then, *and this is very important*, I changed the opacity of the Clone Stamp tool in the options bar to 65 percent. I painted another horizontal layer of sky, this one just under the one that was painted at 100 percent opacity. I painted about 40 percent of the sky this way and stopped just above the top of the horse and the top of the rock talus. At this point, I wasn't very precise and some of the clone spilled over the horse and the rock talus. However, it didn't matter because the new sky was actually going on its own layer, the layer I called **Clouds**, and I would go back later and fix the overlapping areas (see Figure 4.4).

Figure 4.4: By keeping **Clouds** as its own layer, I can go back and edit or enhance it at any time.

6. When I was finished cloning the new sky onto the old, I selected the Move tool (✛) from the toolbar. With the layer called **Clouds** still selected, I put my cursor on the image window, and clicked and dragged the sky around until it was positioned exactly as I wanted.

7. I choose the Eraser tool (⌀) from the toolbar. I selected the following options from the options bar: Brush: Soft Round 100 pixels; Mode: Paintbrush; Opacity: 100 percent; Wet Edges: deselected. On the layer called **Clouds**, I carefully erased the clouds and sky away from the horse, the man, and the rock. (For the detailed areas, I used a Soft Round 35 pixels and a Soft Round 17 pixels brush.)

8. I enhanced the clouds by applying Levels to the **Clouds** layer only (Enhance ➤ Brightness/Contrast ➤ Levels). Finally, I used the Crop tool (⌗) to crop off a small part of the right side of the image, where the cloned sky didn't fit quite to the edge.

9. At this point, I could have flattened my image (Layer ➤ Flatten Image, or Flatten Image from the Layers palette menu), or just saved my image with the two layers intact. Keeping the two layers increases the file size, but I kept them because I wanted the option of going back and tweaking my image, or even restoring the original sky if I wanted.

In some cases, when you are transferring an entire sky from one image to another, it's not a bad idea to use a copy-and-paste technique rather than using the Clone Stamp tool. For this particular image, however, I needed to gradually blend the two skies. The Clone Stamp tool enabled me to do this by giving me the ability to change the opacity as I painted.

Adding a Rainbow

Even just a hint of a colorful rainbow can liven up a sky, especially a black-and-white sky. I took the photograph shown in Figure 4.5 at Higgins Lake in northern Michigan. The docked boat is the *Rainbow*, my father-in-law's prized 100-year-old wooden launch. I didn't have time to wait until a real rainbow appeared, so I had my wife point to an imaginary rainbow and left the rest to Photoshop Elements. Figure 4.6 shows the final image.

Figure 4.5: Waiting for a rainbow. Figure 4.6: After the rainbow is selected from another image, it is pasted onto the new image and then positioned, resized, enhanced, and blurred.

Here's what I did to add the rainbow:

1. I opened both the image of the boat and another image that contained a rainbow (see Figure 4.7). The photo of the boat was shot with traditional black-and-white film and scanned. The rainbow was shot in South Africa on color film, obviously, and also scanned.

Figure 4.7: I "borrowed" this South African rainbow.

2. Using the Lasso tool (⌇), I selected the real rainbow, giving my selection generous room all around. I then copied and pasted the selected rainbow onto the image with the lake and the boat. I named the layer that was automatically created when I pasted, **Rainbow**.

3. On the **Rainbow** layer, I selected the Free Transform command (Image ➢ Transform ➢ Free Transform) and slightly stretched and rotated the rainbow, moving it into position under a dark cloud.

4. To intensify the rainbow, I selected the Sponge tool (⬭) from the toolbox and from the options bar set it to Saturate Midtones. I set the Opacity option at 75 percent and chose a Soft Round 100 pixels brush. With the Rainbow layer active, I clicked and brushed over the rainbow until I got the color saturation I wanted. I then used the Eraser tool (⌇) to erase the excessive blue that came over with the initial copy-and-paste. As a final step, I then applied a strong Gaussian blur to make the rainbow look more realistic.

When I printed a copy of the image for my father-in-law, he just assumed that the rainbow had magically appeared and he got a picture he'd always wanted.

Changing the Time of Day

Photographers and artists love morning and evening light. It's when the sun is angled to the horizon and the shadows are long and dramatic. Sunset light is especially pleasing when the light passes through a thick layer of particulates, such as smog, moisture, or dust. Midday light, on the other hand, is much more difficult to work with. Depending on the time of year and the place, the light is harsh, and shadows are short and intense.

With Photoshop Elements, you can imitate the golden light of a sunset or even change day to night. Here are some specific examples with techniques you can use on your own digital images.

Midday to Sunset

Figure 4.8 shows a beautiful scene taken in San Francisco around 3 P.M. by professional photographer Monica Lee.

Figure 4.8: This photo is beautiful but could benefit from a warm sunset light. (Photo by Monica Lee.)

I thought the photo might benefit from a warmer, more golden sunset light, and with Monica's permission I set out to change the time of day. Here's what I did using Photoshop Elements:

1. I opened the image and made a new layer called **Sunset Light** (Layer ➢ New ➢ New Layer). I set my layer Opacity to 56 percent and the Mode to Color Burn.

2. I selected an appropriate color for my warm tint. I did this by clicking the foreground color selection box in the toolbox. This brought up the Adobe Color Picker, the default color picker. Here I chose a color with the following RGB values: R = 255, Green = 204, and Blue = 102 (see Figure 4.9).

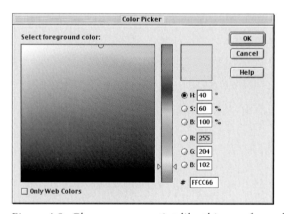

Figure 4.9: Choose a warm tint like this one from the Adobe Color Picker.

3. I selected the Gradient tool () from the toolbox. I chose the following settings from the options bar: Gradient Picker: Foreground to Transparent; Type of Gradient: Linear Gradient; Mode: Normal; Opacity: 100 percent (see Figure 4.10). Then, with the empty **Sunset Light** layer selected, I applied the Linear Gradient tool to the image. I did this by holding the Shift key and dragging the cursor from the bottom of the image window half way up, just past the top of the row of houses. Holding the Shift key while I did this constrained the angle to 45 degrees. (I used the Linear Gradient tool to apply the warm tint, but you can also apply the tint selectively by using the Airbrush ( ) or Paintbrush ( ) tools. Just be sure to apply the color to a layer of its own, using the color values from step 2 and the **Sunset Light** layer specifications from step 1.)

Figure 4.10: Set the Gradient tool options as shown.

4. After I applied the warm tint, I noticed that the sky looked too light for the late hour I was trying to imitate. To darken the sky, I created a Levels adjustment layer and adjusted the entire image so the background darkened appropriately. I then selected the Gradient tool and kept the same settings as described in step 3. However, I clicked the Default Colors icon ( ) (you can also use the shortcut key *D*) to set the colors in the color selection box to their default colors in the toolbox, and reset my foreground and background colors to black-and-white. I then used the Gradient tool on the adjustment layer to create a mask that prevented the levels adjustment from affecting the foreground (see Figure 4.11). More information on this technique is provided earlier in this book (↪ "Complex but Powerful: Layer Adjustments with Masks" in Chapter 2.)

5. The result is shown in Figure 4.12.

Figure 4.11: Note the Layer options for **Sunset Light** *and the adjustment layer mask.*
Figure 4.12: The new image now bathed in sunset light.

Morning to Sunset

Figure 4.13 shows a shot I took of the ancient Mayan ruins in Tikal, Guatemala. Even though it was early morning and the jungle mist hadn't cleared, the light had a bluish tint.

Figure 4.13: This jungle scene lacked warmth.

I wanted the image to feel warmer, more tropical, so I did the following:

1. With the Tikal image open, I made two copies of my background layer and named these layers **Sharpen** and **Blur**. (The easiest way to duplicate a layer is to select the layer and drag it to the New Layer button (□) at the bottom of the Layers palette.) I created a new layer and called it **Tint**. (The easiest way to create a new layer is to click the New Layer button.) Figure 4.14 shows my Layer palette. The layer order is important.

Figure 4.14: Note the layer blending and opacity settings for the selected **Tint** layer. Refer to the text for the **Sharpen** and **Blur** blending and opacity settings.

2. To the layer called **Blur**, I applied a strong Gaussian blur (Filters ➤ Blur ➤ Gaussian Blur) and set the Radius setting to 5.7. I left the **Blur** layer blending Mode to Normal and set the layer Opacity to 58 percent.

3. To the layer called **Sharpen**, I applied an Unsharp Mask (Filters ➤ Sharpen ➤ Unsharp Mask). I used the following settings: Amount: 100 percent; Radius: 1.9 pixels; Threshold: 0 Levels. I then set the **Sharpen** layer Opacity to 61 percent and left the blending Mode at Normal.

4. I filled the **Tint** layer with a light orange tint. To do this, I clicked on the foreground color selection box in the toolbox and then selected in the Adobe Color Picker a color with the following RGB values: R = 255, Green = 204, and Blue = 102. I selected Fill from the Edit menu and chose the settings from the dialog box shown in Figure 4.15. You can also use the Paint Bucket tool (🖌) to fill the **Tint** layer. Just be sure your Fill option in the option bar is set to Foreground and not Pattern. (I want to acknowledge Photoshop master Brad Johnson for concocting this particular tint, which I use often.)

5. I set the Mode of the **Tint** layer to Color Burn, and the Opacity to 44 percent, and I was done. The final image is shown in Figure 4.16.

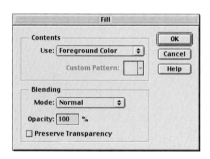

Figure 4.15: Fill settings. Figure 4.16: The final image.

It may seem counterintuitive to apply both a Sharpen and Blur effect to the same image, but rather than canceling each other, the combination of the two effects gave my image a soft, dreamy look and yet kept much of the sharpness in some of the detailed areas. I also could have modified the effects of these two layers by using the Eraser tool (✐) and selectively erasing each effect from certain areas.

Shooting Digital: The Rules of Good Composition

Regardless of whether you are shooting a digital camera or a film camera, the rules of good composition remain the same. Somewhere in your picture there should be a focal point. This can mean arranging your shot to include a blooming branch in the foreground, or a large rock in the middle ground, or a dramatic sky in the background. Don't make the common mistake of assuming that, simply because a scene looks breathtaking to the eye, it will work as a photograph. Without a strong focal point, the camera translates the scene into a mush of small objects that are visually boring. Because most digital cameras don't capture very high resolution, shots without careful composition are especially uninteresting.

Day to Night

Figure 4.17 is a still frame grabbed from a Lexus 2001 TV ad. The shot was taken during the day, but the director, Melinda Wolf, decided afterward that it should have been shot during the night. Special-effects wizard Michael Angelo was called. Before working on the actual footage, Michael used Photoshop to show the director what the scene might look like at night. Michael used Photoshop 6 to originally create this image, but he kindly modified his procedure to show how it could be done using Photoshop Elements (see Figure 4.18).

Figure 4.17: This is how the shot looked during the day. Figure 4.18: This is how it would have looked at night.

This is what Michael did to get the results in Figure 4.18:

1. He made a duplicate layer and called it **Night**. To duplicate a layer, select the layer and drag it to the New Layer button (⬚) at the bottom of the Layers palette.

2. With the **Night** layer selected, Michael removed the color by choosing Enhance ➤ Color ➤ Remove Color. Then he selected Enhance ➤ Hue/Saturation and selected the Colorize option in the dialog box. He tinted the image blue by sliding the Hue slider to the right. He left the Saturation in the middle set at 50. Then he darkened the overall image by sliding the Lightness slider to the left. Because he selected Preview in the dialog box, all his changes were visible on the actual image and he could easily modify his settings to get exactly what he wanted (see Figure 4.19).

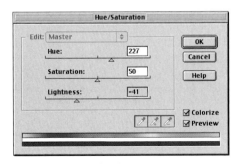

Figure 4.19: Michael's Hue/Saturation settings.

3. He created a duplicate layer of **Night** and called it **Lens Flare**.

4. To the **Lens Flare** layer, he applied the Lens Flare filter (Filters ➤ Render ➤ Lens Flare). See Figure 4.20 for the settings he used. He dragged the flare over one of the headlights and selected OK. He repeated these steps, selecting the Lens Flare filter again to apply another "headlight."

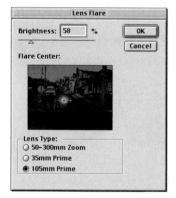

Figure 4.20: Settings for the Lens Flare filter.

5. He duplicated the **Lens Flare** layer and called this layer **Final**. On this layer, he used the Dodge tool (🖌) from the toolbox to paint the reflection of the headlights in the pavement.

The conversion of a single frame from day to night was a piece of cake for Michael compared to what he had to do to convert the entire film footage into night. That was a task for another program and a subject for another book!

Working with the Midday Sun

Figure 4.21 shows a field of wheat shot in the middle of the day by field biologist Laura Laverdiere of the Syngenta Crop Protection company. She used a digital camera to document the effects of different fertilizers and insecticides. The midday sun washed out much of the color, making it more difficult to see the difference between the healthy and unhealthy plants. Figure 4.22 shows the same field after Laura used Photoshop Elements to fix the shot.

Figure 4.21: The midday sun washes out color. *Figure 4.22: With a little help from Photoshop Elements, this is now a useful image. (Photos by Laura Laverdiere.)*

Making this right was a simple matter:

1. Laura applied Auto Levels to her image (Enhance ➤ Auto Levels).
2. She slightly increased the saturation (Enhance ➤ Color ➤ Hue/Saturation).

Adding Lighting Effects

Look at the image in Figure 4.23. The light is flat and monotonous. If we could just part the gray veil and bring out the sun, it might help. Well, with Photoshop Elements and its Lighting Effects filter, we can (see Figure 4.24).

Figure 4.23: This photo is waiting for a little divine intervention. Figure 4.24: The sun, thanks to the Lighting Effects filter. (Photos by Monica Lee.)

Here is what I did to create the image shown in Figure 4.24:

1. I made a copy of the background layer.
2. I selected the Lighting Effects Filter (Filter ➤ Render ➤ Lighting Effects, or use the Filters palette to apply the Lighting Effects). This brought up the dialog box shown in Figure 4.25.

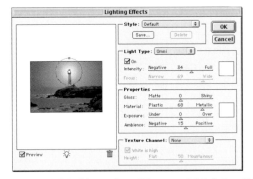

Figure 4.25: Photoshop Elements' Lighting Effects filter dialog box.

3. For Style, I chose Default.
4. For Light Type, I choose Omni, which created a light that shined in all directions. I selected the On check box (below the Light Type) and an Intensity of 34. Still in the Light Type section of the dialog box, I clicked in the color box and then chose white from the Color Picker.

5. I adjusted the Omni light by dragging the center circle in the preview window just over the top of the lighthouse. I played with the size of the light by dragging one of the handles defining the edges of the light until I got what I wanted.

6. To set the light properties, I dragged the corresponding sliders and chose the following:
   - For Gloss (which determines how much a surface area reflects), I left the slider at a neutral 0. (Matte creates a dull reflection, whereas Shiny creates a high reflectance.)
   - For Material, I slid the slider more toward Metallic.
   - I kept my Exposure at 0.
   - For Ambiance, I moved the slider toward the positive, which increased the overall brightness of my image.
   - I left the color of the Ambience light white. (To change the ambient color, click the color box to the right of the Ambient slider and use the Color Picker that appears.)

How did I come up with these choices? To be honest, it was a lot of trial and error. Any time I made a choice, the image in the preview window changed, reflecting that choice. I played around until I got the quality of light that looked appropriate.

7. After I was finished, I clicked OK.

As you can see, the Lighting Effects filter opens many opportunities for changing the quality and direction of light in your digital image. It takes some time and experimentation to fully master its potential, but the extra effort is worth it.

Working around a Difficult Angle

Photographer Monica Lee got a call from her client at Pacific Bell. Pac Bell wanted her to be at Pt. Richmond at 8:45 A.M. to take a quick shot of a boat that the company was sponsoring for the gala opening of the yacht season. When she arrived, the boat was at the wrong angle to the rising sun. There was no time to turn the boat or to position herself differently without either walking on water or using a second boat. She leaned on a pole and tried her best, but because of the angle of the sun, the shadows still filled the faces, and the AstroTurf hanging off the side of the boat was deep in shadow.

Figure 4.26: Photoshop Elements can help when you have no choice but to shoot from the wrong angle, at the wrong time of day. (Photo by Monica Lee.)

Here's what I did to make the photo shown in Figure 4.26 more useable:

1. I made a new Levels adjustment layer. To do this, click the New Adjustment Layer button (▢) at the bottom of the Layers palette and choose Levels.

2. I adjusted the Levels until the AstroTurf and the faces were more visible.

3. As you can see in Figure 4.27, the rest of the image was now unacceptable. I selected the Airbrush tool (✐) from the toolbox and chose black as a foreground color from the foreground color box. On the adjustment layer, I painted the "mask" over the areas that I didn't want affected by the Levels adjustment layers. You can see the mask in Figure 4.28. More information on creating a mask for an adjustment layer is presented earlier in this book (☞ "Complex but Powerful: Layer Adjustments with Masks" in Chapter 2).

Figure 4.27: With a Levels adjustment layer, the faces and AstroTurf are fine, but the rest of the image is blown out. Figure 4.28: Masking the Levels adjustment layer makes the rest of the image OK.

4. As a final step, I made a copy of the background layer and turned off the visibility of the original background layer. On the copy of the background layer, I selected the Burn tool (✋) from the toolbox and slightly darkened the sky and other areas of the image, including the lettering on the banner. I worked on a copy of the background layer because I wanted to keep the original image intact and available for future reference.

The result is shown in Figure 4.29.

Figure 4.29: Now the image looks as if it were shot under better lighting conditions.

Making a Bluer Pond and Greener Grass

It was a bad day for the golf course shown in Figure 4.30. The pond was brackish, and the grass looked like it hadn't been watered for weeks. Even the sky was blah. Web producer Sean Parker couldn't wait for the water to clear or the grass to get greener. He got to work using Photoshop Elements and turned things right around (see Figure 4.31).

Figure 4.30: The golf course before using Photoshop Elements. *Figure 4.31: The golf course after using Photoshop Elements.*

This is what he did to go from Figure 4.30 to Figure 4.31:

1. Sean opened the image and created a duplicate layer of the background layer. (He always works on a duplicate layer so he can flip back and forth between the images and see how natural his changes look.)

2. He then selected the pond by using the Lasso tool (✐) from the toolbox and feathered the selection with a setting of 4 pixels (Select ➤ Feather). He selected the Color Cast eyedropper tool and clicked around the pond until he got the blue he wanted (Enhance ➤ Color ➤ Color Cast).

3. He then inverted this selection (Select ➤ Inverse) and used Levels to increase the contrast and heighten the colors of the rest of the image (Enhance ➤ Brightness/ Contrast ➤ Levels).

4. He then selected the grass in the foreground with the Lasso tool and feathered this selection 4 pixels. He increased the color saturation of this selection (Enhance ➤ Color ➤ Hue/Saturation).

5. He selected the area under the trees and used the Replace Color command (Enhance ➤ Color ➤ Replace Color) to replace the brown with green. More information on using the Replace Color command is provided later in this book (☞ "Changing a Product's Color" in Chapter 5).

Removing Unwanted Objects

Many times a picture is perfect, except for a power line or an unwanted sign or, for that matter, an unwanted person who wanders into your shot. Sometimes all it takes to get the picture right is a little Photoshop Elements blur here, or a burn there. Other times you'll need to remove the object entirely, and that's when the Clone Stamp tool or cut-and-paste techniques come in handy. In this section, I'll show you a couple of ways to remove unwanted objects.

Removing a Tarp from the Golden Gate Bridge

Photographer Monica Lee needed a shot of the Golden Gate Bridge, but on the day she picked to shoot it, the Highway and Transportation District wasn't cooperating. As you can see in Figure 4.32, they placed a yellow tarp right in the middle of the bridge. Monica got the shot, and I helped her remove the unwanted blemish.

Figure 4.32: Who put that yellow tarp in the middle of my picture? (Photo by Monica Lee.)

This is what I did:

1. I made a selection from a nearby part of the bridge by using the Rectangular Marquee tool ( ) (see Figure 4.33). I copied this selection and pasted it on a layer that I called **Fix**.

Figure 4.33: I made a selection from a clean part of the bridge.

2. I used the Move tool (◥₊) from the toolbox to slide the fix into place over the yellow tarp. It didn't match up perfectly, so I selected the Free Transform command (Image ➤ Transform ➤ Free Transform) and turned the fix slightly so it did fit (see Figure 4.34).

3. I then used the Clone Stamp tool (♨) to remove the last bits of yellow on the bottom.

The results are shown in Figure 4.35.

Figure 4.34: I used the Free Transform command to position the pasted fix.   Figure 4.35: The fixed image.

Removing a Person

My wife, Rebecca, writes and photographs a monthly column for *Parents Press*. Mostly she takes pictures of our daughter and the daughter of her coauthor, or photos of other known kids. If an unknown child slips into a photograph, Rebecca is required by the magazine to get a model release before the magazine can use the picture. Occasionally she gets a shot that she wants to submit but that doesn't have a model release.

That's what happened in Figure 4.36. The person sliding down the slide is our daughter, so no problem using her image for the magazine, but who is the person behind her? Using Photoshop Elements, I made the image publishable, as shown in Figure 4.37.

Figure 4.36: The child in the background is recognizable. *Figure 4.37: After using the Burn tool, the child is no longer recognizable.*

Here's what I did to remove the unknown person:

1. I made a duplicate layer of the background.
2. I selected the Burn tool (☜) from the toolbox and selectively darkened the boy's face until it was unrecognizable.

For other pictures that contained unwanted or unusable faces, I've used the Blur tool (◊) to achieve a similar goal. You can also use the Mosaic Tiles filter (Filters ➤ Texture ➤ Mosaic Tiles) to achieve a *Cops*-like look.

Adding Selective Focus

Field biologist Laura Laverdiere is not hindered only by the difficulties of shooting under a midday sun. The digital camera she uses doesn't give her much creative control. For example, the camera is fully automatic, and it's impossible for her to choose a lens aperture and thereby increase or decrease the depth of focus. She gets around this limitation by using Photoshop Elements' Gaussian Blur filter selectively to create a sense of depth. By doing this, she calls attention visually to the critical parts of her image.

Figure 4.38 shows a chemically damaged leaf that Laura wanted to stand out. To emphasize the leaf, she did the following:

1. She created a duplicate layer and called this layer **Blur**.
2. With the Lasso tool, (⌒) she made an outline around the chemically damaged leaf and feathered this selection 3 pixels (Select ➢ Feather). Then she chose Select ➢ Inverse from the menu bar.
3. She applied a strong Gaussian blur with a 4.4 pixel setting to the selection (Filters ➢ Blur ➢ Gaussian Blur). She deselected her selection by typing the keyboard command Ctrl/Command+D. The results are shown in Figure 4.39.

Figure 4.38: A narrower depth of focus would be helpful.   *Figure 4.39: Now the damaged leaf jumps out. (Photos by Laura Laverdiere.)*

By working on a duplicate layer, Laura kept her original image intact. Also, if she wanted to selectively remove the Gaussian blur effect, all she had to do was use the Eraser tool (⌖) selectively on the Blur layer, and the unblurred areas in the background layer would be revealed.

Using Statue Fill Flash

Photoshop Elements' Fill Flash command—which I used earlier in the book (👉 "Using Digital Fill Flash" in Chapter 3) to illuminate two faces—works just as well on inanimate objects, as shown in Figures 4.40 and 4.41.

Figure 4.40: Before Fill Flash. 💿 *Figure 4.41: After Fill Flash.*

Here's what I did to fix the photo of an outdoor statue I took in Prague on a dreary day:

1. I opened the image.
2. I selected Enhance ➤ Fill Flash and adjusted the slider until I got the effect I wanted.

I love Photoshop Elements' Fill Flash. I really do.

Scanning Digital: Digitizing without Owning a Scanner

You don't have to own an expensive slide scanner to digitize your 35mm or APS film. A variety of retail outlets will take your film and in return give you a floppy disk or a CD containing a digitized version of your work. Just keep in mind that although these services are economical and convenient, they may not provide the image resolution you need.

The Kodak Picture CD, which is widely available at most photo finishing outlets, provides a 1536 × 1024 pixel file in the JPEG file format, which has less resolution than what is produced by many digital cameras. This resolution is adequate for monitor viewing or for making small prints. However, for higher-resolution scans I recommend stepping up to the Kodak Photo CD process. Kodak Photo CDs are more expensive than Picture CDs, and services that offer them are less widespread. (For a listing of businesses in your area that provide Photo CD service, go to **www.kodak.com/US/en/digital/products/photoCD.shtml**.) However, the Kodak Photo CD process scans and stores your negative or slide in a proprietary format, which allows for a single image to be stored in up to six different resolutions, ranging from 192 × 192 pixels all the way up to 2048 × 3072 pixels.

Photoshop Elements is especially good at opening these files via the File ➢ Open menu commands. Just go to the Photo CD file folder named **Photo_CD** and open the images from a folder titled **Images**. (Mac users: Do not open your images from a folder titled **Photos**, which contains images saved in the PICT format and intended for screen display, not hardcopy output.) A Kodak PCD Format dialog box appears after you select an image, offering you choices of resolution and color profiles and thereby making it possible to open an image that meets your exact requirements.

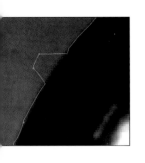

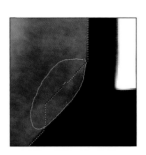

It doesn't matter *if you are selling your son's Power Ranger set on eBay or a vintage sports car through a community bulletin board. A professional looking image will help sell you or your stuff. Sure, it helps to have a fancy photo studio or a high-end advertisement budget. But you can go a long way to make a product shot taken with a consumer digital camera in your living room look better just by using various Photoshop Elements tricks and techniques. In this chapter, you'll learn how.*

5

Better Product Shots

Separating a Product from Its
    Background
Changing a Product's Color
Changing a Product's Texture
Adding Motion Blur
Changing Scale and Perspective
Fixing Keystoning
Improving the Background
Adding Depth
Creating Lighting Effects
Softening Highlights and Glare
Adding a New Label
Making a Product Smile
Simplifying a Product Shot

Better Product Shots

Separating a Product from Its Background

Just about anything you do to enhance or fix a product shot begins by using various selection or eraser tools to separate the product from its background. Only after you do this can you effectively do the following:

- Fix or replace a distracting background
- Colorize, texturize, or add motion blur to the product
- Add depth through a drop shadow or other layer effect

How hard is it to use Photoshop Elements to do this? It depends. I've been handed digital photos of products taken against a white or single-colored background and with a few clicks of the Magic Eraser tool finished the job in a few seconds. Other times, I've been handed a shot of a product placed against a busy background and spent way too much time using many of Photoshop Elements' selection and eraser tools to get the job done right.

Don't be discouraged if your results are less than perfect or if you feel you are taking an inordinate amount of time. The whole time you are trying, you are building skills and experience that will make the job easier next time. If you become really frustrated—and that is an appropriate alternative—you might even consider reshooting the product against a plain-colored background, which will make your Photoshop Elements work go easier and faster.

Note: When you choose and apply one of the several selection tools to an active layer, you'll get a dotted border that looks like an army of marching ants. Technically this is called a *selection marquee*, but I like to think of the little dots as protective ants, keeping the outside at bay. Any tool or task that you apply while the ants are in place will affect only the selected areas. For example, if you choose a Gaussian blur, the effect will apply only to the area that is bounded by the selection marquee. You can easily reverse the selection by choosing Selection ➤ Inverse from the menu bar or by using the keyboard command Ctrl/Command+Shift+I. Then, for example, when you apply a Gaussian blur, it will affect only the areas outside your original selection.

The relevant selection tools for this chapter include the Rectangular Marquee tool (▢), Elliptical Marquee tool (◯), Lasso tool (◯), Polygonal Lasso tool (◺), Magnetic Lasso tool (◺), and the Magic Wand tool (✎). More details on these and other selection tools are provided later in this book (⌇ "Selection Tools" in Zooming In).

When It's Easy

The image shown in Figure 5.1 makes me smile with joy. It's a shot taken with a digital camera of a plastic toy figure against a single-color background. All it needs is a few clicks with the Magic Eraser tool to remove similar pixels within a predetermined range. This will separate the toy figure from its background, and I can go on and make a really interesting shot.

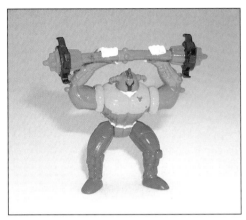

Figure 5.1: It's easy to remove a background when it's a single color. It doesn't matter if the color is slightly graduated.

Here's what I did to remove the background:

1. I chose the Magic Eraser (✍) from the toolbox. The Magic Eraser shares toolbox space with the Background Eraser (✍) and the other eraser tools. You can flip through the eraser tools by using the keyboard command Shift+E.

2. In the options bar, I used the following settings:
    - Tolerance: 60. I came up with this number after some trial and error. The default setting is 32, but when I used this number the Magic Eraser sampled too few variations of color and erased only a small part of the background (see Figure 5.2). When I tried a Tolerance of 85, it sampled too many colors and actually ate away, or erased, much of the foreground object as well as the background (see Figure 5.3). A tolerance of 60 wasn't perfect because it still required a few clicks in different parts of the background to do the job, but it was close enough. Theoretically, if my background had been exactly one color, a Tolerance setting of 1 would have removed all the background with one click. However, I've noticed that making a photo with no color or tonal variations in the background is difficult. Even when you use a perfectly white or single-colored background, the slightest variations in lighting result in different tonal values.

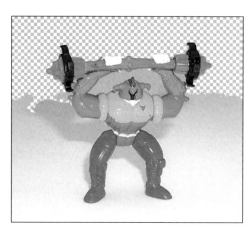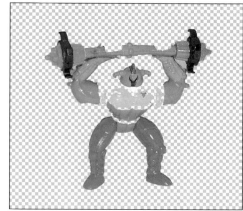

Figure 5.2: A Tolerance setting of 32 was too little. *Figure 5.3: A Tolerance setting of 85 was too much.*

- Anti-aliased: selected. This keeps a smooth transition between erased and non-erased parts.
- Contiguous: selected. This setting, which is the default, is very important. If I hadn't left it this way, the Magic Eraser would have assumed that I wanted to erase all similar pixels in the image and not just pixels contiguous to the one I clicked on. This means that, regardless of the Tolerance setting, if there had been a similar color anywhere in the image, even within the boundaries of the toy figure, these colors would have been erased as well.
- Use All Layers: selected. In this case, I had only one layer, so it didn't matter whether I selected this option. However, it would have made a difference if I had more than more layer and wanted to sample the erased color by using data combined from all visible layers.
- Opacity: 100 percent. I wanted to erase completely to transparency. A lower opacity would have erased the pixels to partial transparency. Frankly, for the purposes of erasing a background in preparation for other tasks, I can't think of a reason why you should choose anything less than 100 percent.

3. After I set my options, I clicked first on the top part of the image. As you can see in Figure 5.4, this only partially erased the background. Next I clicked lower in the image and got what you see in Figure 5.5. I continued clicking in the areas outside the parameters of the plastic toy figure until I got what you see in Figure 5.6.

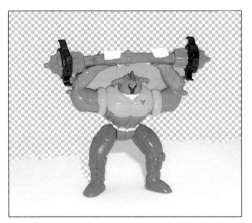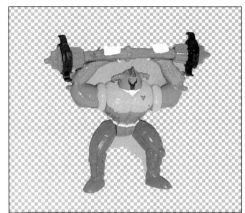

Figure 5.4: One click of the Magic Eraser erased part of the image. Figure 5.5: Another click erased more of the image.

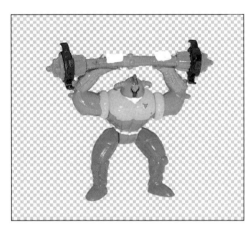

Figure 5.6: The Magic Eraser gets the job done.

When you use the Magic Eraser (or Background Eraser) on a background layer, as I did, you'll notice that the name in the Layers palette is automatically changed from **Background** to **Layer 0**. That's because a background layer can't contain transparency, and by changing its name its properties are also changed.

Note: What is a *transparent layer?* It's helpful to think of an illustration in a physiology book that shows the various parts of the human body in several translucent overlays. Viewed together, the layers make up the complete human body. But lift the layers and you can view each component–skin, muscles, skeleton, and internal organs–separately as well. This is basically what's happening when you place an object on a Photoshop Elements' transparent layer. The object, or technically, a grouping of pixels, is surrounded by a sea of transparency that is designated by a translucent checkered pattern. This pattern can be removed or changed (Edit ➢ Preferences ➢ Transparency) to make the transparent areas more or less obvious. If the layer that contains transparency sits above another layer, the non-transparent areas of the lower layer show through.

Note: In this chapter, I'll show you ways to create and use layers that contain transparency. Keep in mind that a background layer cannot contain transparency. If you cut or delete from a background layer, it will fill with the background color as defined in the color selection box located at the bottom of the toolbox. If you have a background layer and want transparency in that layer, you'll need to change the name of the background layer to something else. To do this, double-click on the layer in the Layers palette and either leave the default name, **Layer 0**, or type something else and click OK. You can also choose Layer ➤ New➤ Layer from Background from the menu bar.

By the way, what is the difference between the Magic Eraser and the Magic Wand (✎)? Not much. The Magic Eraser finds pixels of similar value and automatically *erases* them, either to transparency or, if the transparency is locked in the Layers palette, to the selected background color. The Magic Wand finds pixels of similar value and *selects* them.

In the preceding example, I could have used the Magic Wand to select the background and then hit the Delete key or chosen Edit ➤ Cut from the menu bar and I would have gotten the same effect (🖙 "Selection Tools" in Zooming In). Because one click of the Magic Wand wouldn't have been enough, just as it wasn't enough with the Magic Eraser, I then would have held the Shift key while clicking on other areas, thereby adding new selections without deselecting the preceding ones. Of course, to cut to transparency I also would have had to rename my background layer something else.

When It's a Little More Difficult

Look at Figure 5.7. The designer of the wine label, Lisa Friedman, didn't want me to get rid of the background; she just wanted me to tone it down a little so she could use the image to promote her design work. Because the background is filled with texture, this image is more difficult to work with than the preceding one.

Just for fun, let's try using the Magic Wand to select the background. (Forget the Magic Eraser because Lisa basically liked the background and didn't want to replace it.) I tried various Tolerance settings, but the Magic Wand always seemed to select pixels inside the bottle as well. There were just too many similarities in tone between the bottles and the background for the tool to work efficiently. In Figure 5.8 you can see the results when I choose a tolerance of 44.

Figure 5.7: The bottles and the background aren't very distinct. Figure 5.8: No matter what I did, I couldn't get the Magic Wand to select just the background.

Because the Magic Wand wasn't so useful, I decided to use a combination of two other selection tools, the Magnetic Lasso and the Lasso, which both share a spot in the toolbox.

Let's start with the bottle on the right and the Magnetic Lasso tool. Because the edges of this bottle are fairly well defined, the Magnetic Lasso's selection border should easily and automatically snap into place.

This is what I did to select the bottle on the right:

1. I selected the Magnetic Lasso tool (⚲) from the toolbox, and chose the following options from the options bar:
   - Feather: 0. This is the default setting.
   - Anti-aliased: selected. This is also the default setting.
   - Width: 40. The range here is 1–40, and I chose 40 because the image is relatively simple and has well-defined edges. This number means the Lasso is looking in a 40-pixel radius from the cursor for edge values. In other words, I don't need to be right up close to the edge I wish to select with the cursor. I can be within a 40-pixel range, and the cursor will still find the edge. This means I can be looser with the cursor and work a lot faster. Lower width values are critical when you are working on images with soft edges that are adjacent to other soft edges. In those cases, if you used a higher value, the Magnetic Lasso would easily get "confused" and place

anchor points on edges that you didn't want selected in the first place. With lower values, you need to be very precise in placing the cursor, and that definitely will slow you down.

- Edge Contrast: 30. The range here is 1–100 percent, and I choose 30 percent after some trial and error. Higher values are usually fine for very defined edges. I chose a relatively low number because the shadow areas around the top and bottom of the bottle were less defined, and when I selected a higher percent the Magnetic Lasso didn't do a good job of finding the edges.

- Frequency: 57. I left this at its default. This specifies the rate at which the Magnetic Lasso sets fastening points. A higher value anchors the selection border in place more quickly.

2. I started on the lower-right side of the bottle by clicking the mouse. This set the first fastening point, which anchored the selection border in place. Next, I moved the pointer along the edge of the bottle. As I moved the pointer, the active segment snapped to the strongest edge in the image based on my Width settings. As you can see in Figure 5.9, fastening points were periodically set based on my Frequency setting. I also set fastening points manually by clicking the mouse. For a close-up view, I used Ctrl/Command+spacebar+click to magnify my image and then held the spacebar to activate the Hand tool so I could scroll around the image.

A couple of times, as I was moving the Magnetic Lasso around a corner, my fastening point jumped way off the edge (see Figure 5.10). I did one of two things: I simply hit the Delete key, which brought me back to the last fastening point, where I tried again. Or I just left the mistake alone, knowing I was going back later anyway and fine-tuning the selection.

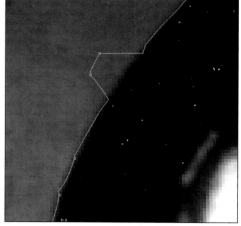

Figure 5.9: This magnified view shows the fastening points and selection border of the Magnetic Lasso tool. I've increased the contrast of the image so you can see the points and border better. Figure 5.10: This magnified view shows a fastening point gone awry. I'll go back later and fix it with the Lasso tool.

3. After I circled the bottle and was ready to close the selection border, I double-clicked. (You can also press Enter/Return, or click anywhere outside the document window.)

I then turned to the bottle on the left. Before I began using the Magnetic Lasso tool, however, I changed one important setting in the options bar. I selected the Add to Selection icon ( ). If I hadn't done this, after I clicked inside the image window my previous selection would have been deselected. I followed the preceding steps, keeping all the other options in the options bar the same. In some places, the edges of this bottle weren't as clearly defined as the other bottle, and the Magnetic Lasso was way off. After I was finished, I double-clicked.

Now that both bottles were selected and ready for fine-tuning, I turned to the Lasso tool. The Lasso tool lets you draw both straight-edged and freehand selections. And although it takes a steady hand to use it effectively, the Lasso tool gives you more of a sense of being in control than you might have with the Magnetic Lasso or Magic Wand.

This is how I fine-tuned selecting the bottles:

1. I selected the Lasso tool (◯) from the toolbox. Because I wanted to subtract from the selection, I chose the Subtract from Selection option (▣) in the options bar. (You can also hold down the Alt/Option key. A minus sign appears next to the pointer.)

2. I then clicked and dragged the cursor around the area that I wanted to subtract, following the edge of the bottle closely. After I released the cursor, the selection was updated to reflect the boundaries of my new selection. See Figure 5.11.

Note: To add to a selection, either choose Add to Selection from the options bar or hold down the Shift key. A plus sign (+) will appear next to the pointer.

Figure 5.11: Subtract from a selection by choosing Subtract from Selection and circling the area you want deselected.

I like the Magnetic Lasso a lot, but it takes getting used to. The first time I used it, I had no trouble. I was working on an image with clearly defined edges. However, not long after that I had a really frustrating experience with it. I was working on an image that didn't have clearly defined edges, and the selection border was constantly snapping into the wrong place. I didn't seem to have any control over where it was going; I felt I had stuck my fingers into a wad of bubble gum and couldn't shake it loose. I suggest that you spend some time getting to know more about this tool in the Adobe Online Help or elsewhere in this book (↜ "Selection Tools" in Zooming In).

Changing a Product's Color

With a product selected or deleted from its background, changing the product's color is easy. Let's try this on the plastic toy image shown in Figure 5.6. Its background is deleted, and the plastic toy is alone on a transparent layer.

Changing Color via the Hue/Saturation Command

Figure 5.12 shows the effect of changing the colors via the Hue/Saturation controls (Enhance ➤ Color ➤ Hue/ Saturation). All I did was slide the Hue slider until I got the colors I wanted (see Figure 5.13). Obviously, this method is easy and provides immediate gratification but it's useful only if you are trying to globally change or shift colors. If you want to change just one color or a specific range of colors, you'll find the following method a lot more useful.

Figure 5.12: Globally change color with the Hue/Saturation controls. Figure 5.13: Slide the Hue slider to change the color.

Changing Color via the Replace Color Command

Figure 5.14 shows the effect of selectively changing the color via the Replace Color command. This method is much more precise than the Hue/Saturation command because it enables you to create a mask around specific colors and then replace those colors in the image. You can change the saturation lightness of the masked area as well.

This is how I used the Replace Color command:

1. I selected the Replace Color command (Enhance ➤ Color ➤ Replace Color).

2. In the Replace Color command dialog box shown in Figure 5.15, I used the Eyedropper tool (✐) to select the pink colors in the legs and barbell. The black areas in the Preview box are the masked areas. I expanded the tolerance of the mask slightly to include more than the sampled colors by dragging the Fuzziness slider. The black areas in the Preview box expanded accordingly.

3. When I was satisfied that I had masked the areas I wanted, I dragged the Hue slider to get the color just where I wanted. Then I added some saturation with the Saturation slider.

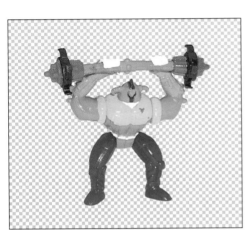
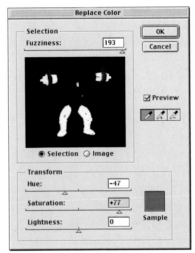

Figure 5.14: With the Replace Color command, I could selectively replace the pink with purple. Figure 5.15: The Replace Color command dialog box.

Changing Color via Painting

You can also selectively paint different colors with the Airbrush or Paintbrush tools. Before you do this, however, you must select the object so the painting or fill area doesn't spill over into the transparent areas.

To select the object in the Layers palette, on the layer containing your product and transparency, Ctrl/Command+click the layer thumbnail. Window users can also simply right-click on the layer thumbnail in the Layers palette. Another way to prevent color bleeding is to lock the transparent pixels. To do this, select the Lock check box in the upper part of the Layers palette.

Figure 5.16 shows what happens when the plastic toy isn't selected or the transparency isn't locked. The blue paint spills all over the canvas. Figure 5.17 shows how selecting or locking the transparency confines the paint to the plastic toy.

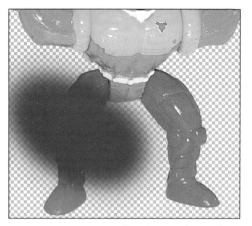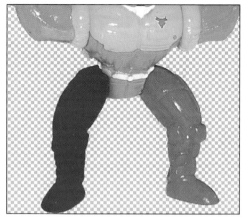

Figure 5.16: Paint spills all over if you don't select or lock the transparency of your image.
Figure 5.17: With the object selected or transparency locked, the paint goes only where you want it to go.

There are many things to consider when you use a brush tool to change or alter the colors. For example, you'll probably want to experiment with different Mode and Opacity settings, and in the case of the Airbrush, Pressure settings. If you leave your settings at their defaults (Mode: Normal, Opacity: 100 percent), you will replace an area that has tonal variations with a single, flat color, which may not be what you want. This is what happened in Figure 5.17.

Here is one simple way to use a brush to change or add colors and still maintain control over how the new paint blends with the old:

1. Assuming that the object you want to paint is already on a transparent layer, select it by Crtl/Command+clicking the layer thumbnail.

2. Create a new layer and name it **Color** (Layer ➢ New). Make sure this layer sits above the layer containing the figure you want to color.

3. Select the Airbrush tool ( ) or Paintbrush tool ( ) from the toolbox and pick a brush from the options bar. Keep the Option settings at their default. Select a color to work with from the foreground color box at the bottom of the toolbox.

4. Paint on the layer called **Color**. Make sure the selection from step 1 is still visible. If it's not, your paint will spill all over the layer and not be confined to the parts of the object you want to paint.

5. When you are finished painting, while keeping the **Color** layer active, experiment with different Mode and Opacity settings in the Layers palette.

The advantage of using this method is obvious. Because you are painting on a separate layer, your original image remains intact. If you don't like what you have, just delete the **Color** layer and start over. Also, you are not confined to one Mode or Opacity setting. You can go back and change these settings at any time until you get just the right blending of new and old colors.

Changing Color via the Paint Bucket Tool

Another simple way to replace color is via the Paint Bucket tool. Figure 5.18 shows an example of a product prototype created by product designer Marcia Briggs for L.L. Bean. Marcia made the line drawing by hand and then scanned it into her computer. Because the client wanted to see the product in various colors, Marcia left the original drawing uncolored, knowing how easy it was to use the Paint Bucket tool to create several versions.

This is what she did:

1. She selected the Paint Bucket tool (🖊) from the toolbox.
2. She left all the options in the options bar set at their defaults. Because she was working with a line drawing with basically no color variations to take into consideration, the Tolerance settings didn't matter. (The Paint Bucket tool looks for adjacent pixels that are similar in color value. The more colors you want to replace, the higher you must set the Tolerance values.)
3. She specified a foreground color from the foreground color box at the bottom of the toolbox. She clicked inside the area where she wanted the color. Then she chose another color and clicked inside another area. She did this until she got the results shown in Figure 5.19.

Figure 5.18: Marcia drew this product prototype and scanned it into the computer.
Figure 5.19: Marcia filled the bag with color by using the Paint Bucket tool.

By the way, even though Marcia was working with essentially a bitmap image, which is an image that contains only black or white, she stayed in the RGB mode (Image ➢ Mode ➢ RGB). Otherwise, she wouldn't have access to any other colors. Also, the Paint Bucket tool doesn't work in Bitmap mode.

Changing a Product's Texture

It's also easy to change the texture of a product or add a pattern after you have selected or separated it from its background. Let's try a variety of Photoshop Elements tools, filters, and fills and see what we come up with.

Adding Pattern via the Paint Bucket Tool

Let's go back to Marcia's bag. With her permission, I've applied a series of patterns by using the Paint Bucket tool. I also changed some of the colors (see Figure 5.20).

Figure 5.20: These patterns were created by using the Paint Bucket tool and setting the Fill option to Pattern.

Here's all I did to produce the patterns shown in this image:

1. I selected the Paint Bucket tool (🪣) from the toolbox.
2. In the options bar, I changed Marcia's Fill setting from Foreground to Pattern and then chose a pattern from the Pattern menu.
3. I clicked inside an area where I wanted the first fill pattern. Then I chose another fill pattern and clicked inside another area. I did this until I had I totally ruined a perfectly good bag.

Adding Pattern via the Fill Command

Look at the pattern shown in Figure 5.21.

To create this pattern, I did the following:

1. I selected the plastic toy by Crtl/Command+clicking the layer thumbnail.
2. I created a new layer and named it **Pattern** (Layer ➤ New). I made sure this layer sat above **Layer 0**, which contained the plastic toy (see Figure 5.22).

Figure 5.21: To create this pattern, I used the Fill command and selectively erased.
*Figure 5.22: With the plastic toy selected, I created a new layer, called it **Pattern**, and made it active.*

3. I selected Edit ➤ Fill from the menu bar, making sure that the layer called **Pattern** was active.

4. I selected Pattern in the Fill Use list and selected the fill of my choice in the Custom Pattern box (see Figure 5.23).

5. I clicked OK. Figure 5.24 shows the results.

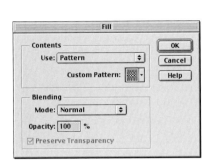

Figure 5.23: From the Fill Use list, I chose Pattern. Figure 5.24: The Pattern filled the plastic toy. I used the Eraser tool to selectively remove it.

The pattern totally filled the plastic toy. To selectively remove the pattern, I selected the Eraser tool (✐) from the toolbox and selected a soft-edged brush from the options bar. On the layer called **Pattern**, I applied the eraser to the areas I wanted removed.

Another variation of this procedure is to apply a Texture or Image Effect from the Effects palette. If you use one of these effects, follow the procedure I just outlined, but after step 2 drag and drop the effect you want from the Effects palette onto the image window with the new layer selected. You can also double-click on the effect's thumbnail. Just remember to avoid using any texture from the Effects palette whose name is followed by the word *layer*. For example, if you use the Sunset (Layer) effect, the effect won't fill your selection, it'll fill the entire layer.

Adding Pattern via a Fill Layer

You can also apply a pattern (or, for that matter a solid color or gradient) via a fill layer. Not only is a fill layer nondestructive, but it also can be easily changed at any time.

To use a fill layer:

1. Select your object by Crtl/Command+clicking the layer thumbnail. This is important. If you don't select your object, the fill will completely fill a layer.

2. Choose Layer ➤ New Fill Layer ➤ Pattern (or Solid Color or Gradient). You can also select Pattern (or Solid Color or Gradient) directly from the Layers palette. Just click the Create New Fill or Adjustment Layer icon (◕) at the bottom of the Layers palette.

3.   Choose from the various palette choices (see Figure 5.25).

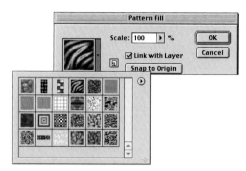

Figure 5.25: When you select Pattern from the New Fill Layer, you get the choices shown here.

4.   After you select your fill, you can go back later and edit the mask to selectively apply the fill (☞ "Making Dull Images Shine" in Chapter 2). Figure 5.26 shows the Layers palette for the image shown in Figure 5.27. Note that Opacity is set at 62 percent, which allows only part of the fill to show through. Note also that I've erased some of the layer mask.

Figure 5.26: Note the edited mask in the Pattern fill layer and the Opacity setting.
Figure 5.27: The final image after selectively applying a pattern fill and setting the layer Opacity to 62 percent.

Adding Pattern via a Filter

Many filters will create a pattern or texture effect. Especially useful are the ones found in the **Artistic, Noise, Pixelate, Reticulation,** and **Texturize** folders. These filters act on the actual pixels of the image, so I suggest that you create a duplicate of the layer containing the object you want to alter and apply the filter to the duplicate. That way, you can selectively erase or change the layer Mode or Opacity settings, as I did in the preceding example.

Here is an example of what I mean:

1. I duplicated the layer containing the plastic toy and called it **Stained Glass Filter.**

Note: To make a duplicate layer, select the layer you wish to duplicate and either choose Layer ➢ Duplicate Layer from the menu bar or select the layer and then drag it to the Create a New Layer icon (⬚) at the bottom of the Layers palette.

2. I applied the Stained Glass filter to the duplicate layer (Filter ➢ Texture ➢ Stained Glass from the menu bar, or drag and drop, or double-click, from the Filter palette).

3. Then from the Layers palette, I set the Mode to Color Burn and the Opacity to 46 percent. You can see my Layers palette in Figure 5.28 and the final image in Figure 5.29.

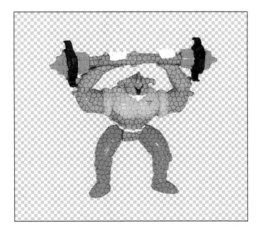

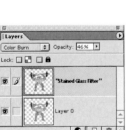

Figure 5.28: Note the duplicate layer called **Stained Glass Filter** *and the Mode and Opacity settings. Figure 5.29: The final image after applying the Stained Glass filter.*

And So On...

I think you get the idea. As you can see, there are many ways to add texture and fills to your product shot, or for that matter, to any digital image. Don't forget to experiment with different Opacity and Mode settings and erase areas in which the fill or texture isn't needed.

Adding Motion Blur

The photo shown in Figure 5.30 is a relatively mundane shot of a very nice vintage car. By removing the background and applying the Motion Blur filter, I gave this static shot some added motion.

Figure 5.30: The original image could use some motion.

Here are the steps:

1. I used the Magnetic Lasso tool ( ) and the Lasso tool ( ) to select the car ("Separating a Product from Its Background," earlier in this chapter). I wasn't precise because I knew that the Motion Blur filter would cover my sloppy work.
2. After selecting the car, I reversed the selection by choosing Select ➤ Inverse (Ctrl/Command+Shift+I) from the menu bar. Now the area surrounding the car was selected.
3. I changed the name of my background layer in the Layers palette to `Citroen`. Then I hit Delete on my keyboard to remove the area around the car and replace it with transparency. If I hadn't changed the name of the layer, my selected areas would have filled with the background color when I deleted.
4. I used the Eraser tool ( ) and the Clone Stamp tool ( ) to touch up the edges and to remove the roof rack (see Figure 5.31). Again, I wasn't precise.

Figure 5.31: After I deleted my selection to transparency, I touched up the edges and removed the roof rack. I wasn't precise.

5. I made a copy of the **Citroen** layer and renamed it **Motion Blur**. Additionally, I made a temporary background layer so I could see the effects of my next step. I did this by selecting Layer ➢ New Fill Layer ➢ Solid Color from the menu bar and made sure the new layer was the bottom-most layer. (You can also click on the Create New Fill or Adjustment Layer icon (●) on the bottom of the Layers palette and select Solid Color.)

6. I selected the layer named **Motion Blur** and ran the Motion Blur filter (Filters ➢ Blur ➢ Motion Blur) and chose the following values: Angle: 41, Distance: 185 pixels. (The effect of the Motion Blur filter will be unsatisfactory if you have locked your transparency in the Layers palette.) Figure 5.32 shows the Layers palette up to this point.

7. I selected the Eraser tool, and on the **Motion Blur** layer I selectively erased the effect. You can see in the final image why I didn't need to be precise in my selecting, erasing, and cloning (see Figure 5.33).

Figure 5.32: With Motion Blur on its own layer, I can selectively erase the effect.
Figure 5.33: The final image.

Shooting Digital: Are You Sure You Want to Erase?

One of the great features of digital cameras is the capability to erase shots you don't like. A word of caution: as you've seen throughout this book, there are many ways to use a digital photo. Think before you erase an accidental shot of the pavement, because it could be used as an interesting background. Think before you erase a picture that is inherently boring but could conceivably be used in a collage. Think before you erase a bad photo of Uncle Jimmy, because the good shot of Aunt Annie next him could be used for something else. Instead of always erasing, consider investing in more memory for both your camera and computer and building a digital library of those potentially useful "throwaways."

Changing Scale and Perspective

Photographer Maggie Hallahan was in Hawaii shooting photos for a medical company, and the art director requested a shot of a man holding an oyster and pearl. He was very explicit and wanted the oyster to fill most of the bottom frame of the image with a man's hand and arm receding into the background. The shot would have been difficult even if Maggie had shot with a view camera with tilts and swings and sophisticated perspective control. Instead, Maggie shot the oyster and pearl with a Hasselbald medium format camera and got the results shown in Figure 5.34. Maggie knew the shot could be fixed later in Photoshop. The final image is still being worked on, but Maggie showed me what needed to be done and gave me permission to use her work as an example of the kind of perspective control you can get with Photoshop Elements' Transform tools.

Figure 5.34: Professional photographer Maggie Hallahan shot this picture knowing it could be fixed later.

Here's what I did:

1. I cropped the image as shown in Figure 5.35.
2. I used a combination of the Magnetic Lasso (🔗) and Lasso (🔗) to select the oyster. I copied and pasted this section (Ctrl/Command+C and then Ctrl/Command+V). I named the resulting layer **Big Pearl**. The Layers palette is shown in Figure 5.36.

Figure 5.35: The cropped image. Figure 5.36: After selecting, copying and pasting the oyster onto its own layer, I increased its scale.

3. With the **Big Pearl** layer active, I selected Image ➢ Resize ➢ Scale and, while holding the Shift key to constrain the proportions, dragged the corner of the bounding box to enlarge the oyster.

4. With the layer containing the cropped image active, I selected the hand and part of the arm as shown in Figure 5.37. I reversed the selection (Select ➢ Inverse or Ctrl/Command+Shift+I) and then I applied a strong feathering to the sky and the rest of arm and body (Select ➢ Feather 10 pixels). Then, to the feathered selection I applied a Gaussian blur. The feathering made the blur appear to recess in a more natural way.

5. Back on the layer called **Big Pearl**, I used the Clone Stamp tool (⚬) to get rid of the gum Maggie had cleverly used to hold the pearl in place. I also used the Dodge tool (⚬) to lighten the pearl. The edges of the oyster looked ragged, so I selected the oyster by Ctrl/Command+clicking the image icon in the Layers palette, reversed this selection (Select ➢ Inverse, or Ctrl/Command+Shift+I), applied a 2-pixel feather (Select ➢ Feather), and hit the Delete key. This softened the edges a little and made the oyster blend more naturally into the background. The final image is shown in Figure 5.38.

Figure 5.37: I made a selection, feathered it, and applied a strong Gaussian blur.
Figure 5.38: The final image.

Fixing Keystoning

Artist Tom Mogensen was given the photo shown in Figure 5.39. It was taken by his friend Len Luke, in a bike shop in Italy. The poster was hanging high on a wall, and Len took the photo by aiming his camera nearly straight up. Because the plane of the camera and the plane of the wall weren't parallel to each other, the resulting photo has a distorted effect called *keystoning*. Keystoning occurs when lines converge rather than remain parallel. Still, Len really wanted a good copy of the poster to hang in the Bike Nook, his bike shop in San Francisco, so Tom helped him out.

Figure 5.39: Len Luke shot this distorted picture of a poster hanging on a wall in a bike shop in Italy.

I know this isn't a product shot per se, but Tom did such a great job of using Photoshop Elements' Transform controls to fix the photo that I thought it would be useful to show how he did it. His method can be applied whenever you have an image, or a part of an image, that contains keystoning. I can imagine this method being used, for example, on a book or rectangular package when the edges aren't parallel as they should be.

Tom straightened the poster out by doing the following:

1. He changed the name of his background layer to **Poster** and expanded his canvas 120 percent (Image ➤ Resize ➤ Canvas Size). He changed the name so the new canvas area would be transparent, rather than colored. With a larger canvas, he had more room to work with.

2. He used the Rectangular Marquee tool (⬚) to select the poster (see Figure 5.40).

Figure 5.40: Tom expanded his canvas by 120 percent and used the Rectangular Marquee tool.

3. He selected Image ➤ Transform ➤ Perspective and dragged the top right corner of the bounding box until the lines of the poster were parallel (see Figure 5.41). Then he applied the transformation by clicking the Commit Transform button (✔) in the options bar. He also could have hit the Enter/Return key or double-clicked inside the bounding box.

Note: If you have trouble determining whether lines are parallel, create a visual crutch to help. Simply make a new layer and then select the Pencil tool (✐) from the toolbox. Select a small brush from the options bar. Hold the Shift key and drag a vertical line near the area you are working. Or you can use the Pencil tool this way: click once to make a single dot, then hold down the Shift key and click to make another dot at the other end. A line will connect the two dots. Now you can use this as a reference when you apply the Perspective control. When you are finished, just trash the layer containing the vertical line.

4. Tom used the Clone Stamp tool (⚒) to fill in the missing edges and applied the Levels command to correct the tonal values of the image. After he was finished, he cropped the image to its edges.

The final image is shown in Figure 5.42.

Figure 5.41: Tom Mogensen fixed the keystone effect by dragging the top corners of the bounding box until the lines were parallel. Figure 5.42: Now the keystoning is gone.

Improving the Background

The background sets the mood, gives a product context, and helps add depth. Sometimes the simplest background is best. Other times a colorful, flashy background is called for. Regardless of what you use for a background, it should complement and not detract from the product.

Simplifying a Complex Background

One of the easiest ways to improve a background is to diminish its effect. Let's apply this to the wine bottles from a previous example (↶ "Separating a Product from Its Background," earlier in this chapter). As noted earlier, the art director basically liked the background but wanted it toned down.

Here's what I did after I selected the wine bottles:

1. I chose Select ➤ Inverse to make the background the active selection. I then slightly feathered this selection 2 pixels to soften the transition between the foreground and background (Select ➤ Feather).

2. The background is too dark, so I adjusted its tonal values and lightened it with the Levels command (see Figure 5.43).

3. This helped, but to give the picture more depth I applied a Gaussian blur to the background (Filter ➤ Blur ➤ Gaussian Blur). I set the Radius at 13.5 pixels.

4. The label still needs selective burning and dodging, and the reflections at the top of the bottles are too harsh. I'll fix the harsh reflections later in the chapter, but as you can see in Figure 5.44, simplifying the background already has significantly improved this shot.

Figure 5.43: Just by applying Levels to the background, the image was improved.
Figure 5.44: Applying a Gaussian blur made the background less distracting.

Creating New Backgrounds

After you have isolated a product from its background, there is no reason why you can't insert any background you want. Backgrounds can come from another photograph or purely from selective Photoshop Elements' effects and a little imagination. Some of the most effective backgrounds are a combination of a real photograph and a Photoshop Elements' filter or effect.

In Figure 5.45, you'll see an example of a background created using a combination of a Gradient fill and an effect.

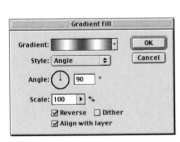

Figure 5.45: This background was quickly created using a Gradient fill and an effect.

Here's what I did:

1. Starting with the car that I previously worked on, I made a gradient background by clicking the Create New Fill or Adjustment Layer icon ( ) at the bottom of the Layers palette and choosing Gradient from the pop-up menu. (You can also select Layer ➢ New Fill Layer ➢ Gradient from the menu bar.)

2. From the various Gradient options, I chose the settings you see in Figure 5.46.

Figure 5.46: I chose the Silver gradient with the settings you see in the dialog box.
Figure 5.47: The Layers palette.

3. Making sure that the **Citroen** layer was active, I applied Colorful Center from the Effects palette. (It's located under Image Effects in the Effects pop-up menu.) You can see in Figure 5.47 that the Colorful Center effect created a duplicate layer and left the **Citroen** layer intact.

The great thing about creating backgrounds this way is that they are totally changeable. I can go back at any time and adjust the gradient or remove the effects layer ("All about Layers" in Zooming In). My original image remains unchanged.

Figure 5.48 illustrates how easy it is to go back and change a background created with a layer effect. I simply selected the first layer in Figure 5.47 called **Gradient Fill** and then from the Layer Styles palette I double-clicked on the effect called Rainbow in the Layer Styles pop-up menu under Complex. The Layers palette for this new image is shown in Figure 5.49.

Figure 5.48: It's easy to change a background if it is created with a layer effect.
Figure 5.49: This is the Layers palette for the image.

Modifying an Existing Background

Figure 5.50 shows a mistake. My digital camera fired unexpectedly. Instead of erasing the blurred image, I used it to create the background shown in Figure 5.51.

Figure 5.50: This was a mistake, but fortunately I didn't erase the image from my digital camera. Figure 5.51: Instead, I used it as the basis for this background.

This is what I did:

1. I opened the image shown in Figure 5.50 and chose Enhance ➤ Auto Levels.

2. I applied the Add Noise filter (Filters ➤ Noise ➤ Add Noise). I used the following settings: Amount: 57, Distribution: Gaussian.

3. I applied the Radial Blur filter (Filters ➤ Blur ➤ Radial Blur) and used the following settings: Amount: 22, Blur Method: Zoom, Quality: Best. The results are shown in Figure 5.52.

Figure 5.52: The image after applying the Add Noise and Radial Blur filters and with a 1368 × 1676 pixel selection.

4. I opened a new image of a bag and noted its pixel dimensions, 1368 × 1676.

5. Now, with the **Mistake** image, I selected the Rectangular Marquee tool (▭) from the toolbox and in the options bar I changed Style from Normal to Fixed Size. Then in the Width box I typed 1368 and in the Height box I typed 1676. I then made a selection, placing the constrained Rectangular Marquee over the area that I wanted. I made a copy of this selection (Ctrl/Command+C).

6. I now pasted the **Mistake** selection into the bag image (Ctrl/Command+V). It fit perfectly. I made sure that the **Mistake** image layer was below the one containing the bag. You can easily move layers into different positions (↩ "All about Layers" in Zooming In).

7. I added a drop shadow to the bag and I was done (↩ "Adding Depth," next).

Adding Depth

After you've found a background, you need to give your image a sense of depth. An easy way to do this is to make a clear distinction between the foreground object and the background. Assuming you've isolated your object from the background, you can do this by creating a drop shadow or other layer style.

Drop Shadows

Drop shadows are commonly used to create a sense of depth. Here's what I did to replace the background, rotate, and add the drop shadow to Figure 5.53.

Figure 5.53: The original digital camera shot.

1. I selected and removed the background by using the Magic Eraser (✎) (☞ "Separating a Product from Its Background," earlier in this chapter). I rotated the image to the right (Image➤ Rotate Canvas 90 Degrees Right).
2. I created a new background by clicking the Create New Fill or Adjustment Layer icon (●) at the bottom of the Layers palette and choosing Color from the pop-up menu. I chose white. (You can also choose Layer ➤ New Fill Layer ➤ Solid Color from the menu bar.)
3. On the layer called **Bag**, I dragged and dropped/double-clicked a drop shadow from the Layer Effects palette. I selected Drop Shadows from the palette pop-up window and chose one called Soft Edge. By clicking the *f* in the layer bar, I got the Style Settings dialog box. From this box, I tweaked the drop shadow by using the settings shown in Figure 5.54. The Layers palette is shown in Figure 5.55.

 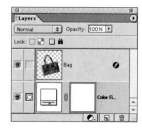

Figure 5.54: These are the settings I used for my drop shadow. Figure 5.55: The Layers palette shows the new background and layer with the drop shadow layer style attached.

The final image is shown in Figure 5.56.

Figure 5.56: The final image.

Outer Glow

You can use other layer styles such as Outer Glow to also make a distinction between the product and its background. To obtain the results shown in Figure 5.57, I started with the previous example and then did the following:

1. I changed the color of the background from white to black by clicking on the layer thumbnail in the **Color Fill** layer and choosing black from the Color Picker.
2. I deleted the drop shadow effect from the layer called **Bag** by selecting that layer and then choosing Layer ➤ Layer Style ➤ Clear Layer Style from the menu bar. You can also clear the styles by dragging/double-clicking on Default Style in the Layer Styles palette.
3. I applied an Outer Glow from the Layers Styles palette pop-up menu to the layer called **Bag**. I chose the outer glow called Simple. I used the settings shown in Figure 5.58.

Figure 5.57: Use Outer Glow styles to add depth to your image. Figure 5.58: These are settings I used for my Simple Outer Glow.

Creating Lighting Effects

Effective lighting can give a product shot dimension and drama. If the interesting lighting isn't there to begin with, you can use Photoshop Elements' Lighting Effects filter to create it. Figure 5.59 shows an original shot and Figure 5.60 shows that shot altered by lighting effects.

Figure 5.59: The lighting is even but uninteresting. *Figure 5.60: With the help of the Lighting Effects filter, the image is more dramatic.*

This is what I did to create the effective lighting:

1. I selected the Lighting Effects filter (Filter ➤ Render ➤ Lighting Effects).
2. I applied the settings shown in Figure 5.61 and clicked OK.

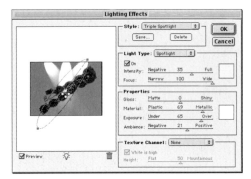

Figure 5.61: These are the settings I used for the Lighting Effects filter.

Softening Highlights and Glare

Figure 5.62 shows a close-up of the wine bottles from a previous example (☞ "Separating a Product from Its Background," earlier in this chapter). You can tell that the light source for the photograph was direct and harsh and not the soft, diffused lighting often used by professional photographers. Fortunately, it is easy to fix this in Photoshop Elements.

All I did to get the results shown in Figure 5.63 was select the Blur Tool (◌) from the toolbox and then click and drag it several times over the spots of light. I selected a soft-edged brush in the options bar and left the Pressure set at 50 percent. The Mode was Normal.

Figure 5.62: The reflections are harsh and need to be softened. Figure 5.63: With the help of the Blur tool, the reflections are softer, more diffused.

Adding a New Label

Will Rutledge is a professional photographer, and manager of QVC Inc.'s photo studio. QVC is an electronics retailer mostly known for its cable shopping channel. As you can imagine, Will shoots a lot of products. He mostly uses a high-end digital camera and he often uses Photoshop to fix a photo because something isn't quite right with the product. Take, for example, the photo shown in Figure 5.64. One of the lipstick cases didn't have a label. However, Will had another, similar shot of a different lipstick case that did (see Figure 5.65). He used Photoshop to cut and paste the label from one photo to the other. Although he used Photoshop to do the job, everything he did can be done in Photoshop Elements as well.

Figure 5.64: The vertical lipstick case didn't have a label and it needed one. Figure 5.65: Will used the Polygonal Lasso tool to select the label.

Here's what Will did to fix the photo:

1. With both images open, Will used the Polygonal Lasso tool (⬝) to select the label from the image that had one. Figure 5.65 shows a close-up of the lipstick case and Will's selection.

 Note: The Polygonal Lasso tool is similar to the Magnetic Lasso tool; however, you manually set endpoints for each straight segment (↪ "Selection Tools" in Zooming In).

2. He then copied (Ctrl/Command+C) and pasted (Ctrl/Command+V) the selection onto the second image. He used the Move tool (⬝) from the toolbox to position the label in place. (See Figure 5.66.)

3. Will then used the Eraser tool (⬝) to erase parts of the pasted label so it blended nicely.

The final image is shown in Figure 5.67.

Figure 5.66: Will copied and pasted the label on this image, and then used the Move tool to put it in place. Figure 5.67: The pasted label blended nicely after Will erased parts of it. (Photo by Will Rutledge. Copyright 2000 QVC. Courtesy of Stacey Schiefflin of Models Prefer Cosmetics.)

Making a Product Smile

Will Rutledge also took the product shot shown in Figure 5.68, this time for QVC's annual report. He was given creative license to make the image fun, and that is what Will did to make the image shown in Figure 5.69.

Figure 5.68: A typical shot of an electrical outlet. (Photo by Will Rutledge. Copyright 2000 QVC.) Figure 5.69: A not-so-typical shot of an electrical outlet, helped along by the 3D filter.

1. Will used the Lasso tool (⌇) to select one of the rectangular slots.

2. He copied and pasted his selection onto a separate layer. He rotated the slot until it was horizontal by using Image ➢ Transform ➢ Free Transform (see Figure 5.70).

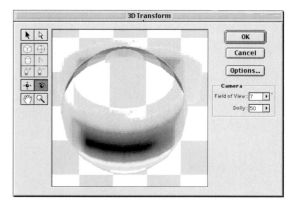

Figure 5.70: After copying and pasting the vertical slot, Will used a Transform command to rotate it to a horizontal position. Figure 5.71: The 3D filter mapped Will's selection to a sphere. When he rotated the sphere, he got a smile.

3. With the layer containing the pasted, rotated slot selected, he opened the 3D filter (Filters ➢ Render ➢ 3D Transform).

4. In the 3D Transform filter dialog box, Will selected the Sphere tool (⊕) and drew a circle tightly around the rectangular slot in the preview window. He then clicked the Trackball tool (☻) and in the preview window rotated the ball until he got a smile. Then he clicked OK. (See Figure 5.71).

5. Finally, Will used the Move tool (▶✛) from the toolbox to position his smile in place and then used the Eraser tool (⬦) and Clone Stamp tool (♨) to make the smile completely replace the old slot.

Who says life always has to be so serious?

Simplifying a Product Shot

Converting a complex product shot into a simple line drawing can be useful for brochures or instructional material. To simplify the shot shown in Figure 5.72, I applied the Photocopy filter with the foreground color set to black (Filter ➢ Sketch ➢ Photocopy). I also set the Detail at 14 and the Darkness at 33. The result is shown in Figure 5.73.

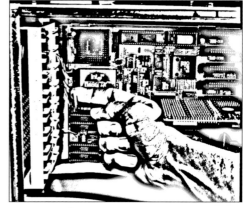

Figure 5.72: The original photo. (Photo by Maurice Martell.) Figure 5.73: A much simpler image after applying the Photocopy filter.

Shooting Digital: Creating Your Own Mini Photo Studio

It doesn't take a lot of money or equipment to set up a mini photo studio in your office or home. With this setup, you'll be able to shoot perfect photos of small objects such as books, coins, jewelry, small appliances, or other objects that you want to place on an online auction or prepare for a flyer or ad.

The basic components are:

· A digital camera
· A white, seamless backdrop and a means to hold it
· Two diffused light sources

Look at the following diagram. The seamless paper is draped over a table. It's important for it to drape smoothly, or it will catch light and create unwanted shadows. Also notice how the object to be photographed is set back, away from the edge of the paper. This also keeps shadows at a minimum. Two diffused lights are enough for most situations. You can diffuse a light source with a sheet of thick, translucent plastic or a window screen. Move the lights around and try to make the light fall as evenly on the product as possible.

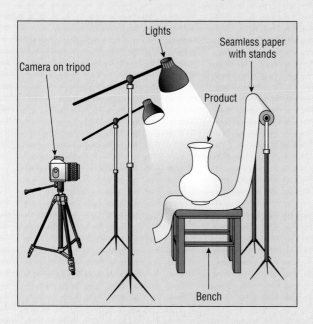

Lights
Seamless paper with stands
Camera on tripod
Product
Bench

When you shoot, experiment with different angles. But remember to show as much of the product as you can. The shot should be informative as well as interesting.

Where do you find the equipment for this mini studio? Professional photography supply houses all carry the seamless paper, lights, and stands. Go to my website (**http://www.shooting-digital.com**) for more resources.

Composites are like tapestries

woven together from the fabric of more than one source. They can be relatively simple to create (adding a missing person to a group shot) or complex (combining many images from many sources). Creating a photo-realistic composite tests nearly all your Photoshop Elements skills, from selecting to transforming, from cloning to managing multiple layers. But when you are finished, you'll have a single image visually richer than the sum of its individual parts.

Making Photo-Realistic Composites

Adding Yourself (or Anyone) to a Group Shot

I'm not in the shot shown in Figure 6.1, but I wanted to be. It was one of those typical situations when old friends gather and suddenly someone says, "Hey, let's get a group shot of *everyone*!"

Figure 6.1: I wanted to be in this shot, but someone had to take the picture.

I had my digital camera but no tripod and I couldn't find anything high enough to put the camera on top of for a self-timer shot. Instead, my wife took a shot with me in it, and then I took another shot with my wife in it. I left my spot open in the second shot so I could simply copy and paste myself from one image into the other.

Here's how I did it:

1. I opened both digital images, and starting with the one that didn't include me I adjusted Levels to make the image look right (Enhance ➤ Brightness/Contrast ➤ Levels). I'll call this Image 1, and the results are seen in Figure 6.1.

2. I turned to the second shot, the one with me in it, which is shown in Figure 6.2. I'll call this Image 2. I wanted the exact same Levels settings applied to Image 2 so the tonal values of my upper body would match the others in Image 1. Normally, I would have made a note of my Input Levels settings in my Levels controls in Image 1, and with Levels open for Image 2, typed them into the Levels Input boxes. Instead, I used a neat shortcut that I learned from Bill Rutledge at QVC, Inc. With Image 2 active, I pressed Ctrl/Command+Alt/Option+L. This automatically applied the same Levels setting from Image 1 to Image 2, and I got exactly the results I wanted. Cool. (I could have continued applying Levels this way to an entire batch of similar images, which would have been a real time saver.)

3.   OK, now on Image 2 I used the Lasso tool (✐) to make a loose selection, as shown in Figure 6.3. At this point, I wasn't precise, and in fact, I purposely included other areas of the image to help me position my pasted selection.

Figure 6.2: My wife took this shot with me in it.   Figure 6.3: I made a loose selection with the Lasso tool and copied it.

4.   On Image 1, I pasted my selection (Ctrl/Command+V), which placed it automatically into its own layer. From the Layers palette, I set the Opacity setting to 50 percent so I could see part of the underlying image. I then used the Move tool (►♣) to position the selection into place. I used part of my friend Joe's shoulder that I had included in my pasted selection as a reference (see Figure 6.4).

Figure 6.4: I set my layer Opacity to 50 percent so I could see the underlying image.

5. Next came the tricky part. I reset my layer Opacity to 100 percent and used the Eraser tool (✐) with a Hard Round 19 pixels brush to remove the superfluous areas around my head and shoulders. Then I magnified my image from 100 percent to 300 percent and used a Hard Round 9 pixels brush. At one point, when I was working on the area to my left, I momentarily changed the layer Opacity back to 50 percent so I could tell where the face of the man in front of me ended and my neck and shoulder started. I finished with a Soft Round 13 pixels brush, brushing the edges of my pasted selection lightly to make them blend into the background.

6. I didn't bring my legs over from Image 1, so I just used the Clone Stamp tool (⚒) to clone the shadow that was already there in Image 2. The final image is shown in Figure 6.5.

Figure 6.5: Now the group is complete.

This composite was easy to make because both Image 1 and Image 2 were so similar. It's more work to create a realistic composite when you are working with shots taken at different times, with different lighting, with different film, or at different resolutions. You'll learn more on shooting with composites in mind later in this chapter (☞ "Shooting Digital: Creating Realistic Looking Composites").

MAKING PHOTO-REALISTIC COMPOSITES

Swapping Kids

Children will be children, and some children like to be thrown up in the air and smile, and others don't. Photographer Maggie Hallahan couldn't get the kid in Figure 6.6 to be tossed in the air, look at the camera and smile all at once. What a surprise! But everything else about the picture was fine, so Maggie tried another tact. She shot the photo shown in Figure 6.7, this time with an older child who smiled but wasn't keen on being thrown in the air. Maggie's client was PJA, an advertising and marketing agency in San Francisco that needed the photo for one of their bio-tech clients.

Back at the computer, PJA Photoshop pro Bretton Newsom went to work with Photoshop, putting the best of Maggie's two shots together. I talked with Bretton before he finished the final composite, and he agreed to walk me through the steps he'd taken so far on a low-resolution file. It should be noted that Bretton, like most pros, works with the full version of Photoshop. However, just about everything he did in this example can be duplicated in Photoshop Elements. The only thing that can't be exactly duplicated is Bretton's use of the Quick Mask to make a more precise selection. Photoshop's Quick Mask makes it possible to paint on a "mask" by using the Paintbrush tool, which gives you great accuracy and control; the mask can then be turned into a selection.

Figure 6.6: Everything about this picture was fine, except the kid. Figure 6.7: The child was great but didn't like being thrown in the air. (Photos by Maggie Hallahan.)

Here are the steps Bretton took:

1. He used the Clone Stamp tool (&) to remove the child, as shown in Figure 6.8.
2. He selected the smiling kid in Figure 6.7 and, as mentioned earlier, used a Quick Mask—a function not available with Photoshop Elements—to create a precise selection around the child. Photoshop Elements has plenty of powerful selection tools, and Bretton probably could have done just as good of a job with say, the Magnetic Lasso (⚲), albeit with a little more time. Recall that I've already shown you several ways to make selections (☞ "Separating a Product from Its

Background" in Chapter 5). After the kid was selected, Bretton copied the selection and pasted it into its own layer in the first image, as shown in Figure 6.9. He used the Move tool (⊕) to position the pasted selection into the arms of "mom."

Figure 6.8: Bretton used the Clone Stamp tool to remove the child. Figure 6.9: After selecting and copying the child, Bretton pasted the smiling child into the arms of "mom."

3. As you can see in Figure 6.9, the woman's arm is covered. Bretton copied and pasted part of the woman's arm and shoulder, as shown in Figure 6.10. He placed the layer containing the arm and shoulder above the layer containing the smiling child, which put the arm and hand in the correct position relative to the child. You can see Bretton's Layers palette in Figure 6.11.

Figure 6.10: Bretton made a copy of the woman's arm and shoulder and pasted it onto its own layer. Figure 6.11: Bretton's Layers palette. Note the arm and hand layer is above the child.

4.   As a final (for now) step, Bretton added a slight shadow on top of the dress, as if it came from the outstretched arm. The "final" image is shown in Figure 6.12.

Figure 6.12: The final composite.

After this low-resolution "comp" is approved by the client, Bretton will go back and work on a high-resolution copy of both images to make a perfect version suitable for print.

Note: This chapter focuses on creating photo-realistic composites. But what about composites that are just for fun? Mark Ulriksen, a freelance illustrator for *The New Yorker* magazine who is best known for whimsical portraits often derived from photo composites, says that when creating a composite, you should think of your Photoshop Elements' image window as a stage and all the images you want to use as your props. Let's say you just came back from a family vacation to the Grand Canyon. Your "props" might include a shot of the Grand Canyon, a close-up of the kids, a red-tailed squirrel, and your favorite hamburger stand. You might start by using the Grand Canyon shot as the background. Then pick another image, or prop if you will, that represents the most memorable part of your vacation. That great meal, the squirrel that ate from your kids hands, whatever. Place that image in the front of the stage and make it big so it takes on significance and importance. Now place the other images, or props, in relationship to the dominate image or prop. Use Photoshop Elements' transform tools to play with the size of each image, and use the Move tool to change the relationships between the objects. Experiment and, most importantly, have fun.

Expanding Your Image

Figure 6.13 is also Maggie's work. The image is another composite consisting of two shots taken in Hawaii for PJA: the man in one photograph, and the beach in another. Once again it was Bretton Newsom who did the Photoshop work of copying and pasting the man onto the beach. I won't go into the details of how Bretton created the composite because he essentially used the same techniques described in the previous example. However, I'd like to use this image to illustrate a couple of techniques that Bretton uses when he needs to extend the edge of an image and make it look realistic. This situation comes up often when creating photo-realistic composites, so these techniques are very useful.

Figure 6.13: To extend the edge of a composite such as this one, you'll need special techniques to make the addition look realistic. (Photo by Maggie Hallahan.)

Using the Hawaii shot as an example, here is what he does:

1. He uses the Rectangular Marquee tool ([⃞]) to select an area that's the size equivalent to the needed addition. To see the size of your selection, use the Info palette found in the palette well. The numbers in the lower-right corner actively read out the measurements as you adjust the Marquee. Using the Info palette's options pop-up menu, you can change the measurements to read out in pixels, inches, centimeters, points, picas, or as a percentage. You can also change the measurements by clicking the crosshair icon in the Info palette. Figure 6.14 shows the rectangular selection, and Figure 6.15 shows the Info palette, indicating the selection size is 1 × 6.517 inches. You can also set the size of the marquee in the selection tool options bar. Just choose Fixed Size from the Style list box and type the numerical values in the Width and Height boxes.

Figure 6.14: Start with a rectangular selection of the area you want to extend. Figure 6.15: Use the Info palette to read out the size of the selection marquee.

2. He then copies (Ctrl/Command+C) and pastes (Ctrl/Command+V) the selection. It automatically goes onto its own layer.

3. To expand the canvas area, he selects Image ➤ Resize ➤ Canvas Size. This brings up the dialog box shown in Figure 6.16. He moves the Anchor point to the leftmost center position and adds an inch (or whatever is needed) to the Width box. For this example, he left the Height alone. Generally, he adds a little more area than is called for and crops away the extra when he is done.

4. Using the Move tool (⊹), he slides the pasted selection over, as shown in Figure 6.17.

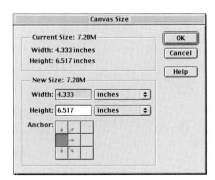

Figure 6.16: The Canvas Size dialog box provides a way to extend the edges of your canvas.

Figure 6.17: Slide the selection over by using the Move tool.

At this point he, uses one of two methods:

- He uses the Eraser tool ( ) with a small, soft-edged brush to shave a very small amount off the edges of the adjacent sides. He doesn't drag the Eraser tool by hand along the edge as you might imagine; the tool is only as precise as your hand is steady. Instead, he holds the Shift key to constrain the Eraser tool to a 90-degree angle, and then he clicks and releases with the Eraser tool on one of the edges, at the very top of the image. Then he moves the cursor straight down to the bottom of the image and, still holding the Shift key, clicks once again. The Eraser tool erases everything between the two clicks. Then he does exactly the same thing to the adjacent side, remembering to select the layer that contains that side (see Figure 6.18). Now when he uses the Move tool or, for more precise control, the arrow keys, to slide the two sides together, they fit like a hand in a glove. In the spots where the blend is noticeable, he uses the Clone Stamp tool ( ), cloning and stamping in horizontal sweeps to spread pixels of similar values (see Figure 6.19).

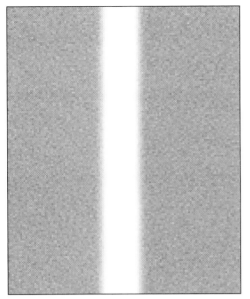

Figure 6.18: Slightly erasing the edges with a soft-edged brush makes them fit together seamlessly. Figure 6.19: Now the edges slide together like a hand into a glove. In spots where the match isn't perfect, the Clone Stamp tool will finish the job.

- His alternate method is to flip the pasted selection horizontally (Image ➤ Rotate ➤ Flip Horizontal). Now the edge of the pasted selection mirrors the edge of the original image and lines up almost perfectly. Again, where the match isn't perfect, he uses the Clone Stamp tool to fix it. See Figure 6.20.

Figure 6.20: When the pasted selection is flipped horizontally, the edges are mirrors of each other and fit almost perfectly. Again, the Clone Stamp tool fixes anything that isn't perfect.

Seamlessly Pasting

One of the biggest challenges in composite making is pasting a selection seamlessly into another image so it looks natural without a halo or jagged edges. It's a lot easier when you are pasting a selection into a busy background, as I did in the first example in this chapter, and more difficult when you are pasting to an area of continuous tone, such as a sky.

I use one method with pretty good success. I'll demonstrate by selecting, copying, and pasting the Doggie Diner head from Figure 6.21 to the street shot shown in Figure 6.22.

Figure 6.21: This is one component of my composite. Figure 6.22: And this is the other component of my composite.

Figure 6.23 shows a close-up of what happens if I simply make a selection, copy it, and paste it into the street shot.

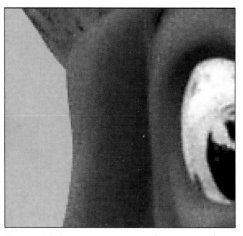

Figure 6.23: By using a simple copy and paste, I get the jagged edges shown here.

Now I'll try something different:

1. I make a selection just as before, by using the Magic Wand selection tool (✦). One click on the white background with a Tolerance of 15 pretty much does it, except I'll use the Lasso tool (⌁) to select some of the white areas in the Doggie Diner's hat that were missed by the Magic Wand.

2. I reverse my selection (Select ➢ Inverse) and shrink it by 2 pixels (Select ➢ Modify ➢ Contract). This tightens up my selection and reduces the chance that I'll copy unwanted background areas.

3. I add a 3-pixel feather (Select ➢ Inverse, Select ➢ Feather), as shown in Figure 6.24.

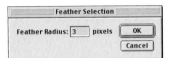

Figure 6.24: The Feather Selection dialog box.

4. I copy (Ctrl/Command+C) and paste (Ctrl/Command+V) the selection into the street scene. I use the Move tool (▶✛) to position it where I want. Because I slightly shrunk my selection and feathered it, the edges of the Doggie Diner head now blend more naturally into the new background.

5. As you can see in Figure 6.25 and in the close-up in Figure 6.26, the paste is almost seamless. Where it is not, I can use the Eraser tool (⌧) with a combination of both hard-edged and soft-edged brushes to make it perfect.

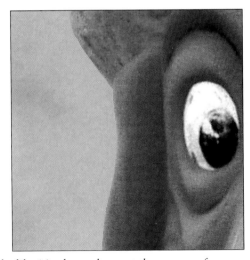

Figure 6.25: Now the Doggie Diner head looks like it's always been at the corner of Stockton and Greenwich Streets. Figure 6.26: Even on closer examination, the deception is barely visible.

Pre-visualizing a Hotel

Photo-realistic composites are extremely important in the world of architecture. Architects can use a composite not only to show a client what a potential building or remodel will look like, but also as a good tool for convincing a design review board to approve a project by showing the effect that it will have on a neighborhood.

David Mlodzik is one of those rare architects who is not only versed in design but is also computer and high-end digital-imaging literate. An increasingly growing part of his business is providing other architects and the construction community with design visualization and graphic services.

Figure 6.30 shows one of his recent projects for a Hilton hotel. At the time David started work on the project, the hotel didn't even exist. He took the design done by the San Francisco firm RYS Architects, and used a 3D rendering and animation program to create several views of the hotel. Then he turned to Photoshop. Although he worked in the full version of Photoshop, everything he did is possible using Photoshop Elements.

Here are the steps he took:

1. He scanned the site photograph shown in Figure 6.27.

Figure 6.27: The site photograph. (Photo by David Mlodzik.)

2. He copied and pasted the hotel into a layer with the site photograph. The rendering had a black background, which David removed by using the Magic Wand selection tool (✎) and then cutting to transparency.

3. David applied a slight Gaussian blur to the hotel rendering to make it look more realistic (Filters ➢ Blur ➢ Gaussian Blur).

4. As you can see in Figure 6.28, the hotel sits in front of the McDonald's in the site photograph. David created a copy of the background layer containing the·site photo, and to that layer he erased the areas shown in Figure 6.29 by using the Eraser tool (✐) and various selection tools to Select/Delete.

Figure 6.28: When it's pasted in, the hotel sits in front. Figure 6.29: David used various erase techniques to make room for the hotel.

5. As you can see in Figure 6.30, the hotel looks like it's always been there. Figure 6.31 shows David's Layers palette.

Figure 6.30: The final composite. Figure 6.31: David's Layers palette.

Note: If you want to create a composite from several images and are willing to give up some control, try using Photomerge (File ➤ Photomerge). It's fast, it's easy, and it's very fun. I'll tell you more about using this Photoshop Elements filter later in the book (☞ Chapter 8).

Shooting Digital: Creating Realistic-Looking Composites

Recently I got a call from a company in Sweden that wanted a group shot of their board of directors for an annual report. The only problem was that one of the directors, futurist Paul Saffo, lived in California and wasn't about to make the long trip just for a photo opportunity. Would I shoot a picture of Saffo here, and they'd Photoshop him into the group later?

When you attempt to come up with a photo-realistic composite as I did for this one, there are several things to consider. Ideally, all the images should be shot with the same kind of camera and lens and from the same perspective. In my case, I had to rent the same kind of lens they used in Sweden. Unless you want to spend a lot of time trying to match the film grain or the resolution of the digital file, use the same type of film, or if using a digital camera, use the same resolution. As you can see in the following picture, it worked out just fine. And neither Saffo, nor for that matter, I, had to endure a long plane ride.

If you are in the business *of selling a home or property, you'll need photographs that bring out marketable features and diminish or remove detractive ones. You may have already mastered the use of a digital camera, but that is only a start. In this chapter, you'll learn how to use Photoshop Elements to take your digital image the extra step and make it ready for a flyer, an ad, or the Web.*

7

Better Real Estate Shots

Straightening a Slanted Looking
    Building
Transforming a Kitchen
Removing a Construction Sign
Smart-Blurring a Background
Balancing the Light
Removing Wires

Better Real Estate Shots

Straightening a Slanted Looking Building

Look at just about any real estate magazine or newspaper section and you'll see photos of buildings with sides that appear to converge rather than remain parallel. This is an effect called *keystoning*, and it occurs when the plane of the camera and the plane of the building are not parallel to each other. You already encountered a variation of this phenomenon earlier in the book, when you saw a poster on a wall that was shot at an angle (☞ "Fixing Keystoning" in Chapter 5).

Sophisticated 4 × 5 view cameras have backs that tilt and swing to compensate for keystoning, and you can buy expensive 35mm camera lenses that correct this type of distortion as well. You also can avoid keystoning by positioning your camera so that it is level with the plane of the building. However, this isn't always possible, and Figure 7.1 illustrates my point. The shot was taken with a digital camera with a wide-angle lens, and in order to fit the entire building into the shot I had to step back a good distance. The ground sloped behind me, and I ended up shooting upward toward the building, which created the keystoning effect. Fortunately, it's not hard to fix shots like this if you use the Perspective command (Image ➢ Transform ➢ Perspective).

Figure 7.1: The sides of this building are not parallel.

Here's what I did:

1. I copied the background layer containing the building (Layer ➢ Duplicate Layer). I turned the visibility of my original background layer off so it wouldn't confuse me later when I applied the Perspective command. (Turn a layer's visi-

bility off by deselecting the eye icon in the leftmost side of the Layers palette.) I created a copy for a couple of reasons: first, I wanted to keep my original image intact, and second, Transform commands aren't an option when you are working on a background layer.

2. After duplicating the layer, I applied Auto Levels and increased the saturation (☞, "Making Dull Images Shine" in Chapter 2).

3. I then selected View ➢ Show Grid to give me a series of 90-degree vertical references. The grid makes it a lot easier to determine when the sides of the building are straight. Figure 7.2 shows the grid, which I customized (☞ the following Note). Using the grid is an alternative to another method I described earlier in the book, when I used the Pencil tool to draw a 90-degree reference line on a separate layer (☞ "Fixing Keystoning" in Chapter 5).

Figure 7.2: A grid provides a series of 90-degree lines, which I can use as reference points when I try to straighten the building.

Note: To change the pattern and color of the grid, select Edit ➢ Preferences ➢ Grid. You can select a preset color or a custom color. You can choose solid, dashed, or dotted lines. You can also vary the spacing of the major grid lines and the frequency of minor grid lines.

4. I selected the Perspective command (Image ➢ Transform ➢ Perspective). If you hold down the Alt/Option key when you do this, a new layer containing the transformed image will be automatically created. If you are not concerned about the original image appearing in the background as you adjust the perspective controls, this can save you time. However, when using the Alt/Option method, it's not possible to turn off the visibility of the original layer before you commit the transform. I find it distracting when the original shows through, and that's why I chose to manually create a duplicate layer and turn off the visibility of the original layer as described in step 1.

5. I didn't change any of the default choices in the Transform options bar. These options are more applicable to other transform commands, which by the way, can also be accessed via the options bar.

Note: In the Transform options bar, Rotate (↱) selects the Rotate transform, Scale (⬓) selects the Scale transform, and Skew (▴) selects the Skew transform. You can also switch to other Transform commands by holding down the right mouse button/Ctrl key and clicking anywhere on the image window. A pop-up window appears with your options.

6. To illustrate how the Perspective command works, I'll give you an example by first using it in the wrong way. Figure 7.3 shows what happens when I place the pointer on the bounding box handle in the upper right and click and drag it inward. Figure 7.4 shows what happens when I change the perspective by going the opposite way. Figure 7.5 shows the right adjustment as confirmed by the vertical grid lines.

7. When I was finished, I clicked the OK button (☑) in the options bar. You can also press Enter/Return.

BETTER REAL ESTATE SHOTS

Figure 7.3: This is what happens when I drag the bounding box inward. Figure 7.4: This is what happens when I drag the bounding box too far the other way.

Figure 7.5: By aligning the sides of the building with the grid lines, I can see this is about right.

Transforming a Kitchen

When the real estate market is hot, Sally Rogers shoots hundreds of photos a month with a digital camera. She documents property both from an indoor perspective and an outdoor one. She shoots big buildings and small buildings, commercial and residential. As soon as she is finished shooting, the images are quickly downloaded into her computer and prepared for newspaper ads, flyers, and the Web. Sally's job is demanding because it requires attention to both quality and speed. She does her best to get the shot right in the first place, but that's not always possible considering her schedule.

Figure 7.6 shows a not-so-uncommon mistake: the picture wasn't framed properly. In the days before Photoshop Elements, she'd have to live with the mistake, reshoot, or decide that the kitchen wasn't that important after all. Nowadays Sally just starts up her computer and gets to work.

Figure 7.6: This kitchen looks like it was in an earthquake. (Photo by Sally Rogers.)

Note: Just about all real estate shots will benefit from the basic image processing techniques found earlier in this book (↪ Chapter 2 and Chapter 4). Another relevant topic is how to make panoramics from a sequence of photos (↪ Chapter 8).

Here is what she did to straighten the kitchen:

1. She made a copy of the background layer, turned off the visibility of the original layer, and turned on the grid, just as I did in the preceding example.
2. She then selected Image ➢ Transform ➢ Free Transform from the main menu bar.

3. As she positioned the pointer in the upper-right bounding box, it turned into a curved arrow (⟳). Then she rotated the image until the lines in the cabinet lined up with the vertical lines of her grid (see Figure 7.7). For some images, rotating them like this will rotate parts of the image off the edge of the canvas. If this happens, you'll need to enlarge your canvas area (Image ➤ Resize ➤ Canvas Size) before applying the Transform command.

4. When she was finished, she clicked the OK button (☑) in the options bar. You can also press Enter/Return.

5. As you can see in Figure 7.7, the rotation fixed the kitchen but created a skewed image frame. She used the Crop tool to crop the image, as shown in Figure 7.8.

Figure 7.7: After using the Free Transform command, the kitchen appears mostly level.
Figure 7.8: Sally used the Crop tool as a final step.

Note: Nowadays most real estate photographs end up on the Web. Later, I'll tell you about converting your photos to the Web-friendly JPEG file format (↪ "Converting GIFs to JPEGs" in Chapter 11). I'll also give you more general information on digital images and the Web (↪ Chapter 10).

Removing a Construction Sign

Sally does the best she can to shoot around clutter or objects that detract from the property. In the case of Figure 7.9, she couldn't avoid the bright red construction sign in front, which gave the false impression that the building was still under construction.

Figure 7.9: The red construction sign is distracting. (Photo by Sally Rogers.)

Here is what she did:

1. She created a duplicate of her background layer. She'll work on the duplicate and save the original layer for future reference.

2. She selected the Clone Stamp tool (⚐) from the toolbox and magnified her image 400 percent. She positioned the red construction sign in the middle of her image window. (You can move an image that is larger than the image window around by holding down the spacebar. The cursor turns into a hand. Then, when you click and drag, the image moves with your cursor.)

3. She used a Soft Round 13 pixels brush and started on the red cones, sampling or "cloning" parts of the road and sidewalk by holding the Alt/Option key while clicking on them, and then painting the sampled areas over the cones (see Figure 7.10). Then she sampled parts of the wall and the sidewalk and painted them over the sandwich sign, this time using a Hard Round 5 pixels brush because the work in this area required her to be more precise. Then she turned to the sign itself, sampling and using parts of the window and window frame to cover it. At times, the clone didn't look quite right. Ctrl/Command+Z quickly reverted the step. As a final step in removing the sign, Sally selected a Soft Round 35 pixels brush and a Soft Round 9 pixels brush and cloned the intact tree and trunk over what remained of the sign (see Figure 7.11).

4. She then zoomed back to 100 percent magnification (by double-clicking on the Zoom tool) and tightly cropped the image. She adjusted the contrast of her image with the Levels controls and increased the saturation with the Saturation controls until she got what she wanted, as shown in Figure 7.12.

If you zoom in tightly, you'll see that the clone job isn't perfect. Zoomed out, however, most people wouldn't notice.

Figure 7.10: Sally started with the red cones, using the Clone Stamp tool to replace them with parts of the sidewalk and street. Figure 7.11: Sally cloned the tree on the left over the area where the red sign used to be.

Figure 7.12: The final image after cropping and applying Levels and increasing saturation.

Note: The secret to using the Clone Stamp tool is not to get too caught up in the details. Zoom in to see what you are doing. But then periodically zoom out to see how your work looks in a normal view. It's also useful to turn away from the monitor from time to time. When you look back, you'll have a different perspective. The fact is, after spending so much time working with the Clone Stamp tool, you'll be tuned into every tiny mistake, mistakes that most people probably won't even notice.

Smart-Blurring a Background

In the photo shown in Figure 7.13, Sally wanted to highlight the staircase, not emphasize the view out the windows. Shooting-wise, there wasn't much Sally could do except cover the windows completely. At first, Sally tried selecting the entire window area and applying a Gaussian blur. She got what you see in Figure 7.14. The Gaussian blur blurred everything, including the window frame. She considered selecting each glass part of the window individually and applying the Gaussian blur, but that would have taken too much time. Instead she turned to the Smart Blur filter, which gave her a lot more control over the blur, enabling her to blur the background and leave the window frame alone.

Figure 7.13: Sally wanted to diminish the view out the windows. Figure 7.14: A Gaussian blur blurred everything, including the window frame. (Photos by Sally Rogers.)

To use the Smart Blur filter, she did the following:

1. She used the Polygonal Lasso tool ( ) to select the entire window area.

2. She selected the Smart Blur filter (Filters ➢ Blur ➢ Smart Blur). By playing with the relationship between the Radius and Threshold settings, she got the effect she was looking for.

Sally's Smart Blur settings are shown in Figure 7.15. The final effect is shown in Figure 7.16.

Note: The Smart Blur filter's Radius setting specifies the area the filter covers when looking for pixels of dissimilar values. In some cases, a higher number doesn't produce more blur as you might expect. It all depends on the value of adjacent pixels and your Threshold setting. Increasing or decreasing the Threshold setting determines how different the pixel values must be before they are affected by the Radius setting. You can also choose between speed and quality with the Quality setting. The High setting will slow the processing but produce a better result. Normal mode is the default, but for special effects you can also choose Edge Only and Overlay Edge.

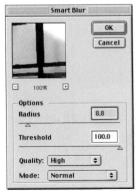

Figure 7.15: Sally's Smart Blur settings. Figure 7.16: The result after applying the Smart Blur filter.

Balancing the Light

Figure 7.17 shows a room separated from a brightly lit atrium with a thin shoji screen. A lot of light was pouring in from the adjacent room, creating a tricky lighting situation—especially considering the limits of the relatively inexpensive digital camera Sally was using. To balance the light, Sally used one of Photoshop Elements' most effective and easy-to-use commands, Fill Flash.

Figure 7.17: The light needs balancing. (Photo by Sally Rogers.)

Note: Architects use before and after photo montage techniques to help create visual references for clients and approval boards. An example of these kinds of composites appears in the preceding chapter (↝, "Pre-visualizing a Hotel" in Chapter 6).

This is what she did:

1. She selected the Fill Flash (Enhance ➢ Fill Flash).
2. She used the settings shown in Figure 7.18.

The results are shown in Figure 7.19.

Figure 7.18: The Fill Flash settings. *Figure 7.19: The results.*

Removing Wires

Telephone or electric lines are just about everywhere, and it's nearly impossible to shoot a home or building in a such a way as to avoid them. Sometimes these lines can easily be removed by using the Clone Stamp tool and a "Nudge" technique that I'll explain shortly. I say *easily removed* with the following qualification: our eyes are very sensitive to horizontal lines. Take a telephone line that runs horizontally in an image and rotate it so it is vertical, and it's less likely that you'll even notice it. Our innate sensitivity to horizontal lines also means that if you try to remove such a line from your image, you must do it carefully, in a way that leaves no trace. I suggest that if you have a choice between doing the job poorly or leaving a vestige of our modern life, choose the latter.

Having said all this, let's look at two simple techniques for removing a pair of horizontal wires shown in Figure 7.20.

Figure 7.20: Power and telephone lines are hard to avoid but easy to remove.

The first method requires the Clone Stamp tool, which by now you must agree is one of the most powerful tools in Photoshop Elements' arsenal. This is how I used the tool to get rid of the wires on the left side of the image:

1. I selected the Clone Stamp tool (⊛) from the toolbox and kept the default settings in the options bar.

2. I started with a Hard Round 19 pixels brush and then changed the size of the brush to a Hard Round 5 as I worked on the wire near the windowsill and the wire near the top of the roof. I chose a hard-edged brush because I wanted to keep the texture of the stucco intact. A soft-edged brush would have diffused the edges and blurred some of the details.

Note: To get near-instant access to the brush palette, hold down the right mouse button/ Ctrl key and click anywhere on the image window area. The palette will appear on the screen, and you can chose a new brush. This method is especially handy because you can easily match the size of your brush to the area you are working on.

The Clone Stamp tool worked great, as you can see in the close-up in Figure 7.21. I could have kept using it to remove the rest of the wires. In order to demonstrate a slightly faster alternative, however, I'll use the "Nudge" method to remove the rest of the lines.

Figure 7.21: I used the Clone Stamp tool to remove the wires that crossed the building.

To use the Nudge method, I followed these steps:

1. I made a selection of both wires by using the Polygonal Lasso tool. I feathered this selection 5 pixels (Select ➢ Feather), as shown in Figure 7.22. I used the arrow keys on my keyboard to move just the selection outline slightly below the power lines, as shown in Figure 7.23.

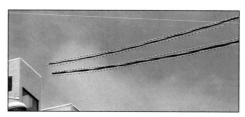 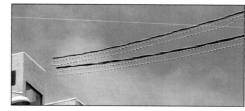

Figure 7.22: I made a selection using the Polygonal Lasso tool and feathered it 5 pixels.
Figure 7.23: Then I used the arrow keys to move the selection down.

2. While holding the Alt/Option+Command keys, I used the arrow keys to nudge the selection of the sky up. This copied my selection and offset the duplicate by 1 pixel (see Figure 7.24). I kept nudging the selection until the power lines were replaced by sky. There was a little streaking in the clouds, but after deselecting my selection, I went back and quickly fixed it with the Clone Stamp tool. The final image is shown in Figure 7.25.

Figure 7.24: Holding the Alt/Option+Command keys while using the arrow keys duplicates a selection and offsets it by 1 pixel. Figure 7.25: The final results.

The Nudge method works especially well when the line to be removed crosses areas of continuous tones. It doesn't work so well in complex areas, where the copying and shifting of pixels are more noticeable.

Shooting Digital: Focus on Marketable Features

You can do a lot with Photoshop Elements to fix a photograph that is lacking. However, you can save time by shooting with certain points in mind in the first place. Here are a few tips:

- If you are using a typical digital camera, you can avoid keystoning by shooting a building straight-on level. This may require the use of a ladder or it may mean scouting out a higher vantage point, such as the roof of another building or a hill.

- When shooting, focus on marketable aspects of the property, such as hardwood floors, new appliances, a beautiful deck, or a view.

- To avoid window glare, use a polarizing filter. You'll need to rotate the filter until the glare is gone. Remember that polarizing filters are most effective when used at a 90-degree angle off axis to the sun. This means the lens is less effective if the sun is directly behind you or in front of you, and most effective when the sun is to the left or right. Polarizing filters can also help increase color saturation in many outdoor shots.

- Shoot around clutter or just remove it before shooting. If your camera has manual aperture and focus controls, you can control the depth of focus and blur a distracting background or foreground.

- Because you are shooting with a digital camera and film costs are not an issue, shoot the same scene from several different angles. You can edit the best shot later.

8

Until recently, *it took an expensive camera or a time-consuming cut-and-paste procedure to produce images that offered a field of view beyond 90 degrees. That's all changed with Photomerge. All you need are two or more sequential, digital images taken with just about any kind of camera, and Photomerge will automatically blend and stitch them together into a panoramic that is both beautiful and informative. This chapter shows you how to use Photomerge to create panoramics and other types of photo montages as well.*

Creating Panoramics with Photomerge

Photomerge Dos and Don'ts

Photomerge—and the capability to stitch multiple images together—is new to the Photoshop family. At this time, it is available only through Photoshop Elements, although it is expected to migrate to future versions of Photoshop.

Photomerge does a very good job of creating panoramics on certain sequenced photographs, especially ones that were shot with the capabilities of Photomerge in mind. To avoid a lot of frustration and to help you manage your expectations about what Photomerge can and cannot do well, I suggest you keep the following dos and don'ts in mind:

- Do follow some simple shooting rules and suggestions for better, quicker stitching (☞ "Shooting Digital: Planning for Photomerge," later in this chapter).
- Do increase your computer's RAM or allocate more RAM to Photoshop Elements (Mac). At this time, Photomerge works entirely in RAM.
- Don't work with image files larger than 3MB unless you have 75MB or more of RAM available for Photoshop Elements.
- Do expect mixed results depending on the content of your image.
- Do expect better results from images that contain a modest amount of edge detail, such as a building with windows.
- Don't expect great results from images that have large expanses of similar tonal values, such as a landscape with sky.
- Do expect to spend time later in Photoshop Elements using the Clone Stamp tool (♣) and the Burn and Dodge tools (✆) (◉) to clean up areas where the merge wasn't perfect.
- Do keep an open mind for lucky mistakes that occur when Photomerge doesn't do what you expect it to do.
- Do use Photomerge for things other than panoramics—for instance, collages.
- Do know that future versions of Photomerge will be better, and periodically check Adobe's website (http://www.adobe.com) for up-to-date information.

Now let's get into the actual work of using this tool.

Creating a Priceless View

I can understand why people in the real estate business will be enthusiastic about Photomerge. Take Figure 8.1, for example. It's a view of San Francisco from my front window with the Golden Gate Bridge in the background. I'm told that when we want to sell our house, we should include this view in flyers for potential buyers. The photo is actually a collection of six shots, assembled using Photomerge, and it would have been impossible to get this shot any other way.

Figure 8.1: This view was created by stitching together six sequenced frames. The six frames are included on the CD.

To create the panoramic, I mounted my Olympus E-10 digital camera on a tripod and zoomed in on the scene by using the camera's maximum focal length, which is approximately equivalent to 140mm on a 35mm camera. I chose a long focal length purposely. I wanted to compress the perspective and at the same time create a wider angle of view. If I had used a wider focal length to create the images for my panoramic, the picture would have been totally different. The buildings would have seemed much farther away, which isn't how it looks to the naked eye.

To maintain a consistent exposure for each frame, I selected an Olympus function button that locked my auto exposure. Many digital cameras don't have this locking feature, but if the exposure doesn't vary from frame to frame, Photomerge creates a smoother stitch. I shot one frame, then rotated the camera and took another, then rotated the camera and took another, repeating this six times until I covered the scene. I used visual references to overlap each shot by about a third but I wasn't particularly precise, and the variations didn't seem to affect the final Photomerge results.

After transferring my digital files to the computer, I did the following:

1. I opened Photomerge from the file menu (File ➤ Photomerge). I chose Add from the Photomerge dialog box and then navigated to my six source files. On the Mac, I selected all six image files by Shift+clicking each one individually, and you can do the same on a PC. Figure 8.2 shows the Photomerge dialog box after I had selected the six files. (You can remove files by using the Remove button.)

Figure 8.2: The Photomerge dialog box after selecting six images.

2. In the dialog box, I deselected Attempt to Automatically Arrange Source Images. You can try leaving this option checked. Many times, Photomerge will do a good job of automatically creating a panoramic, especially with certain types of images. And it's no big deal if Photomerge can't do the job; it'll give you a chance to place the images yourself. I chose to deselect this option so I could show you the process step by step.

3. I changed the Image Size Reduction option to 25 percent. I chose 25 percent based on trial and error. The camera produced digital files that are 10.8MB each. I allocated 100MB of RAM to Photoshop Elements and yet, even with a 50 percent image size reduction, Photomerge choked. Instead of boosting my RAM, I opted to use the 25 percent image size setting, which worked fine.

4. After selecting OK, I waited while Photomerge went through an automatic process of opening, resizing, and placing the six images into a single file. When it was done, the dialog box shown in Figure 8.3 appeared.

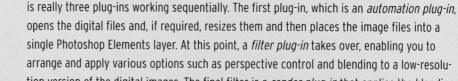

Note: If you watch Photomerge in action with the History palette open, you'll see that it is really three plug-ins working sequentially. The first plug-in, which is an *automation plug-in*, opens the digital files and, if required, resizes them and then places the image files into a single Photoshop Elements layer. At this point, a *filter plug-in* takes over, enabling you to arrange and apply various options such as perspective control and blending to a low-resolution version of the digital images. The final filter is a *render plug-in* that applies the blending and perspective calculations to the final images. You can stop the Photomerge process at any point by simply pressing Esc (PC) or Command+period (Mac).

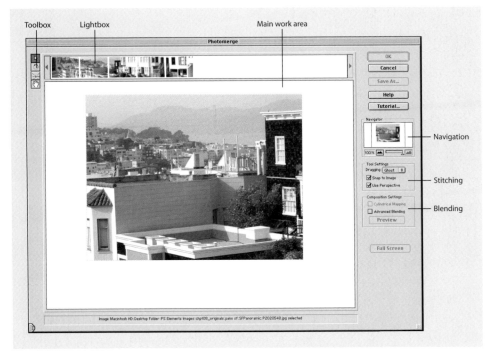

Figure 8.3: The work area in this Photomerge window consists of a toolbox, lightbox, a main work area, and various navigation, stitching, and blending options.

5. Now I was ready to start arranging my images and building my panoramic. You'll see only five thumbnails in my lightbox because I've already dragged one of the center images to the main work area. To create the panoramic, I selected the Use Perspective check box and set the Dragging option to Ghost. I then dragged the thumbnail representations from the lightbox to the main work area, placing each one adjacent to the next. As similar parts of the adjacent images overlapped, something remarkable occurred. When Photomerge detected similar areas, it automatically snapped them together. The more edge detail it had to work with, the easier it was for Photomerge to line up the adjacent images. Because I had selected Use Perspective, Photomerge automatically corrected perspective and attempted to compensate for the natural distortion between images. (If you have perspective turned off, Photomerge still looks for similar edges and snaps the images together, albeit without any perspective compensation.) Because I had selected Ghost as my Dragging choice, parts of the underlying image showed through, making alignment easier (see Figure 8.4).

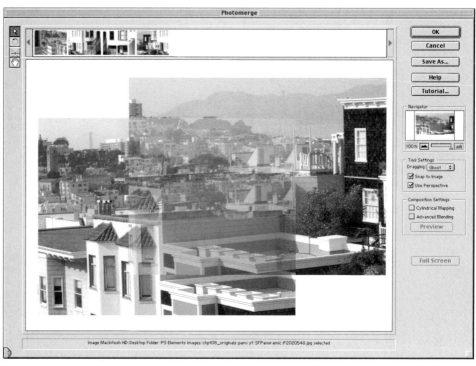

Figure 8.4: With the Dragging option set to Ghost, you can see parts of the underlying image and therefore more easily line up the images.

Note: Setting the Dragging option to Blend isn't nearly as useful as setting it to Ghost. By using Blend, you can't easily see where one image starts and the other begins, so aligning the images is more difficult.

Just because Photomerge can't find and snap edges of different images together doesn't mean it can't do perspective compensation. If Photoshop is having trouble aligning your images, try the following: While clicking and dragging one image on top of another, hold down the Ctrl/Command key. When you release the mouse, Photomerge will bypass the attempt to find similar-edge pixels and go right to the perspective algorithm.

6. The fact is, at this point, I didn't like the resulting image (see Figure 8.5). The perspective didn't look right, so I tried to fix it by setting a different vanishing point. By default, if Use Perspective is selected, Photomerge makes the first image you drag to the work area the vanishing point, and outlines it in a light blue border when it is selected. It's helpful to think of the *vanishing point* image as a base image, or one that sets the perspective for all the others. For example, if the vanishing point image is in the middle, as it is in this example, the images on either side will be transformed so that they lead the eye toward the center. If you look again at Figure 8.5, you'll see the bow tie configuration that I am talking about.

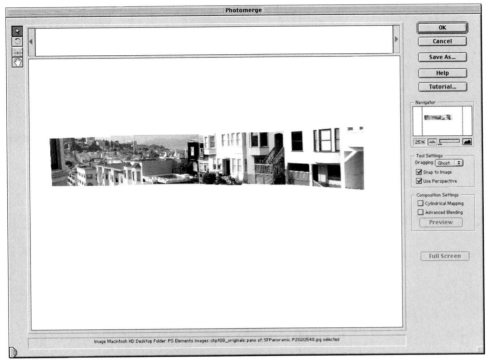

Figure 8.5: The vanishing point is near the middle, outlined by blue.

Note: It's easy to forget where your vanishing point is. To find it, simply hold down the Alt/Option key and roll your mouse over the frames. The vanishing point image has a light blue border, and all the other images have red borders.

To try another vanishing point, I simply selected the Set Vanishing Point tool ( ) and clicked on another image in the work area. In Figure 8.6, I made the image on the left the vanishing point. See what happens to the perspective? In an attempt to correct the perspective to the new point of view, the images to the right of the vanishing point are transformed in size and shape. As you can see, Photomerge wasn't successful in transforming the perspective of all the images to this new vanishing point. To deselect the vanishing point completely and start over, I selected the Select Image tool ( ) and dragged the vanishing point image away from all the other images. When I did this, the other images snapped back to their original perspectives. I deselected the Use Perspective option and repositioned the former vanishing point image, to get what you see in Figure 8.7. In this case, using no perspective control and therefore no vanishing point worked better.

Figure 8.6: The vanishing point is to the left. Figure 8.7: Now the perspective control is turned off.

Note: Deselecting the Use Perspective option doesn't automatically revert your composition. You have to detach the vanishing point image completely from the rest of the panoramic, then deselect Use Perspective.

To move your images from the work area back into the lightbox, hold the Alt/Option key. The Cancel button changes to New. Select New and start editing your composition again.

7. Next, I tried different blending options. Advanced Blending differentiates between areas of detail and areas of similar tones or colors. When it detects a lot of detail, Advanced Blending applies a sharper blending transition. When it detects similar tones or colors, it applies a more gradual blending transition. In some cases, Advanced Blending can compensate for different exposures in adjacent frames. On these types of images, if you don't use Advanced Blending, you'll see very obvious diagonal banding. In my image, Advanced Blending added a sharp shaft of light shooting down from the top of my middle frames. Its occurrence didn't make any sense, so I attributed the flaw to a bug in the software. I turned Advanced Blending off, and the artifact disappeared and the blending was just fine. (You can get a preview of the effect of Advanced Blending by selecting the Preview button from the Photomerge window.)

8. When I was finished editing my panoramic, I selected Save As. This command saved all my settings and my arrangement as a PMG file in the same folder as my source images. You have to keep the PMG file in the same folder as the source files. If you move it, you won't be able to reopen your work. To open the PMG file, choose File ➢ Photomerge and click Open in the Photomerge dialog box, then navigate to the PMG file and click Open.

9. After saving my Photomerge file, I selected the OK button and waited while Photomerge merged the higher resolution versions of my images. Up to this point, Photomerge had worked on and displayed only screen resolution versions of the images. The time it takes for this transformation depends on the size of the final image and the computer processing speed.

10. With the final panoramic open as a new Photoshop file, I adjusted the Levels controls and used the Clone Stamp tool (⚒) to clean up some of the background. Then I cropped the irregular-shaped image into a rectangle and I was done.

Shooting Digital: Planning for Photomerge

You'll get better results with Photomerge if you shoot with the following suggestions in mind:

- Use a tripod and keep the camera level. If you can't use a tripod, plant your feet firmly and keep the camera as level as possible as you turn from your waist. If your camera has one, use the optical viewfinder rather than the LCD. Holding the camera firmly to your eye helps maintain consistency.

- If you are using a zoom lens, don't zoom while you shoot your sequence. Keep a consistent focal length. If you are using a film camera, rectilinear wide-angle lenses are OK. Don't use fish-eye lenses.

- If your camera is capable, use the exposure lock to maintain a consistent exposure between frames. If you have only an automatic setting, avoid scenes with wide variations in lightness and darkness.

- Don't use a flash in one frame and not in the others.

- Use the camera's viewfinder to previsualize the panoramic before shooting. Turn your head slowly and imagine how the panoramic will look. Pay attention to the way the light changes from the start of the panoramic to the end. Avoid extreme fluctuations of light and dark.

- When you shoot, allow a one-third to one-half overlap between frames. Use a visual reference to imagine a spot one-third to one-half of the way in the viewfinder, then rotate the camera to that spot for the next shot. If you overlap more than one-half between frames, the blending will suffer. If you don't have at least one-third of a frame overlap, it's still possible to manually assemble the panoramic, but the Attempt to Automatically Arrange Source Images option likely won't work.

Creating an Interior Panoramic

How many times have you tried to shoot an interior photo and couldn't get back far enough to fully capture the room? Cutting a hole in the wall behind you might help, but that solution is not very practical. Using an expensive super-wide-angle lens might help, but many of these lenses create a fish-eye look. If you are shooting with a digital camera, forget it. At this time, the widest available lenses for digital cameras aren't very wide.

Professional photographer and panoramic/virtual reality expert Scott Highton encounters logistical problems like this all the time. It's his business and passion to push the boundaries of photography, to take it places it could never go before the advent of the computer. The shot in Figure 8.8 is an example. Scott created the panoramic of a large satellite control room of a major telecommunications company by stitching together three sequenced images with Photomerge. By doing this, he got a fully corrected shot that would have been virtually impossible otherwise.

Figure 8.8: This interior panoramic is made up of three images stitched together with Photomerge. (Photo by Scott Highton.)

This is how he shot the images, and how he used Photomerge to stitch them together.

To shoot the images:

1. Scott set a 35mm camera on a tripod and used an 18mm rectilinear lens. (The *rectilinear lens* is a corrective lens that makes straight lines appear straight in wide-angle images.) He used a medium-speed print film, which gave him a lot of exposure latitude.

2. Using a specially marked tripod head, he shot a sequence of 12 consecutive images at 30-degree intervals, going well beyond the 120-degree view you see in Figure 8.8. Scott used all 12 images and another software program to stitch together a 360-degree panorama for a QuickTime VR presentation, but that's another story. (To see Scott's VR work, go to **www.highton.com**.)

3. He processed the film and had the film digitized onto a Kodak Photo CD.

Scott then took three of the images that covered the field of view he wanted and in Photoshop Elements he did the following:

1. He selected Photomerge (File ➤ Photomerge).
2. He chose Add from the dialog box.
3. He selected the three images.

4. He deselected the Attempt to Automatically Arrange Source Images option and set the Image Size Reduction setting to None. (His files were only 1.13MB each.)

5. Scott started with the central image by dragging and dropping the thumbnail into the main work area. With Use Perspective selected, this image automatically became his vanishing point image. He then placed the other images on either side of the vanishing point image. As you can see in Figure 8.9, the images came in sideways. Scott used the Rotate Image tool (◌) to turn the images 90 degrees. Holding down the Shift key while turning constrains the move to 45-degree increments. Because the images could be rotated only one at a time, turning them was time-consuming and Scott wished Photomerge offered some way to turn all the images with one command. The images also came in out of order. That's because Photomerge doesn't follow the sequence of the images in the first Photomerge dialog box but attempts to sequence the images based on their filenames or numbers. Although this may be annoying, you can always rearrange the order of the thumbnails in the lightbox by clicking and dragging.

6. Because the images contained a lot of edge detail, they snapped right into place. The perspective transformation worked well also, and even matched up the lines in the ceiling. Scott used Advanced Blending with good results (see Figure 8.10). The process went smoothly, but Scott found the navigational controls lacking. He couldn't use the standard Photoshop Elements keyboard commands to magnify or reduce the image in the main window, only the Navigator. It helped when he discovered that he could click and drag his work around the window by holding the spacebar.

Figure 8.9: When an image comes in like this, use the Rotate Image tool to correct it.
Figure 8.10: Photomerge corrected the perspective and blended the three images together nicely. The light blue box shows the vanishing point image. (Photos by Scott Highton.)

7. Scott saved the composition by using the Save As button and then clicked OK.

8. The final panoramic was nearly perfect. Scott had to only crop, apply the Levels command, apply a slight Unsharp Mask, and he was done.

Creating an Epic Panoramic

Only a very expensive panoramic camera could have matched the results that Scott Highton got in Figure 8.11 with a conventional camera and Photomerge. A fish-eye lens would have covered the same field of view but with a huge perceived distortion.

Scott created this moving panoramic of the Lincoln memorial in much the same way he created the interior shot described in the preceding section. His shooting technique was basically the same, and once again, he shot this as a 360-degree panoramic that could be turned into a QuickTime VR as well. His Photomerge settings were also the same; he kept the Use Perspective and Advanced Blending settings on. As you can see in Figure 8.12, he set his vanishing point directly in the middle.

Figure 8.11: This is actually five images stitched together. Figure 8.12: The vanishing point is in the middle. (Photos by Scott Highton.)

Although this image looks great at first, on closer examination it reveals some of the limitations of Photomerge on this type of image. If you look at Figure 8.13, for example, you can see where Photomerge had trouble matching a column. This is because of the lack of edge contrast that Scott had so much of in the previous example. You can also see in Figure 8.14 where Photomerge had trouble correcting the perspective. Still, even with its flaws, it's a dramatic image.

 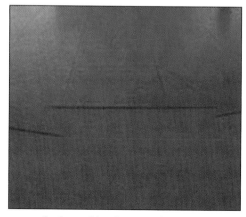

Figure 8.13: Photomerge had trouble aligning the column because of the lack of edge detail. Figure 8.14: It also had trouble correcting the perspective.

Making Handheld Panoramics

I don't want you to get the impression that the only way to use this cool tool is by shooting very carefully in a controlled way. Driving past a vineyard in Napa, California, I stopped and snapped four quick shots, holding the digital camera by hand. As you can see in Figure 8.15, Photomerge did a fine job stitching the images together. My settings are shown in Figure 8.16.

Figure 8.15: This is actually four handheld shots, stitched together with Photomerge.

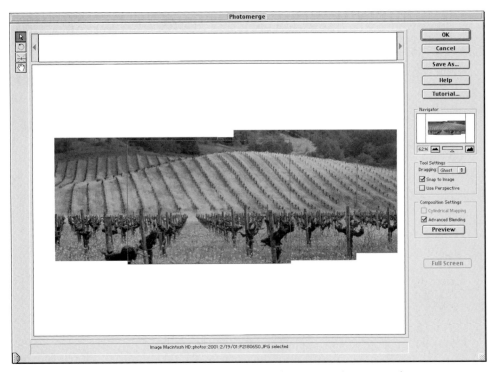

Figure 8.16: These are the Photomerge settings used to create the vineyard panoramic. Notice that I didn't select Use Perspective.

Note: To create 360-degree panoramics, follow these steps: Shoot a 360-degree sequence. Then use those images to make three separate 120-degree panoramics with Photomerge; make sure Cylindrical Map is selected and Use Perspective is deselected. (Photomerge handles only 120 degrees or fewer at a time.) Next, load the three 120-degree panoramics into Photomerge and stitch them together, again with Cylindrical Map selected and Use Perspective deselected.

Making Vertical Panoramics

A panoramic doesn't have to be horizontal. You can shoot and stitch a vertical panoramic as well. That's what I did in Figure 8.17. The image of the Transamerica building had everything going for it, from the way I shot it with a tripod and carefully allowed a generous overlap between shots to the amount of edge detail. Photomerge worked beautifully after I deselected Use Perspective and Advanced Blending (see Figure 8.18). I couldn't get any vanishing points to work properly, and Advanced Blending produced the same glitch that I noticed in one of the earlier examples.

Just to emphasize that Photomerge works better on some images than others, I shot a similar series of images of nearby Coit Tower, which didn't have as much edge contrast as the Transamerica shot. As you can see in Figure 8.19, Photomerge didn't do as good of a job matching up the tower edges. Figure 8.20 shows my Photomerge settings.

Figure 8.17: This nearly flawless vertical panoramic was quickly created using Photomerge.

Figure 8.18: The settings for the Transamerica shot; notice that I deselected Use Perspective and Advanced Blending.

Note: It's frustrating when you spend a lot of time building a panoramic in Photomerge only to be informed at the end that the program can't complete the task because of a lack of memory. You can avoid the hassle of having to completely redo your work by selecting Save As in the Photomerge dialog box. Now, if you run out of memory, reselect Photomerge from the File menu, set the Image Size Reduction to a lower percentage, *then* select Open and *not* Add. Navigate to the folder that contains the Photomerge file designated by a **.pmg** extension, open it, and select OK. This time, with the lower resolution setting, it should work. If it doesn't, repeat the last steps and choose an even lower percentage before reselecting the PMG file.

Figure 8.19: Without a lot of contrast and edge detail to work with, Photomerge has a difficult time aligning the tower.

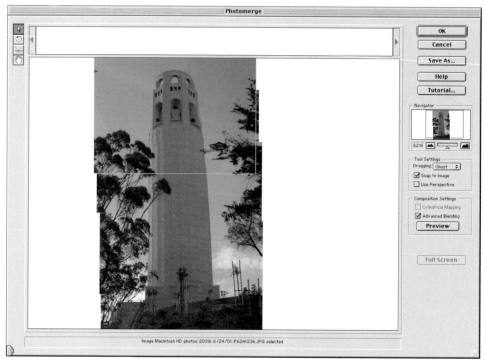

Figure 8.20: The settings for the Coit tower shot.

Showing Baseball's Big Picture

Until recently, illustrator Mark Ulriksen spent a lot of time kneeling on the floor, trying to assemble batches of 3 × 5 inch prints with tape and scissors to create a panoramic. When he was finished, he'd use the patched work as a basis for many of his illustrations that appear in *The New Yorker* magazine.

I talked Mark into trying Photomerge on a series of eight images he took of the San Francisco Giants at spring training in Arizona last year. He shot the images with a 35mm film camera and used a normal focal length. He didn't shoot with Photomerge in mind, and in many cases the images don't overlap at all. Still, as you can see in Figure 8.21, he managed to create a fun panoramic that could easily be used as a basis for one of his illustrations. Now that Mark's tried Photomerge, I don't think he'll ever use tape and scissors again. Figure 8.22 shows one of Mark's attempts at changing the vanishing point and his Photomerge settings.

Figure 8.21: Mark Ulriksen created this panoramic from eight images by using Photomerge. It's not perfect, but creating it with Photomerge was a lot easier than using tape and scissors. Figure 8.22: Mark played with different vanishing point settings until he got the image he liked.

Photomerging a Collage

There is no reason why your images need to be in sequence to use Photomerge. I brought six images into Photomerge and played with different arrangements until I got the Hockneyesque image you see in Figure 8.23. Sure, I could have created the montage by cutting and pasting the images into their own Photoshop Elements layer. If I had done this, though, the process wouldn't have been nearly as fun. Every time I'd want to move a particular image, I'd have to go to its layer, select it, and then move it. Using Photomerge was much faster and more satisfying. Figure 8.24 shows the images as they appeared in the Photomerge window with my settings.

Figure 8.23: This Hockneyesque collage was created in Photomerge.

Figure 8.24: The settings for my collage.

Scanning Digital: Creating Scanograms with a Flatbed

Flatbed scanners are mostly used to scan flat art, but there is no reason why the boundaries can't be stretched to include inanimate objects such as flowers, coins, and jewelry. If the cover of the flatbed doesn't completely close, you may have to play around with different scanner color and brightness controls. Also, be careful when placing hard objects on the scanner glass so you don't scratch it. The following image is a beautiful example created by photographer Michelle Vignes. She simply placed a whole head of garlic on her flatbed scanner and scanned.

Aa Bb C

cD Dd E

e Ff G

g Hh Champagne I

Many times *you'll want to add type to your digital image. In some cases, type takes a relatively minor role, say as a small photo credit or caption in the corner of your digital image. Other times, as in a poster or a flyer, the type is big, bold, colorful, and dominant. Creating all kinds of type is easy with Photoshop Elements' Type tool, which makes type that is fully editable so you can go back to your layered PSD file at any time and make changes. This chapter covers the basics of this powerful tool and shows a few of the myriad ways you can take type further. It also introduces the Shape tool, which can be used to set type apart from a background image.*

9

Taking Type Further

Adding a Photo Credit
Making Headline Type
Making Type More Readable
Using Shape Tools to Accent Type
Warping Type
Filling Type with an Image
Making Volcano Type
Adding Effects to Type
Applying Liquify to Type

Taking Type Further

Adding a Photo Credit

Let's start with the relatively simple task of creating a photo credit. By walking step by step through the process, you'll see how the Type tool actually works. It's a fairly intuitive tool to use, especially if you are familiar with word processing software. However, until you've grasped some of the basic concepts behind the Type tool and used it a few times, it won't always work the way you might expect it to.

Figure 9.1: To create a photo credit, find an area with similar tones and then use a contrasting color and an easy-to-read font.

Here's how I made the text shown in Figure 9.1:

1. I selected the Type tool (**T**) from the toolbox. If I click and hold the Type tool icon, two choices appear: horizontal or vertical type. I chose horizontal for this example, but the choice is not critical because I can always go back and change the orientation later in the options bar.

Note: Type is fully editable as long as it remains as a type layer. If you simplify the type layer, the type becomes rastorized and has the same properties as any other bitmap element in your image. You can simplify a layer via the Layers palette pop-up menu or by selecting Layer ➤ Simplify Layer from the menu bar. Why simplify a type layer? There are certain things you can't do to a type layer, such as apply Perspective and Distort commands or use any of the filters or paint tools. I suggest that you make a copy of your type layer and simplify the copied layer. That way, you can always go back to the original type layer and make changes.

2. Before you type, you need to choose a font and a font style, size, and color. You also need to make sure that the other options in the Type tool options bar are appropriate. For example, be sure that you select the Create a Text Layer button (T) in the options bar. If you've inadvertently selected the adjacent button, Create a Selection (☷), the Type tool won't create editable type, it will create outline type (☞ "Filling Type with an Image," later in this chapter.)
Here's what I chose for the following options:

- Font: Arial. This is a sans serif type that is legible even when it's small.
- Font Style: Regular. I want the type to be readable but not necessarily dominant. The other options—Bold, Italic, and Bold Italic—draw more attention to the type.

Note: You must have the bold, italic, and bold italic versions of your font loaded in your system for these options to be available. You can always choose a faux bold or faux italic, from Show Text Options (⅞) in the options bar. Keep in mind that these faux fonts are only crude approximations of an actual font and are machine-made without considering nuances such as spacing and aesthetics.

- Font Size: 14pt. The size that you use depends on the size of your image. As a rule of thumb, 72pt. type is approximately 1 inch high in an image that is 72dpi. My image is 144dpi, so the pixels are packed relatively tighter, which reduces 72pt. type to about half an inch. Having said this, the fact is I'm never exactly sure how big my type will look. I experiment until I get the size I want.
- Font Color: Black. I chose a contrasting color to the underlying tonal values. You can change it to any color by clicking on the color swatch.
- Anti-aliased: Selected. This smoothens the edges of the type. It also adds more colors and therefore adds file size. The increased file size is inconsequential unless your image is destined for the Web (☞ "Creating Web Type" in Chapter 10).

Grabbing Digital: Taking Screen Captures Further

Both the PC and the Mac have built-in commands that create a snapshot of your entire desktop window and save the image as a PICT file. On the PC, press Ctrl+Print Screen for the entire screen, or Alt+Print Screen for the focused window. To quickly paste the screen capture into Elements, you can select File ➤ From Clipboard. On the Mac, simply press Command+3. Third-party alternatives give you much more control over your screen captures. Check out SnagIt by TechSmith for the PC, or Snapz Pro by Ambrosia Software for the Mac. Both enable you to capture the entire screen, a dialog box, a menu, or a selection of your choice. They give you the capability to capture video frames as well.

Note: Before adding type to your digital image, consider your choice of fonts. If you plan to use small type, say as a photo credit or caption, use a font that holds up and is readable small. Usually, so-called *sans serif* fonts are best for this because they are simpler and don't contain decorative flourishes, or *serifs,* at the beginning or end of a character stroke. Two popular and commonly available sans serif fonts are Arial and Helvetica. If you are using type as a headline for a poster or flyer, the font can be either serif or sans serif as long as it is readable from a distance. Myriad is one popular headline font. If you plan to fill your type with an image or texture, use the bold version of a heavy font such as Verdana, Myriad (both sans serif), or Georgia (serif). It's a good rule of thumb not to mix more than two fonts on a single image. If you've chosen an appropriate font, you also won't need to embellish it with too much color or gaudy effects. Photoshop Elements uses the fonts installed in your system folder. The actual fonts that are available to you will vary accordingly.

3. After selecting my options, I placed my cursor in the upper-right side of the image and clicked. I chose an area consisting of light, flat tones so my black type would be easily visible. When I clicked my mouse, an insertion bar in the shape of an I-beam appeared at the point of clicking. I then typed in my letters. The baseline of my type lined up with the small line through the bottom of the I-beam. The I-beam also marks a point of reference for any alignment choices you make in the options bar.

As you can see in Figure 9.2, when my letters came to the edge of the image, they didn't automatically wrap to another line. They continued off the edge. I could have pressed the Enter/Return key when I got to the edge of the picture, which would have created a new line, but instead I continued typing. When I was finished, I pulled the cursor away from the type until it turned into the Move tool pointer ( ), at which time I dragged the type into position. You can also move type in 1-pixel increments by using the arrow keys. To move the type in 10-pixel increments, press Shift at the same time you use an arrow key.

Note: If you are in Committed mode and your type is selected, you can quickly change the color of your type with the following shortcuts: Alt/Option+Backspace/Delete will fill the type with the foreground color. Command+Backspace/Delete will fill it with the background color. If you are in Edit mode, you can use only the foreground shortcut.

Photo by George Washin

Figure 9.2: Type will not wrap to the next line as it does with conventional word processing software. It will continue off the edge of the image unless you hit the Enter/Return key. In this case, I just dragged the single line of type into position.

TAKING TYPE FURTHER

> **Note:** After type has been *committed*, you can drag it at any time into different positions. Just select the Move tool (▸✥) from the toolbox and click on the type. This automatically selects the type layer, and a bounding box appears around the selected type. Clicking outside the bounding box deselects the type. Place the pointer inside the bounding box and drag the type into position. Be sure that the Auto Select Layer and Show Bounding Box options are selected in the Move tool options bar.

4. Moving the type automatically committed it. I could have committed it before this, however, by selecting the OK button (☑) in the options bar. I also could have selected the Cancel button (☒), which would have discarded the type layer. Selecting the Cancel button discards a type layer only if the type has not been previously committed.

> **Note:** Photoshop Elements type can exist in one of three basic modes: Edit, Committed, and Simplified. When type is in *Edit* mode, all you can do is edit; you can't use other Layer commands from the Layer menu. When type is *committed*, you can edit and apply just about any of Photoshop Elements tools and commands, including a layer effect. However, in order to use any of the painting tools or filters, you must first *simplify* the type layer.
>
> How do you know which mode your type is in? One way is to look at the Layers palette. If the layer thumbnail contains a *T* and the layer contains the word *Layer* followed by a number, you are in the Edit mode. If the layer thumbnail contains a *T* and the layer contains other words or type, it is a committed layer. If the layer thumbnail doesn't contain a *T*, it is a simplified layer. Another way of telling is through the Type tool options bar: If the Cancel and OK buttons are showing, you are in Edit mode. If not, you are in Committed mode. If your type has been simplified and you try to use the Type tool on it, the Type tool will just create a new type layer. You can't edit simplified type.

What do you do if you want to go back and change your type? Here's what I did to get from Figure 9.1 to Figure 9.3:

1. I made sure the Type tool was selected.

2. I placed the cursor over the type I wished to edit. The cursor turned into an I-beam insertion point. I placed the insertion point at the end of the word *Washington* and clicked. This automatically selected the type layer. I then typed a copyright (©) symbol and 2001. At this point, I could have chosen a new font or font style or even changed the color of the type in the options bar. I also could have changed the orientation from horizontal type to vertical by selecting the Text Orientation (T͢) button, but I didn't.

3. When I was finished, I pulled the cursor away from the type and moved the type into position. Doing this automatically committed my new text.

Photo by George Washington © 2001

Figure 9.3: Edit your type by selecting the Type tool and clicking on the type.

As I said, the basics of the Type tool are pretty simple. Let's move on.

Making Headline Type

Headlines are meant to be bold and catchy, and often they consist of just one or two words that reinforce the theme or message of the underlying image. The secret to a good headline is readability and simplicity. Take a look at Figure 9.4.

Figure 9.4: You can create 100pt. type such as this, or larger, by typing the number directly into the Set Type Size box in the Type options bar.

This is how I created the *Relax* headline:

1. With my target image open, I selected the Type tool and selected the following options in the options bar:
   - Font: Apple Chancery.
   - Font Type: Chancery.
   - Font size: 100pt. The secret here is not to feel restricted by the 72pt. maximum displayed in the pop-up window. You can type in any number you want.
   - Font color: Red.
2. I then clicked on the sky and typed the word *Relax*.
3. I moved the cursor outside the type area, and it turned into the Move tool pointer. I dragged the headline into place, which also committed it.

That's it for now. In the next section, I'll show you ways of making the headline even more readable.

Making Type More Readable

Sometimes type needs a little help to make it stand out from a busy or colorful background. Photoshop Elements has as many techniques to distinguish type from the background as there are stars in the galaxy. Here are a couple of examples that should spark your imagination.

Adding a Drop Shadow and Embossment

Figure 9.5 shows the result of adding two layer styles to the word *Relax*, making it easier to read and more interesting.

Figure 9.5: By adding a drop shadow and emboss layer style from the Layer Styles palette, the type is more readable.

To create this effect, I did the following:

1. In the Layers palette, I selected the type layer containing the word *Relax*.
2. In the Layer Styles palette, I chose Drop Shadows from the pop-up menu; I then chose the Low drop shadow. Figure 9.6 shows the effects so far.

> **Note:** You can remove an effect by clicking the Default Style button in the Layer Styles palette, or by selecting the Step Backwards button (↩) from the shortcuts bar, or by choosing Layer ➤ Layer Style ➤ Clear Layer Style.

3. Next, in the Layer Styles palette, I chose Bevels from the pop-up menu; I chose Scalloped Edge. Figure 9.7 shows the effects so far.

> **Note:** Layer Styles effects are cumulative. Attributes of a second style are added to the attributes of a first style, and so on. Unfortunately, you can remove layer styles only sequentially. You can't, say, remove the third of five layer styles and keep the rest. You have to use the Step Backwards command to remove the last layer style, then remove the next-to-last layer style, and so on. If you upgrade to the full version of Photoshop, layer styles are more manageable.

Figure 9.6: By adding a simple drop shadow, the type is already more readable. Figure 9.7: The embossment makes it even better looking. ◎

4.   In the Layers palette, on the type layer containing the word *Relax*, I double-clicked the *f*. This brought up the dialog box shown in Figure 9.8. I slightly increased the Shadow Distance but kept the Bevel Size.

Figure 9.8: In the Style Settings dialog box, you can control the fine points of a layer style.

Using a Gradient

As you can see in Figure 9.9, when you place type with a single color against an area containing a similar color or contrast, part of the type becomes unreadable. You can use a Gradient fill to make your type readable across a wider spectrum of color and contrast (see Figure 9.10).

Figure 9.9: Black type disappears in the shadow area. Figure 9.10: By applying a Gradient fill to the type, it is more readable.

This is what I did to make the type more visible:

1.   I needed to fill my Foreground and Background boxes on the toolbox with contrasting colors so that I could use those colors later to make the Gradient tool work properly. To do this, I used the Eyedropper tool ( ) to select a dark area from my image. When I clicked on the cursor, that dark color became my Foreground color. I then used the Switch command ( ) to turn the Foreground color into a Background color. You can also type *X* to exchange the colors. Or you can hold down the Alt/Option key with the Eyedropper tool selected to set the background color. I used the Eyedropper tool again to find a contrasting tone, clicked, and it became Foreground color.

2. On the text layer, I Ctrl/Command+clicked on the Layer thumbnail. This selected the type. If I didn't select the type and then applied the Gradient fill, the fill would fill an entire layer and not just my type.

3. I selected Gradient from the pop-up menu that appeared when I clicked the Create New Fill or Adjustment Layer button ( ) at the bottom of the Layers palette. From the Gradient dialog box that appeared, I selected a linear gradient type and chose the Foreground to Background gradient fill from the Gradient Picker pop-up palette. (Now you see why I needed to go through step 1.) I then positioned my cursor on the words *Photo by Ana Mikaela* and dragged back and forth across the text until the gradient looked right. Dragging like this across the type sets the starting and ending points of the gradient.

4. I linked the two layers together so I if I moved my type layer, the gradient would move with it. To link the two layers, I selected the type layer in the Layers palette. Then, in the gradient layer, I clicked in the column immediately to the left. As you can see in Figure 9.11, the link icon now appears in the column next to the gradient layer.

Figure 9.11: My Layers palette showing the linked **Gradient Fill** *layer.*

Using a gradient like this requires a little work, but once you get the hang of it, it really opens a lot of possibilities. You can choose different colors or different gradients and get completely different looks for your type. Just keep in mind when you're ready to print your work that some printers might not capture the fine detail of the gradient. If you are having trouble, merge your gradient and type layers, and then apply a very slight Add Noise filter (Filter ➢ Noise ➢ Add Noise). Use the Monochromatic and Gaussian settings, and this should help.

Using Shape Tools to Accent Type

Shape tools provide an easy and quick way to create a simple background that will help make your type stand out from the rest of the image. Shape tools include the Rectangle, Rounded Rectangle, Ellipse, Polygon, Line, and Custom shape tools. They are all found in the same spot in the toolbox, along with the Shape Selection tool.

When you use a shape tool, Photoshop Elements places the shape of choice onto its own layer by default. You can go back at any time and edit a shape's color in the options bar or via the Layers palette. You can also apply layer styles to a shape as well as apply transformations to it. However, a shape layer is similar to a type layer in that you must simplify it before you can paint or apply filters to it.

Figure 9.12 shows examples of different shapes that are particularly useful for placing type against. As you can see in Figure 9.13, the shape layer must reside under the type layer, or else the type won't be visible.

 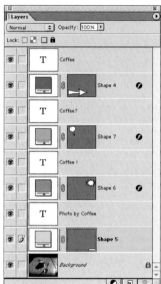

Figure 9.12: Here are just a few of the ready-made shapes that can be used to make your type stand out. *Figure 9.13: Note that the type layers must be above the shape layer; otherwise, the type won't be visible.*

Here's how I made the various shapes:

- The Yellow shape was created by using the Rectangle tool filled with yellow. I didn't use any Layer Effects.
- The Green shape was created by selecting the Custom shape tool and navigating to the Thought 2 shape found in the Talk Bubbles category. (You access this category—and all categories—by clicking the down arrow button next to the word Shape in the options bar. Then click the right arrow, in the upper-right corner of the new window.) I then flipped the shape to a horizontal position (Image ➤ Rotate ➤ Flip Horizontal). I also applied a Glass Button: Lime Green Glass Layer Effect.
- The Blue shape was created by selecting the Custom shape tool and navigating to the Arrow 1 shape found in the Arrows category. I applied a Bevels: Simple Shape Inner Layer Effect.
- The Red shape was created by selecting the Custom shape tool and navigating to the 10 Point Star shape found in the Default category. I applied a Drop Shadow: High Layer Effect.

Warping Type

I can't believe how easy it is to warp type. In the old days, you'd never consider using a bitmap program such as Photoshop Elements to do this. You'd use a vector program such as Macromedia FreeHand or Adobe Illustrator. Now, in just a few simple steps you can distort type into an arc or a wave and make it conform to a particular shape. That's what I did to create a 50th wedding anniversary card for my parents, as shown in Figure 9.14.

Figure 9.14: *The type in this image was warped to conform to the shape of the photograph. Warped type is completely changeable.*

Note: When you warp type, you warp all the characters in a particular type layer. You cannot warp individual characters within the same type layer.

To get this effect, I did the following:

1. I selected the Type tool and typed in the text.
2. I committed the type and then applied a drop shadow and bevel from the Layer Effects palette.
3. With the Type tool selected, I clicked on the type and selected the Create Warped Text button (𝗧) from the options bar.
4. In the Warp Text dialog box, I selected Arc from the Style options. I slid the Bend slider until the type assumed the general shape of my photograph. I didn't touch the Horizontal or Vertical Distortion sliders. (see Figure 9.15).

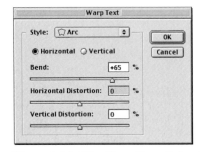

Figure 9.15: *The Warp Text dialog box and options.*

Filling Type with an Image

You can blur the distinction between type and image by creating type out of an image (see Figure 9.16).

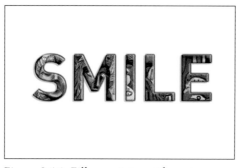

Figure 9.16: Fill your type with an image.

To create type from an image, follow these steps:

1. Open an appropriate image, such as the one in Figure 9.17.
2. Select the Type tool and then select the Create a Selection button (𝚃) in the options bar.
3. Choose a bold font wide enough to adequately show your fill. For this example, I chose Myriad Bold as the font style and 500pt. as the font size.
4. Type in the area you wish to use as fill. A red background will appear, showing the selected areas (see Figure 9.18).

Figure 9.17: Choose an image with lots of color and texture as fill for your type.
Figure 9.18: When you type, a red background appears, showing you the selected areas.

5. Commit your type, and the text will appear as a selection. Now make a copy of the selection (Ctrl/Command+C), and paste the selection to its own layer (Ctrl/Command+V).
6. At this point, your type is simplified, meaning you can't use the Type tool to change it. However, you can use just about any other tool or filter to further enhance the type. For the type shown in this example, I applied a drop shadow and bevel from the Layer Effects palette.

Making Volcano Type

Type can be especially effective if it draws on a theme or quality of an image. That's what National Geographic web designer Valerie Robbins did, as shown in Figure 9.19. Valerie created the special look by using several Photoshop layer styles that aren't included with Photoshop Elements. I've taken the liberty, with her permission of course, to show you how to get a close approximation (see Figure 9.20).

Figure 9.19: Valerie Robbins made this explosive type largely with Photoshop's layer effects. (Background photo copyright Carsten Peter. Screen grab courtesy The National Geographic Society.)   Figure 9.20: I tried to duplicate Val's work with Photoshop Elements.

This is what I did to come up with the approximation:

1. I started with Val's original type, as shown in Figure 9.21. The font, by the way is DIN, black, set at 144pt. I changed the type to a variation of the red found in the volcano, as shown in Figure 9.22.

Figure 9.21: I started with Val's original type.   Figure 9.22: I changed it to red.

2. I then tried to re-create Val's layer effects, knowing that I didn't have Photoshop's Satin, or Stroke, or Color Overlay layer effects to work with. I started with a Low Drop Shadow, then I applied a Simple Pillow Emboss, and a Simple Inner Glow. When I was finished, I double-clicked the *f* in the type layer and played with my settings in the Style Settings dialog box until I got something close to Val's work (see Figure 9.23).

Figure 9.23: I changed the Lighting Angle and the Bevel Size and left the other settings alone.

Adding Effects to Type

Photoshop Elements has several effects that can enhance your type. Effects, unlike layer styles, are not changeable. They also simplify your type layer, so it's best to always create a copy of your type layer before applying an effect.

Figure 9.24 shows a few examples of type treated with effects.

Figure 9.24: Type treated with different effects.

Applying Liquify to Type

If you really want to have fun with your type, use the Liquify filter. You'll need to simplify the type layer before doing so, but once your type is in the Liquify filter work area, you'll have trouble deciding when to stop.

Artist Tom Mogensen used about every technique outlined in this chapter to create the wine label shown in Figure 9.25 for his friend Ellen Deitch. I won't go into all the details of what he did, but I was particularly impressed with his treatment of the word *Champagne* and how he used the Liquify filter to create a ripple with the letter *C*.

Figure 9.25: Tom Mogensen used a variety of type tricks to create this wine label.

This is what he did:

1. He duplicated the type layer containing the warped word *Champagne* (Layer ➢ Duplicate Layer).

2. He flipped the duplicate type layer and moved the flipped *Champagne* in a position below the original warped type (Image ➤ Rotate ➤ Flip Vertical), as shown in Figure 9.26.

3. He used the Type tool to create a large C and applied an Outer Glow Layer style to it. He positioned the C over the C in *Champagne*. He duplicated the C type layer and positioned the duplicate C over the C in the flipped copy of the word *Champagne*, as shown in Figure 9.27.

Figure 9.26: Tom flipped a copy of the word Champagne and dragged it below the original type. Figure 9.27: The bottom C will soon get liquified.

4. He simplified the layer containing the duplicate C and selected the Liquify filter.

5. With the Liquify filter Reflection tool ( ), he lightly brushed the letter to get the effect shown in Figure 9.28. As a final step, he played with his Layers palette Opacity settings to make the reflected word *Champagne* and the Liquified letter C look right.

Figure 9.28: The Liquify filter Reflection tool distorted the letter C as shown.

By the way, as shown earlier, there is an effect called Water Reflection. If Tom had used this effect, he would not have had as much control over the final look of his work.

Note: If you want type to be visible outside the image area, you'll need to expand the canvas. To do this, choose Image ➤ Resize ➤ Canvas Size and enter the desired dimensions in the Width and Height boxes. Give yourself plenty of room; you can crop later. If you want an equal amount of extra canvas surrounding your image, leave the Anchor set in the middle position.

There is a big difference *between preparing images for the Web and preparing images for print. The Web is a screen medium, meaning anyone who views your images will see them at 72dpi on systems with different display capabilities and specifications. It's also a medium with limited bandwidth, which means file size is an important consideration. This chapter focuses on creating and preparing images for the Web so they look great on as many display systems as possible and download quickly as well. This chapter also walks you through the creation of essential design components, such as navigational buttons and web page backgrounds. You'll even learn how to use the Web Photo Gallery automation command, which is a remarkably easy way to create a ready-to-go website complete with thumbnails and HTML links.*

10

Working with the Web in Mind

Choosing GIF or JPEG
Making GIFs
Building Web Page Backgrounds
Creating Navigational Graphics
Creating Web Type
Making a Web Photo Gallery

Working with the Web in Mind

Choosing GIF or JPEG

Before you begin optimizing your digital images for the Web, you'll need to decide on a file format. The two graphics file formats of choice for the Web are *GIF* and *JPEG*, which are both widely supported by just about any web browser in the world.

One other graphic file format, *PNG*, is also supported by some web browsers. PNG combines the best of JPEG (24-bit color support) and the best of GIF (transparency and lossless compression) without the drawbacks. It also fixes the gamma problem that exists between platforms, so images look the same on any platform. For all these reasons, PNG is slowly gaining acceptance in the web community. Photoshop Elements is capable of creating PNGs, but for now I suggest that you stick with the more universally supported GIF or JPEG format.

Before you start, you also need to set your Photoshop Elements preferences to reflect the special requirements of the Web. Select Edit ➤ Color Settings and set your option to No Color Management. Select Edit ➤ Preferences ➤ Saving Files and turn off the image preview options, especially if you are creating JPEG files. By doing this you'll make the File Browser work slower but you'll also reduce the file size and eliminate the chance of creating a corrupt file. Select Edit ➤ Preferences ➤ Units and Rulers and select Pixels, the preferred measurement unit of the Web's bitmap world. For more on setting Photoshop Elements preferences, refer to the beginning of the book (☞ "Setting Preferences" in Chapter 1).

So which file format should you choose, GIF or JPEG?

Both the GIF and JPEG formats give you ways to control the file size of your web graphics, a critical feature considering the Web's limited bandwidth capabilities. JPEG does this by compressing and actually throwing away data it considers unnecessary. GIF controls file size through a combination of lossless compression and color reduction.

The GIF file format, however, supports only up to 256 colors. It can simulate more colors through a process called *dithering*, but this often results in a grainy or rough-looking image. Most digital images consist of millions of colors, so you can see right away that GIF is not necessarily the best choice for a photograph or continuous tone image. On the other hand, GIF gives you precise control over which colors you choose to use. This can be important if your image is a graphic, for example, containing large expanses of color that you want to blend seamlessly into an HTML-designated background color. It's also possible with the GIF file format to define selected areas as transparent, which can make an irregular-shaped graphic or image appear to float without a rectangular border on a web page. Finally, you can use the GIF file format to create simple animations. I'll get into both transparency and animation later in the chapter.

The JPEG file format supports millions of colors and compresses an image much more than a GIF ever could. However, with the JPEG file format you don't have precise control over the individual colors, and because data is actually thrown away, there is some loss of quality. The loss of quality is especially noticeable in images that contain a lot of detail. That's why the JPEG format is generally not used on images that contain type. Of course, as you will soon see, there are exceptions.

Figure 10.1 is an image saved in the JPEG file format. It is a 640 × 320 pixel photo composite created by designer/artist Valerie Robbins and it is a perfect candidate for the JPEG format because it contains continuous tones and lots of color. Using Photoshop Elements to convert the image to the JPEG file format, I got a very decent file size of 25.83KB without any noticeable loss of quality. When I converted the original PSD file to the GIF format, it compressed to only 119.4KB. Figure 10.2 shows the GIF version. If you look closely at it, you will see that the GIF image doesn't look very good either. It's rough and grainy. In the next section, I'll show you ways to turn your photo into a GIF with better results.

Figure 10.1: In the JPEG format, this photo composite by Valerie Robbins compresses to 25.83KB with no noticeable difference in quality. Figure 10.2: When saved as a GIF, the file size is 119.4KB, and you can see the degradation in quality.

Figure 10.3 is also saved in the GIF file format. It's a 249 × 279 pixel web graphic created by Valerie Robbins. Figure 10.4 shows the palette and the 34 colors that make up the graphic. (You can always see the palette of a GIF by choosing Image ➢ Mode ➢ Color Table.) The file size of the GIF graphic is 15.1KB and converting it to a JPEG would have likely resulted in a slightly smaller file size with an acceptable loss in quality. However, if it had been a JPEG, Valerie wouldn't have had precise control over the background color, which was critical because that color needed to exactly match the background color of her web page.

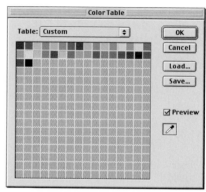

Figure 10.3: This works well as a GIF because it contains fewer than 256 colors—34 to be exact. (Illustration by Valerie Robbins for the site **www.philanthropyroundtable.org.***)*
Figure 10.4: The colors that make up the graphic as displayed in the color palette.

Of course, rules are made to be broken. Figure 10.5, for example, is a 620 × 450 pixel graphic Valerie created for her own website, **www.buttercupstudios.com.** As you can see, it contains type but it also contains important tonal subtleties. To keep these subtleties, Valerie saved the graphic as a JPEG, and it weighed in at only 23KB. Sure, the type might have appeared crisper if she had saved the graphic as a GIF, but in the case of this particular image, it didn't matter so much.

Figure 10.5: Even though this graphic contains type, it works fine as a JPEG.

For the sake of simplicity, let's just say this:

- Use JPEG for photographic images and continuous tone art.
- Use GIF for graphics that contain type, a limited number of colors, or for those special situations when you want transparency or an animation.

The next section shows you how to create great looking GIFs. The next chapter is devoted entirely to the JPEG file format.

Making GIFs

The secret to making great GIF images lies in your choice of a color palette, the number of colors you use, and how much dithering, if any, you apply.

Before I show you how to do this by using the Save for Web and the Save As methods, let me just take a moment to illustrate how critical color palettes are to the GIF file format. Look once again at Figure 10.3, the graphic created by Valerie Robbins. Next to it in Figure 10.4 is its color index, or palette, showing exactly which of the up-to 256 possible colors are actually present. Believe it or not, Figure 10.6 shows the same exact image, but this time I've applied a different color palette, or index, to it. Figure 10.7 shows the new color palette, and as you can see, the image changes accordingly.

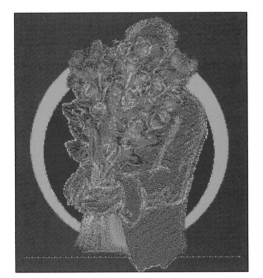
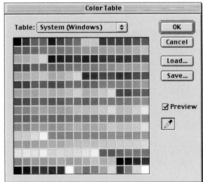

Figure 10.6: With a different color palette, this is totally different image. Figure 10.7: The new color palette.

Keep this example in mind as you proceed through the next steps.

Using Save For Web

Let's work on an appropriate image for the GIF file format. Figure 10.8 shows a headline designer Val Robbins created for one of my websites, **www.shooting-digital.com.** The graphic contains text and colors that Val wanted precise control over. I'll use the Save for Web method to convert it to the GIF file format. The Save for Web plug-in features side-by-side viewing capability so I can easily compare my original with the optimized version. It also gives me several other preview options that I'll discuss later.

Figure 10.8: I'll make this PSD graphic a GIF by using the Save for Web plug-in.

First, I'll prepare the graphic in a quick and simple way that will result in a GIF that is ready to be placed on a website and displayed by just about any web browser in the world. Afterward, I'll use the Save for Web palette, Dither, and Color options to "tweak" the same image and create a GIF that takes up less kilobytes but still looks great.

Keep in mind that once a graphic is open in the Save for Web plug-in, none of Photoshop Elements' regular tools and commands are available. That's why I resized Valerie's graphic to the desired dimensions before proceeding.

After the graphic was properly sized, I did the following:

1. I chose File ➢ Save for Web. This opened a new window, as shown in Figure 10.9. As soon as my image appeared in the window, the plug-in automatically began optimizing it for the Web. It applies the last-used settings or the default setting if you are using it for the first time. You can stop the optimizing by typing Esc/(Command+period).

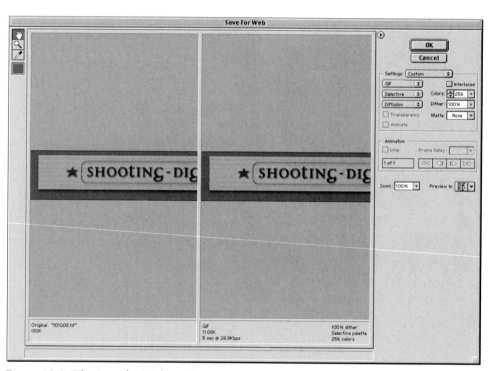

Figure 10.9: The Save for Web work area.

2. For this example, I kept the default GIF settings:
- Palette: Selective
- Dither option: Diffusion
- Colors: 256
- Dither amount: 100 percent

I left the Interlaced box unchecked. Interlace creates a GIF that loads on a browser window gradually, in successive passes. However, it also adds file size so it is best avoided. Because my graphic didn't contain any transparent areas, Transparency was not an option. (Again, I'll get to the whole issue of GIF transparency and choosing a matte color later in this section.)

3. By zooming in, I could see that I had an optimized image that looked just as good as the original. I could also see by the numbers below the optimized version that the file size was 11.08KB. This number is accurate, unlike file sizes found in Photoshop Elements' main window, which are approximations.

> **Note:** You can zoom in for a closer examination of your optimized image by selecting the Zoom tool (🔍) and clicking on the image. You can also zoom in by selecting a percentage from the Zoom pop-up menu. If you right-click (Windows) or hold Control while clicking anywhere in the Save for Web window (Mac), you'll also have access to view controls. To preview your graphic as it would look in a browser window, click the Browser icon (in the Preview In box) on the right of the Save for Web window.

4. I selected Save, and Save for Web automatically added the GIF extension and returned me to the main Photoshop Elements window.

If you duplicate what I've just done in this example with just about any GIF-appropriate image, you'll be fine. But for now, let's fine-tune this image and optimize it even more.

This requires some experimentation and understanding of the various palette and Dither options. If you click on the Palette pop-up menu, you'll see several other choices besides the Selective palette, including Perceptual, Adaptive, Web, and Custom:

- **Perceptual** is much like Selective, in that it creates a custom color table based on the colors in your image. Selective favors so-called web-safe colors (more on them later), and Perceptual gives priority to colors that are more visible to the human eye.

- **Adaptive** also creates a custom palette based on the colors found in the image.

- **Web,** on the other hand, is a fixed palette containing only the 216-color table common to both Windows and the Mac. Frankly, there are very few cases when this palette is appropriate, and I'll get into those later.

- **Custom** isn't exactly a palette in the same way the other choices are. This setting forces the Save for Web plug-in to keep the current color table, created previously by one of the other palettes, and not to add any new colors to the palette when changes to the Dither or Colors options are made. The number of colors, however, can be reduced.

The three relevant choices then are Selective, Adaptive, and Perceptual, and I suggest you try each one on your image and see what they do. The results vary from image to image depending on the content and colors contained in the image, so I can't give you any other advice except to experiment. In the case of Val's graphic, the Selective palette turned out to be the best.

The next thing to do is choose different Dither settings. Dithering is an issue only if your original image contains more than the maximum 256 colors supported by the GIF format. In this case, dithering creates a smooth gradation between adjacent colors by using the existing colors to create patterns that the eye merges into a single new color. This gives the appearance of extending the Color palette beyond 256 colors. Up close, however, the patterns become obvious, and the image looks grainy or speckled. Without dithering, the sharp contrast between colors will result in *banding*, which is not very attractive. Dithering always increases the file size.

The Dither options include No Dither, Diffusion (default setting), Pattern, and Noise. Most of the time, a Diffusion dither is your best choice and creates the smoothest transition between colors. However, once again, you can experiment to see what works best for your particular image. You can also control the amount of dithering with the Dither option. The default is 100 percent, but you can lower that number. As you do, the file size will be reduced accordingly.

I chose No Dither because Val's graphic contained fewer than 256 colors and so dithering wasn't necessary.

The next choice is Colors, and this is where you can get some real file size reduction. If you leave the default set to 256 colors, a color index that contains 256 colors will be created, regardless of whether you need that many. If you choose the Auto option from the Colors pop-up menu, Photoshop Elements will determine the optimal number of colors in the color table for you. You can also incrementally reduce the number of colors until your image becomes unacceptable. That's what I did with Val's graphic. I started with 256 colors, stepped down to 128 colors, and compared the optimized version with the original. Because there was no difference, I kept going, down to 64 colors. Still no difference. At 32 colors, I began to notice some degradation in the drop shadow areas so I went back to 64 colors, confident that I had optimized my file size as much as I could. The final file size? I went from 11.08KB to 7.49KB, a 30 percent reduction.

Note: To embed your Save for Web settings into the original Photoshop Elements file, hold down the Alt/Option key. The OK button turns into a Remember button. If you select Remember, the next time you open the Photoshop Elements file with the Save for Web plug-in, it will apply the same settings that were applied at the time you chose Remember. If you don't do this, the next time you open your Photoshop Elements file, it will apply the most current optimized settings.

Note: When you view the same image on a Mac and a PC, it will look different. This means if you create a graphic or image that looks good on a Mac, it will look too dark on a PC. If you create an image or graphic on a PC that looks right, it will look washed out on a Mac. If you are interested in having your work look good on both platforms, you should consider adjusting your brightness settings accordingly. In the Photoshop Elements work area, select Enhance ➤ Brightness/Contrast ➤ Brightness/Contrast. If you are working on a PC, try reducing your brightness by -15. If you are working on a Mac, try increasing your brightness by +15. Once back in the Save for Web plug-in, you can preview your work to see what it will look like on either platform. Click the small arrow in the upper-right of the Save for Web window, and a drop-down menu appears. Choose the platform in which you wish to preview your work. You can also choose Browser Dither, which shows how your graphic will look if it is forced to dither by a browser.

Using Save As

Another way to create a GIF is to use the Save As method. When you use this method, you lose a certain amount of preview capabilities but you'll gain more in the way of options and control.

As with the Save for Web method, there is a quick and easy Save As method, and then a way that takes more time but usually results in a smaller file size.

To use the quick and easy method:

1. While in RGB mode, size your image to the desired size (Image ➤ Resize ➤ Image Size). To make sure you are in RGB mode, select Image ➤ Mode ➤ RGB.

2. Select File ➤ Save As. In the file dialog box, choose CompuServe GIF from the pop-up menu. After you select Save, the Indexed Color dialog box shown in Figure 10.10 appears. You can also open this dialog box by going directly to Image ➤ Mode ➤ Indexed Color. Again, you must start in the RGB mode.

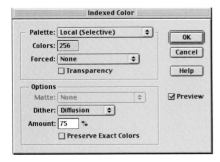

Figure 10.10: When you choose Save As ➤ CompuServe GIF ➤ Save, you get this dialog box. You need to start from the RGB mode.

3. The following settings will give you perfectly acceptable results:
- Palette: Local (Selective).
- Colors: 256.
- Forced: None.
- Dither: Diffusion.
- Amount: 100 percent. (75 percent is the default, and that works fine too.)

By leaving the Preview check box selected, you can see the effect of your choices on the image. Under the word *Preview* in the Indexed Color box, a short dash pulses until the optimizing is complete. You won't have the advantage of the Save for Web side-by-side comparison, and to view your original you'll need deselect the Preview box. Using common Photoshop keyboard commands—Ctrl/Command zooms in and Alt/Option zooms out—you can carefully examine the effects of your settings.

4. After you are finished, click Save.

Now for some details that will help you optimize your image further. You'll see more Palette options in the Indexed Color dialog box than you will in the Save for Web plug-in, including the following:
- **Exact** is an option only if the image contains 256 or fewer colors.
- **System (Mac OS)** uses the Macintosh default 8-bit palette.
- **System (Windows)** uses the Windows system default 8-bit palette.
- **Uniform** is used in scientific work, and I won't even try to describe it.
- **Custom** creates a custom palette by using the Color Table dialog box.
- **Preview** uses the custom palette from the previous conversion.

For most digital images, the three relevant palettes are Adaptive, Selective, and Perceptive. You'll notice the words *Local* and *Master* in front of these three choices. Master is an option only if more than one image is open in the Photoshop Elements window at a time. If you select a palette with the word *Master* in front of it, Photoshop Elements averages all the colors in all the images that are open and creates a "master" palette that it then applies to your image. If this isn't what you want, just be sure to use the palette with the word *Local* in front of it. That way, you'll know you are getting a palette specifically tailored to the image you started with.

As I described in the "Using Save for Web" section, you can experiment with the different palettes, dithering, and colors to come up with an even more optimal image. The only drawback is you won't know your file size until after you save your image.

Paying Special Attention to Web Colors

The 216 colors that can be read by both the PC and the Mac are called *web-safe*, or *browser-safe*, colors. Web-safe colors are an issue only if a display system is not capable of displaying more than 256 colors.

If your digital image or graphic contains colors that are not web safe, and they are viewed on a web browser running on a limited display system, the browser will either replace the color with one that is web safe or simulate the color through dithering.

When it comes to using web-safe colors for your work, I suggest you have three choices:

- You can ignore the whole issue and say good riddance to those viewers who don't have display systems capable of displaying at least thousands, if not millions, of colors. If you choose this option, move on and skip the rest of this section entirely.
- You can get really obsessive and use only web-safe colors, in which case you should read one of my earlier books, *Photoshop for the Web* (O'Reilly & Associates, 2000), in which I devote many chapters to ways to do this.
- You can take a more reasoned approach and use web-safe colors only in areas of large expanses of solid color, such as backgrounds, and don't worry about the other areas where it won't matter if your image dithers or if the colors are slightly changed.

If you decide on option 3, which I think is a good choice, you'll need to start with web-safe colors when appropriate or swap existing non-web-safe colors with ones that are.

You can select browser-safe colors to work with from the Swatches palette found in the palette well, or from the Color Picker, accessed by double-clicking on the foreground or background color boxes (🖱) in the toolbox. Figure 10.11 shows the Web Spectrum found in the Swatches palette. Figure 10.12 shows the Color Picker with the Only Web Colors option selected.

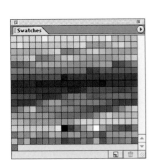
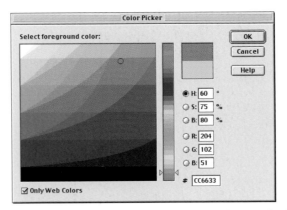

Figure 10.11: The Swatches palette with the Web Spectrum loaded. The 216 displayed colors are considered web safe. Holding the cursor over a swatch displays the color's hexadecimal value. Figure 10.12: The Color Picker with the Only Web Colors box selected. Now only web-safe colors can be selected. Hexadecimal values are also shown.

Note: To extend the web-safe palette, you can use the DitherBox filter to create custom dithering patterns from web-safe colors and simulate a wider color spectrum (Filter ➤ Other ➤ DitherBox). The filter makes it easy to create patterns based on collections of 4-64 web-safe colors and to save the patterns in groups called *collections*. See Figure 10.13.

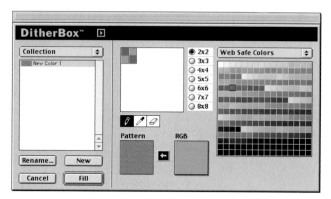

Figure 10.13: The DitherBox filter helps you simulate a wider web-safe color spectrum.

There are several ways to swap non-web-safe colors with ones that are. One way is to follow these steps:

1. Fill the foreground color box with a web-safe color from the Swatches palette or from the Color Picker set to Only Web Colors.

2. Use either Photoshop's Magic Wand (✎), Magnetic Lasso (✎), or manual selection tools to select the area of the image that you want to change.

3. Fill the selected area with the color that you chose from a browser-safe palette (Edit ➤ Fill and Use: Foreground).

4. To ensure that your browser-safe colors don't shift when you apply the Indexed Color command, check the Preserve Exact Colors box in the Indexed Color dialog box. This will be an option only if your choose a Dither pattern.

Another way is to use the Color Table to swap out the non-web-safe color. This works only if you are in the Index Color mode. Here's how:

1. Choose Image ➤ Mode ➤ Color Table.

2. Select the Eyedropper tool (✎) from the Color Table dialog box.

3. Click on the area in your image that you wish to alter. The color box in the Color Table will be highlighted, and your selected color deleted from the box and from the image. Now deselect the Eyedropper tool.

4. Double-click the highlighted color box in the Color Table to bring up the Color Picker. Select the web-safe color of your choice and click OK. That color will now replace your old, non-web-safe color.

5. You can repeat this process on other flat colors that you don't want to dither. Click the OK button when you are finished. Test your image by using the Save for Web preview options.

Of course, you can always apply the Web palette to the entire graphic palette by using the Save As or the Save for Web method. This might or might not produce acceptable results, depending on the colors in your image. With an image that contains more than 256 colors, the results generally are not good.

If you do decide to apply the Web palette to a graphic, you'll end up with an indexed image that contains 216 browser-safe colors. But what if you don't need 216 colors? What if your image contains only 64 colors, or, for that matter, 16? By saving your file with 216 colors, you have created an unnecessarily large file. What to do now? You can get rid of the unused colors by following these steps:

1. Switch from Indexed Color to RGB mode (Image ➤ Mode ➤ RGB).
2. Without doing anything else, switch back to Indexed Color mode. If your image has fewer than 216 colors, the Exact palette should be selected, and the number of colors in the image will be displayed.
3. Click the OK button and save the indexed image as a GIF.

The new image will look exactly the same as the original GIF, while the file size will shrink.

Making Transparent GIFs

By using the GIF file format, you can designate a color as transparent. This means you can make a non-rectangular object appear to float against a background.

You can do this either with the Save for Web or Save As methods. Both methods require that you start in the RGB mode and create transparent areas as indicated by gray and white checkers—or whatever pattern or color you've set your Transparency preferences to.

Figure 10.14 shows another graphic created by designer Valerie Robbins for another one of my websites. If I convert her graphic to the GIF format "as is" with its white background and place it on my web page with a gold background, the graphic will float in a rectangular patch of white. If I remove the white background and replace it with transparency, then the graphic will float against the gold background. The fact is, if I make the white area transparent, it doesn't matter what color my web page background is; the graphic will still appear to float against it.

Figure 10.14: Placed against a gold background, the rectangular shape is obvious.

To create a transparent GIF by using the Save for Web method (starting in the RGB mode), I followed these steps:

1. I used the Magic Eraser (⌦) to delete the white background to transparency. If your graphic is already on a transparent layer, you are ready to go.

2. I chose File ➢ Save for Web.

3. In the Save for Web window, I clicked the Transparency check box. This option is available only if your graphic contains transparent areas. If the box is left unchecked, your transparent areas will appear in the optimized view as white, or whatever color you choose in the Matte color box next to the word *Transparency*. After you click the Transparency check box, the transparent areas in your graphic will be designated by the familiar gray and white checkered pattern.

4. I chose the appropriate palette, dithering, and colors, and optimized the graphic.

5. I used the Save for Web browser preview feature to view the transparent GIF.

At this point, I saw a problem in the browser window. Figure 10.15, which is magnified, shows a halo around the edges.

Figure 10.15: Now I've got transparency but I also have a halo.

Before I get into how to fix this problem, it's helpful to explain a basic fact about the GIF transparency. Variable opacity is not an option in the GIF format. It supports only one transparent color, which effectively means a 1-bit mask. Areas are either transparent or not.

To get around the 1-bit mask limitation, you can have Photoshop Elements create a pseudo multi-bit mask. If you know the color of your web page background, all you need to do is choose that color from the Matte pop-up menu. Photoshop Elements then adds variations of this color to edges of your graphic. If your web background consists of multiple colors, pick a representative color from your background and use that. Creating this pseudo multi-bit mask adds some file size to your GIF, but not much.

Because I know my graphic will be placed on a page with a gold background, I chose Other from the Matte pop-up menu, and then in the Color Picker I chose FFCC33, the hexadecimal value for my color. The selected color is displayed in the Matte box. (If you set the Matte to None, no pseudo multi-bit mask is created. Use None if an aliased look is what you want.)

A blow-up of the edges shown in Figure 10.16 illustrates how Photoshop Elements adds variations of the Matte color to the edges of the graphic. Now when the graphic is placed against the browser background, there is nice anti-aliasing effect that makes the graphic look much better (see Figure 10.17).

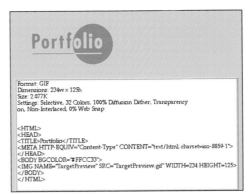

Figure 10.16: When you choose a Matte color, a pseudo multi-bit mask is created, which diminishes the jagged look. Figure 10.17: Now the graphic floats nicely on the page.

You can also use the Save As or Image ➢ Mode ➢ Indexed Colors method to designate transparent areas.

While in the RGB mode:

1. Use one of the Eraser or Selection tools to delete your background or other areas to transparency. Transparency is signified by gray and white checkers.

2. Select Save As or Image ➢ Mode ➢ Indexed Colors.

3. Select Transparency from the dialog box. If you know the background color of your web page, and you want to avoid a jagged or halo effect, have Photoshop Elements create a pseudo multi-bit mask. In the Matte pop-up menu, choose from the preset options or enter a color from the Color Picker. Matte will be available only if your image contains transparent areas.

4. Select the optimal palette, dithering, and color options. When you are finished, click OK. The areas signified by the gray and white checkers will become transparent.

GIFing a Photograph

Although GIF isn't the ideal format for photographs, if you want true transparency or control over certain colors in an image, there are times when you'll want to GIF a photographic image.

If you do this, I recommended that you use the following settings:

- Palette: Perceptual or Adaptive
- Dither option: Diffusion
- Colors: 256
- Dither amount: 100 percent

Furthermore, there is something else you can do to make certain photographs look better, especially photographs of faces. The method that I'll describe doesn't work with the Save for Web plug-in. You'll need to toggle between Image ➢ Mode ➢ RGB and Image ➢ Mode ➢ Indexed Color.

You have to understand that when Photoshop Elements converts an image from the RGB mode to the Indexed Color mode, it treats all parts of the image equally. It doesn't recognize, for example, that you might be more concerned about the foreground of the image than the background. But you're not stuck with this situation—you can "influence" Photoshop Elements to create a palette that best represents the important parts of your image.

Take the photograph shown in Figure 10.18. I applied the standard GIF settings described in the preceding bulleted list, and this is what I got. As you can see by the Color Table in Figure 10.19, the Perceptual palette gave a lot of emphasis to the colorful background and not enough to the important skin tones. It's OK, but I can easily do better.

 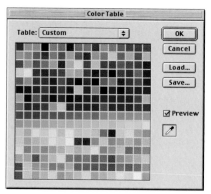

Figure 10.18: By applying the standard GIF settings, I got this. Figure 10.19: The Color Table shows an equal emphasis on the background colors and the face.

All I need to do is simply select the area that I want to emphasize with a selection tool. Now when I convert from RGB to Indexed Color mode, Photoshop Elements will automatically weigh the conversion in favor of the selected area.

This is what I've done to get the image shown in Figure 10.20. I made a selection around the child's face with the Elliptical Marquee tool (⬭), then converted the image to Indexed Color mode. The new palette, shown in Figure 10.21, contains many more of the subtle tonal variations that make the skin tone more realistic. Yeah, the rainbow now has color banding, but the face is the important part.

 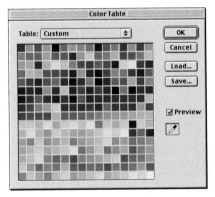

Figure 10.20: By selecting the child's face with the Elliptical Marquee tool and then applying the Indexed Color mode, the conversion is weighed in favor of the selected area.
Figure 10.21: The Color Table displays more skin tones.

Another thing you can do to make a photographic image look better is apply selective dithering. When you command Photoshop to dither an image, it applies the dither pattern to the entire image, even to areas that you might not want to dither, such as areas containing flat colors. Wouldn't it be great if you could "tell" Photoshop to selectively dither a small part of an image and yet keep the other parts intact? You can, by following these steps:

1. In RGB mode, select and copy the part of the image to dither (Ctrl/Command+C).

2. Index the image (Index ➤ Mode ➤ Indexed Color).

3. Paste the copied portion back from the Clipboard to the indexed but undithered image (Ctrl/Command+V). Photoshop automatically dithers the pasted RGB selection, leaving the rest of the image untouched.

By the way, I have CNET's Casey Caston to thank for showing me this very useful method.

Animating GIFs

You can also create simple animations by using the GIF file format and the Save for Web plug-in. Individual animation frames are created from Photoshop Elements layers. You can open an existing GIF animation file and view each frame as a layer in Photoshop Elements. This round-trip GIF animation capability is especially handy if you want to change and edit your animation.

Figure 10.22 and Figure 10.23 are two photographs that Sean Parker—my resident animation guru—turned into a mini-movie complete with motion blur by using the animating capabilities of the Save for Web plug-in. Sean cleverly created new layers based on different blends of the two images to make it look like more than just two photographs were used. Creating additional frames this way is a process referred to in animation as *tweening*.

Figure 10.22: Image 1 of Sean Parker's GIF animation. Figure 10.23: Image 2 of Sean Parker's GIF animation.

This is what he did:

1. He dragged the two images into a new document and positioned them such that little Peter and his grandparents were roughly sandwiched on top of each other. He temporarily changed the layer opacity to 50 percent to help him line up the two images.

2. He then copied Image 1, which has little Peter looking devilishly up at Grandma, three times and set the opacity to the three new layers at 75 percent, 50 percent, and 25 percent respectively.

3. The next step gets a little tricky. The point is to create three new layers by merging the duplicate layers of Image 1 (with different opacities) that Sean created in step 2 with Image 2, which shows Peter grabbing his grandmother's face. To do this, Sean created a new empty layer (Layer ➢ New ➢ Layer). Then, with this new layer selected, he turned off the visibility of all the layers *except* the layers containing Image 2, the new empty layer, *and* the copy of Image 1 set at 75 percent opacity. (To turn a layer's visibility off, click the eye icon on the far right side of the Layers palette. To turn on the visibility, click in the box on the far right side of the Layers palette.)

4. Sean needed to merge the three layers with their visibility turned on into one, and at the same time keep the layer containing Image 2 intact. If he selected

Merge Visible from the pop-up menu to the side of the Layers palette, the three layers would merge into one, and Sean would have lost the layer containing Image 2. Instead, Sean held down the Alt/Option key while selecting Merge Visible. Now the new empty layer became the target for the merge, and the other layers remained distinct and intact. He named this layer **Frame 2 - Image 1 - 75%**.

5. Before creating the next merged layer, Sean threw away the duplicate layer of Image 1 set at 75 percent opacity. This is the layer he just used to create the new merged layer, and he was finished with it. (To throw away layers, click and drag them into the trash icon at the bottom of the Layers palette.)

6. Next Sean created another merged layer. To do this, he created a new empty layer and this time he turned on the visibility of the duplicate of Image 1 that was set at 50 percent opacity, the new empty layer, and the layer containing Image 2. He turned off the visibility of the other layers. Once again, he held down the Alt/Option key while selecting Merge Visible from the pop-up menu. He called this now-merged layer **Frame 3 - Image 1 - 50%**. He threw away the duplicate of Image 1 set at 50 percent opacity.

7. To create the third and final merged layer, Sean created a new empty layer, turned on the visibility of the duplicate of Image 1 set at 25 percent opacity, the new empty layer, and the layer containing Image 2. He held down the Alt/Option key while selecting Merge Visible from the pop-up menu. He named this layer **Frame 4 - Image 1 - 25%**.

8. At this point, Sean had five layers but he needed three more to complete his animation. He created these three layers by duplicating the three layers containing the merged copies of the semi-transparent Image 1 and Image 2. Then he arranged the layers as shown in Figure 10.24. Note that Image 1 is the first layer of the stack. The Save for Web plug-in makes the first layer the first frame in an animation. It doesn't matter if the visibility of a layer is on or off. Save for Web will use the layer as part of the animation regardless.

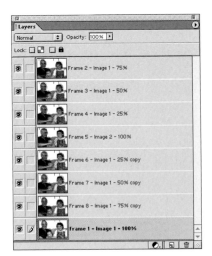

Figure 10.24: Sean's Layers palette showing the "frames" of his animation.

9. With his layers complete, Sean now selected File ≻ Save for Web, as shown in Figure 10.25. He selected GIF as his file format, chose the Selective palette with Diffusion, chose 256 colors, and checked the Animate box. In the Animation settings, he checked Loop so his animation would play continuously, and experimented with the frame rate settings until he got the look he wanted. You can step frame by frame through an animation by using the Animation controls in the Save for Web window. However, to view the animation in action, you need to click the Preview In check box and view your animation in a selected web browser.

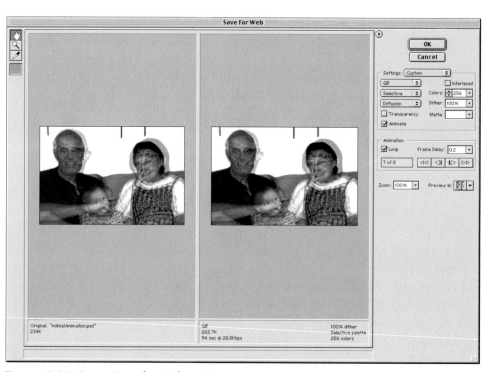

Figure 10.25: Sean's Save for Web settings.

Sean's GIF animation is included on the accompanying CD. The original Photoshop Elements file complete with layers is also there.

Building Web Page Backgrounds

The simplest way to create a web page background is to use HTML-designated colors. However, you can take your web page to another level of professionalism by using Photoshop Elements to create custom backgrounds. This section shows you how to use large images to fill a background and how to create smaller background tiles that automatically tile and fill any size browser window.

The HTML code for adding a graphic to your background page is simple: just add the **BACKGROUND** extension to your **BODY** tag. The tag **<BODY BACKGROUND="***background***.gif">**, where *background* is the name of your background image, tiles the graphic across and down the browser window. Any text or graphics on your page will be displayed on top of the tiled background.

You can use either GIF or JPEG files for background. Just remember to make your graphic small enough through compression or color indexing so it appears nearly instantly.

Creating Tiled Patterns

A simple way to create a background image that loads quickly is to create a square tile made in such a way that it tiles seamlessly.

To do this, you can either use one of Photoshop Elements' ready-made patterns or create one of your own.

To use the ready-made pattern:

1. Create a new Photoshop Elements document 128 × 128 pixels at 72dpi (File ➤ New).
2. Choose Edit ➤ Fill. Then choose Use: Pattern and select any of the custom patterns. Play with different opacity settings in the Fill dialog box. Lowering the opacity diminishes the effect of the pattern on the content of your web page.
3. Select the OK button.

Now you'll need to convert your pattern into a GIF or JPEG by using the methods described earlier in this chapter. To test your pattern and see what it might look like on a web page, use the method described in the upcoming subsection "Testing Your Background Tiles." Figure 10.26 shows a tile created by using this method and the Water pattern from the Custom Patterns palette. Figure 10.27 shows how it will look tiled.

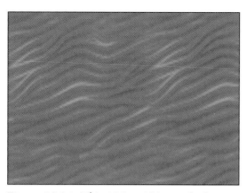 

Figure 10.26: This 128 × 128 pixel tile was created by using the Water pattern set at 65 percent opacity. Figure 10.27: This is how it will look as a background on a web page.

To create a tile completely on your own:

1. Create a new Photoshop Elements document 128 × 128 pixels at 72dpi (File ➤ New).

2. Create your own texture by using various filters applied to a background or foreground color. Try any of the filters found under the Texture, Pixelate, or Render categories. If you use the Clouds and Difference Clouds filters found under Filter ➤ Render and use the dimensions suggested in step 1, your tile will automatically tile seamlessly. You'll need to apply these filters to an image with existing texture, not a flat color. If you use these filters on other dimensions or use other filters, your image might not tile seamlessly. In that case, you'll need to use the Offset filter found under Filter ➤ Other.

3. To use the Offset filter shown in Figure 10.28, do the following: In the Horizontal and Vertical boxes, type values equal to half the dimensions of your tile. For example, with a 128 × 128 pixel tile, use the number 64. This moves the image 64 pixels to the right and 64 pixels down. Next, select the Wrap Around option. This inverts the remaining portion of the image and tiles it in the unused areas. Click the OK button.

4. Use the Clone Stamp tool (⟁) to remove the seam caused by the outside edges meeting in the center, and smooth out the lines. Convert your tile to the GIF or JPEG file format and test it by using the method described in "Testing Your Background Tiles," later in this section. Figure 10.29 shows a tile I created by applying the Grain filter (Filter ➤ Texture ➤ Grain) to a 128 × 128 tile, then the Offset filter as described, and touching up the seams with the Clone Stamp tool. Figure 10.30 shows what it looks like tiled.

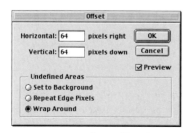

Figure 10.28: The Offset filter helps create tiles that tile seamlessly.

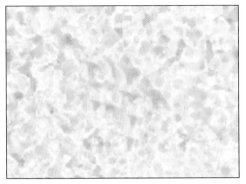 

Figure 10.29: I created this 128 × 128 pixel tile by using the Grain filter and the Offset filter.
Figure 10.30: After some touching up with the Clone Stamp tool, the image tiled seamlessly.

Creating Tiled Strips

Figure 10.31 shows another type of tile, one that gives you a way to control the placement of color so you can have a bright band of color on one side and a solid band of color on the other. Figure 10.32 shows what it looks like tiled.

Figure 10.31: This type of tile gives you a different kind of control. Figure 10.32: By controlling where the colors go, you can create a horizontal or vertical navigational bar.

This is how I created the tile shown:

1. I created a new file, 1200 × 8 pixels (File ➢ New). In the New dialog box, I set the Contents option to White.

2. I used the Rectangular Marquee selection tool (⬚) on the left edge of my image to create a selection 150 pixels wide. I pulled the Info box from the palette well so I could see when my selection was exactly 150 pixels. I feathered this selection 10 pixels (Select ➢ Feather).

3. I then filled the selection with red, by using the Layer ➢ New Fill Layer ➢ Solid Color command.

4. I saved the tile as a GIF and tested it by using the method described next.

You can fill your selection with any color you want or use a pattern. If you want the color to run horizontally across a web page, just create a vertical tile, 8 × 1200 pixels, and fill the top portion of the tile instead. If you want a band of color on the opposite side, you can do that as well.

Testing Your Background Tiles

To see what your tiles look like tiled, you can test them by designating them as a background in an HTML document and observing how they look on a web browser. Or you can use the following method to test them with Photoshop Elements:

1. Use the Rectangular Marquee selection tool (⬚) and select all your tiles or just use the keyboard command Ctrl/Command+A.

2. Choose Edit ➢ Define Pattern. Name the pattern and save it.

3. Create a new file 800 × 800 pixels at 72dpi (File ➢ New). Actually, you can make the file any size you want as long as it is large enough to approximate the size of a browser window.

4. Select Edit ➢ Fill and choose Pattern from the pop-up menu. Find and select your saved defined pattern and click OK. This option will tile your defined pattern to fill the current window in much the same way that a browser would.

Using an Image as a Background

If you use a single image as a background, keep the following suggestions in mind:

- Keep the file size down through heavy JPEG compression or careful color indexing. Unless it is the only graphic on the page, a background image shouldn't be more than 20KB. Some web designers say that a web page should never exceed 50KB total, including the background, all the graphics, and HTML coding. I've compressed JPEG images that were 800 × 800 pixels down to 4KB. Of course, I used some of the methods described in the following chapter to do this (☞ "Optimizing a Digital Image for JPEG Compression" in Chapter 11).

- Make your image at least 640 × 480 pixels and preferably a little larger. Unfortunately, there is no set size to work with, and this is where the drawback to using a single image becomes apparent. Unlike the tiling method described earlier, your image might be too small or too big, depending on the size of the browser window.

- Tone the image down so it doesn't distract from the rest of the page's content. While in the RGB mode, use the Levels or Brightness/Contrast controls to do this. Apply a Gaussian blur filter to diffuse it more.

Creating Navigational Graphics

Navigational aids are an important part of any website. Sometimes a simple HTML word link is all you need. However, if you want to give your web page a unique look, Photoshop Elements provides several easy ways to make an assortment of appropriate shapes that can be customized in almost an infinitesimal amount of ways.

To create all the navigational graphics shown in this section, I started with these two steps:

1. I chose File ➢ New and created an image window 160 × 160 pixels at 72dpi.
2. I selected a shape from the toolbox. To access the various shape tools from the toolbox, position the pointer on the visible shape tool and hold down the mouse button until the tools list appears. You can then select the tool you want.

For the graphic shown in Figure 10.33, I did the following:

1. I selected the Custom Shape tool (♥). In the options bar, I selected a predefined Arrow 9 from the Arrow category found in the Shape pop-up palette.
2. In the new image window, I clicked and dragged the shape to size.
3. From Layer Style in the options bar, I choose the Complex category and Purple Neon. Then from the Glass Buttons category, I chose Teal Glass. Because I used these particular layer styles, it really didn't matter which color was selected in the color box. I left my color black.

If I had wanted to, I could have adjusted various aspects of the layer styles by double-clicking the *f* in the Layers palette. This would have brought up the Layer Styles palette with its various options.

Figure 10.33: The arrow is a custom shape with Purple Neon and Teal Glass layer styles applied to it.

For the graphic shown in Figure 10.34, I followed the preceding steps, except I selected the 10 Point Star from the Default category. From the Layer Style Complex category, I chose Color Target.

Figure 10.34: The star is a custom shape with the Color Target layer style applied to it.

For the triangle shown in Figure 10.35, I followed the same steps, except I selected Sign 4 from the Signs category. I chose red as my color and applied an Inner Ridge layer effect from the Bevels category. I used the Layer Styles palette to adjust the shape of the bevel and the direction of the light. You can rotate the triangle to any direction by selecting the Shape Selection tool ( ) and choosing Image ➢ Rotate and the direction you want to go. You might need to open the Layer Styles palette and adjust your settings to reflect the new orientation.

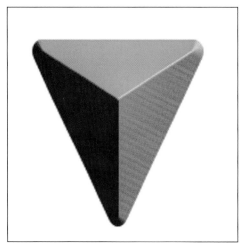

Figure 10.35: The triangle was created by using the Sign 4 custom shape and the Inner Ridge bevel layer effect.

To create the button shown in Figure 10.36, I followed these steps:

1. I selected the Rectangle shape tool (☐).

2. From the Layer Style Bevels category, I chose Simple Inner. I chose red as a color.

3. I clicked and dragged the rectangle to size. I adjusted the look of the bevel by double-clicking the *f* in the Layers palette. This brought up the Layers Style palette, and I played with the various options until I got what I wanted.

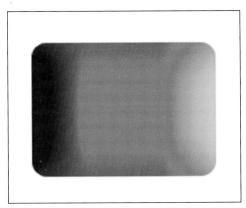

Figure 10.36: The button was created by using the Rectangle shape tool and a Simple Inner bevel layer style.

To create the bullet balls shown in Figure 10.37, I took these steps:

1. I selected the Eclipse shape tool (◯) from the toolbar. You can also select the various shape tools directly from the options bar.

2. From the Complex Layer Style category, I chose Rivet.

3. I held the Shift key and clicked and dragged the eclipse into a centered circle. I then double-clicked the *f* in the Layers palette and adjusted the Layer Style settings to get the effect I wanted.

Figure 10.37: This bullet ball was created by using the Eclipse shape tool and the Rivet layer style.

Creating Web Type

When I refer to *web type*, I don't mean HTML-coded type. I'm talking about type created with Photoshop Elements' Type tool (T) that has been rastorized, or simplified, and then converted to the GIF (or in some cases, JPEG) file format. Web type should be treated just like any other web graphic, taking into consideration web-safe colors and optimal file size. However, there is one additional point to keep in mind: readability.

To make web type readable, you have to consider the limitations of your viewer's display system. Because 72dpi (sometimes 96dpi) is the maximum resolution of your type on the Web, any type smaller than 9pt. will hardly be readable. Anti-aliasing will help make your type more readable. However, as you can see by comparing an anti-aliased letter and one that is not (see Figures 10.38 and 10.39, respectively), anti-aliasing adds file size by increasing the number of colors necessary to make a smooth transition. New colors are introduced, adding potentially non-browser-safe colors that might dither your type. Having said this, the trade-off is generally worth it. Turning off anti-aliasing completely is appropriate only for very small, sans serif type.

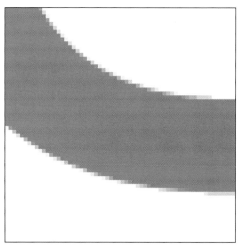 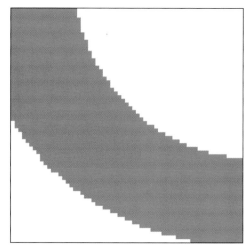

Figure 10.38: This magnified letter has anti-aliasing applied to it. Figure 10.39: This magnified letter doesn't have any anti-aliasing applied to it.

Another way to make your web type more readable is by adding drop shadows and blurring the background area. The Layer Styles palette, found in the palette well, contains several types of drop shadows that you can easily add to your type. You'll find more on creating type in Photoshop Elements in an earlier chapter (๛ Chapter 9).

Making a Web Photo Gallery

With the Web Photo Gallery command, it's easy to convert a folder of images into an interactive online gallery. Photoshop Elements creates both thumbnails and full-size images and even creates HTML pages and navigable links! Photoshop's Web Photo Gallery feature is especially useful when you have a folder full of digital camera shots that you want to present on the Web with speed.

You can choose to display your image files in four distinctly different ways:

- Horizontal Frame, as shown in Figure 10.40
- Simple, as shown in Figure 10.41
- Table, as shown in Figure 10.42
- Vertical Frame, as shown in Figure 10.43

Figure 10.40: Horizontal Frame organizes and displays your images this way.
Figure 10.41: Simple does it this way. Clicking on a thumbnail brings up a new web page with a full screen shot.

Figure 10.42: Table does it this way. The hyperlinked thumbnails are placed in HTML tables on a separate page. You have no control over the background pattern.
Figure 10.43: Vertical Frame does it this way.

You can customize pages as well, selecting from a range of options, including:

- Banner font and font color
- Gallery image's size and JPEG quality
- Gallery thumbnail's font, font size, and caption information
- Custom colors for backgrounds, banner, and hyperlinks

To create the gallery shown in Figure 10.43, I did the following:

1. I placed six photos into a folder and chose File ➤ Automate ➤ Web Photo Gallery. Photoshop Elements generates captions from the filenames of the individual images, so you might want to make sure your filenames use descriptive words or phrases. In the Web Photo Gallery dialog box, you can select Gallery Thumbnail from the Options pop-up menu and then select Use File Info Caption, and the program will use the File Info data if there is any. I deselected Use Filename and chose this option instead.

Note: To add captions and other information such as copyright notices to your images, select File ➤ File Info. From the Caption dialog box, you can choose different options from the pop-up menu. The information you include in the Caption option box will be used, if you choose, by the Web Photo Gallery to generate thumbnail captions.

2. In the Web Photo Gallery dialog box, which is shown in Figure 10.44, I chose the source and destination folders. From the Styles list box, I chose Vertical Frame. I chose Banner from the Options pop-up menu and in the Site Name text box, I named the site Family Vacation, Hawaii. I left the Photographer field blank and typed 2001 as the date. (If you don't put a date in this field, the current date will be automatically generated for you). I set the Font Size option to 5 and left the default Arial as my font.

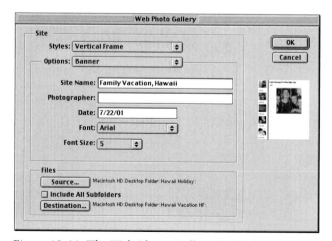

Figure 10.44: The Web Photo Gallery dialog box.

3. I selected Gallery Images from the Options pop-up menu and then, under the Gallery Images options, I changed the size of my images from Medium to Large and left the JPEG quality setting at Medium. This is a great feature. If you want to display really large images, you'll want to select more compression to make the image file size smaller.

4. Under the Gallery Thumbnails options, I left everything at their defaults but changed the captions as described in step 1.

5. I selected Custom Colors from the Options pop-up menu, and under Custom Colors, I changed my background and banner to black and my text to white. Again, this is a great feature. Just be sure to pick your colors carefully. You don't want a black text color and a black background; the type won't be readable.

6. After I set the options and clicked OK, Photoshop Elements did the rest. It opened each image and created both a thumbnail version and a gallery version and, regardless of the original file format, saved the file as a JPEG. It also created an HTML index page and three folders containing the thumbnail images and navigational GIFs, gallery images, and HTML pages. It also generated a separate file called **UserSelections.txt** that stores the settings from the Web Gallery dialog box. This way, if you only change, delete, or add a single new file and don't change any other options, Web Photo Gallery will process only the files it needs to make the update.

The amount of time it takes for Photoshop Elements to process the images varies depending on how many images are in the source folder and the speed of the CPU. You can stop the process at any time by typing Esc/(Command+period).

If you want to, you can always tweak the HTML later. You might also want to go into the HTML pages and edit the banner headline. The Web Photo Gallery adds the filename or number to the banner whether you want it or not. It's also likely that before you place the gallery on a server, you'll need to edit the links to reflect a proper directory path.

Shooting Digital: Lessons from Shooting Sequenced Stills

In one of my earlier lives, I was hired to shoot sequences of still images for a major CD-ROM multimedia project. The script included 50 social dilemmas that the producers needed to establish visually. Instead of shooting with a single image in mind, I needed to shoot many images that helped build narrative sequences. When I shot a curtain, I shot it in different positions. When I shot a door, I shot it open and closed. When I shot people, I tried to capture their eyes both open and shut. It sounds like film, but the model that inspired me was the comic strip, which uses a few related frames to tell a story. The comic strip also taught me that if you give viewers a chance, most of them will fill the space between images with their imagination, so you don't need to show them everything. I shot mostly horizontal images because vertical images didn't fit as well on the screen. I also centered the action and kept the images simple because of the limited resolution of most monitors. Because I was shooting digital, I learned to shoot a lot of images, because developing cost wasn't a factor and many times my outtakes became useful as transition images.

It's remarkable *that the term* JPEG *has made it into the popular vernacular. "Just JPEG it to me" has become almost as common as "send me an e-mail" or "just Photoshop it." Its popularity is for good reason. The* JPEG *file format shrinks full-color or grayscale digital images to a manageable size so they can be stored or e-mailed anywhere. And as Visa and MasterCard are in the financial world,* JPEGs *are universally accepted by most applications and web browsers. In this chapter, you'll learn how to use Photoshop Elements to create a* JPEG *that not only looks great but is the optimal size as well.*

Making Great JPEGs

Understanding the JPEG Format

The more you know about the JPEG file format, the easier it will be to use Photoshop Elements to create great JPEGs. To start, keep in mind that the JPEG file format—and, for that matter, all file formats—organize digital data. The JPEG file format compresses data as well. However, unlike some graphics file formats, JPEG compresses data by sampling images in 8 × 8 pixel squares. It looks for similarities in tone and contrast and then transforms each block into mathematical equations that represent the relevant color and brightness values. You can actually see these blocks by magnifying a highly compressed image (see Figure 11.1). The JPEG file format also "intelligently" selects and throws away high-frequency data that it determines unimportant; this is why the JPEG file format is called a *lossy* technology. Other file formats, such as the PSD or PNG file formats, are called *lossless* because they compress images without throwing away data.

Figure 11.1: This image has been magnified 1200 percent to show the 8 × 8 pixel squares that result from JPEG compression.

With Photoshop Elements, you can control the amount of JPEG compression by a ratio as high as 70:1. Lossless file formats compress by a ratio of only 2:1 or 3:1. The more compression, the smaller the file size, and the more data is thrown away. The secret is to find the right balance between quality and file size, and that's what I will discuss next.

Saving JPEGs

There are basically two ways to create JPEGs by using Photoshop Elements: File ➤ Save As and File ➤ Save for Web. The method you use will depend on where your digital image is headed:

- Use the File ➤ Save As method for most general purposes.
- Use the Save for Web plug-in if you are optimizing a digital image destined for the Web or for other purposes where file size is critical. Because a slight delay occurs between the moment you select the plug-in and the moment it is ready to use, this method is a little slower than the File ➤ Save As method. However, the Save for Web plug-in enables you to view and compare your original image alongside an optimized version of your image and determine precisely the optimal JPEG compression and format settings.

Grabbing Digital: Images from the Web

It's easy to grab digital images directly from the Web and then use them as reference material or even components in a composite. Just remember that many of these images are copyrighted, meaning that if you use them for anything but personal use you must obtain written permission. Although some images are considered public domain, such as the images on the Library of Congress website (**http://www.loc.gov**), you should still check and make sure that no special restrictions are attached to their use.

The method you use to grab these images will vary slightly depending on which computer platform (PC or Mac) and web browser (Netscape Navigator or Microsoft Internet Explorer) you are using. If you are using Netscape or Explorer on a PC, right-click on the image and save the image to the destination of your choice. On the Mac, just click and hold on the image and choose Save This Image or click on the image and drag it to your desktop.

Many of the images may be placed on the Web by using the GIF file format. (You can tell it's a GIF file by the **.gif** extension.) If you are saving these GIFs for whatever reason as JPEGs, see the relevant section in this chapter (↩ "Converting GIFs to JPEGs").

File ➤ Save As Options

To create a JPEG by using this method, choose File ➤ Save As. After the dialog box shown in Figure 11.2 appears (it will look a little different in the Windows version), select JPEG from the Format list box. Make sure that the ICC Profile (PC) or Embed Color Profile (Mac) option is turned off. If it isn't, Photoshop Elements will include color profile settings and add file size to your JPEG image. You can find more information on saving files earlier in the book (☞ "Setting Preferences" in Chapter 1).

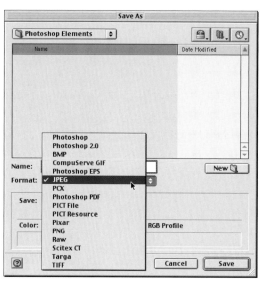

Figure 11.2: When you select File ➤ Save As, you have a choice of different file formats.

Now click the Save button and you'll see the dialog box shown in Figure 11.3. Here you can choose compression settings, JPEG format, and, if your original Photoshop files include transparent areas, even add a colored matte. If Preview is selected, you get a real-time view of the effects of your JPEG settings on your original image. You can zoom in and out by using the standard Photoshop Elements Zoom commands to get a better view of the effects (Ctrl/Command enlarges, and Alt/Option reduces). An approximate file size is also provided.

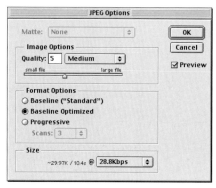

Figure 11.3: JPEG file options. When an image includes transparent areas, the Matte option is available.

Note: In the preceding chapter (⤳ "Making GIFs" in Chapter 10), I explained how to create a transparent GIF graphic that appears to "float" on a web page without showing any rectangular edges. The JPEG file format doesn't support transparency, but you can create a pseudo-transparent look.

If your Photoshop Elements file contains transparent areas, as signified by the gray and white checkered boxes, the Matte option is available, both in the Save for Web plug-in and in the JPEG options box that appears when you choose File ➤ Save or File ➤ Save As. Choose the Matte option and then select a matte color that matches the color of your web page background. Photoshop Elements then fills the transparent areas with this color, blending the edges with variations to make a smooth transition. When you view your graphic on a web page, it will seem to float against the background. Of course, it's not really floating, and if you have a complex background, or you change your mind and use another background color, what seemed transparent will stand out.

Another point to keep in mind is that there is no such a thing as web-safe color in the JPEG file format. Colors shift unexpectedly when JPEG compression is applied. Even if you carefully choose a web-safe matte color for your JPEG, the color, once compressed, will never exactly match another web-safe background color.

You also need to choose from one of the following:

Baseline ("Standard") This is Photoshop Elements' default setting. If you have any doubts about what program will be used to open your image, you should choose this option.

Baseline Optimized I suggest that you choose Baseline Optimized, because you'll get an image slightly smaller in file size with better color fidelity. Most programs and web browsers support this standard. However, some (mostly older) programs have trouble opening a baseline-optimized JPEG.

Progressive I generally don't recommend using this option. The Progressive format contains the same data as the Baseline ("Standard") and Baseline Optimized formats and creates a JPEG about the same file size. However, the data is displayed in a series of scans, and the first scan appears quickly because it is equivalent to a low-quality setting. With each subsequent scan, more data is provided. When you choose Progressive, you can choose the number of scans it takes for the entire image to appear (3, 4, or 5 scans). A Progressive JPEG could be useful if you are creating really large images destined for a web page and you want something to appear on the page immediately. However, Progressive JPEGs are not fully compatible with all web browsers or applications, and using them is therefore risky.

The next step is determining which JPEG quality setting to use.

I suggest that you start with the Medium setting from the pop-up window. This often produces a good compromise between quality and file size. Keep in mind that when I say *Medium*, I am referring to a range of 5–7, as reflected in the slider. Each of these Medium numbers will produce a slightly different sized JPEG. You'll need to fine-tune your choice. If Preview is selected, the results of your choice will be reflected in the image. Use Photoshop Elements' Zoom In command and look for loss of detail or for compression artifacts. Keep in mind that viewers will ultimately see your work at 100 percent, so don't get too hung up on how the magnified image looks.

If Medium isn't good enough, try a slightly higher setting.

As I mentioned earlier, you always lose some data when you compress with JPEG. If you want your digital image viewed at its best, you'll probably settle for only the highest-quality settings. Keep in mind that even when you choose Maximum, there is some loss of image quality that can never be replaced.

If you must use JPEG on images with sharp-colored edges, such as text, you'll get better results if you choose the Maximum, or 12, setting. At this setting, Photoshop automatically turns off Chroma downsampling, a process that works well with photographic images but causes fuzziness or jaggedness around the edges of hard lines. Chroma downsampling samples color areas at a rate of 2×2 pixels rather than 1×1 pixel. This relatively coarse method of throwing away color data results in smaller file sizes but creates 2-pixel jaggies around sharp color boundaries.

Believe it or not, depending on the image, you can produce very good quality at the Low setting. Even the 0 setting can be used on some images. You can adjust the setting to 0 by using the compression slider or by typing a zero in the Quality box.

Compare Figures 11.4 and 11.5 to see the difference in quality between the Low and Maximum settings. The original image was 1.7MB. The Low setting produced a file size of only 44KB, while the Maximum setting produced a file size of 726KB.

Whatever setting you ultimately select, you'll quickly learn that creating the smallest possible file size without sacrificing image quality is a matter of trial and error.

Figure 11.4: An image at the Low setting—44KB. Figure 11.5: An image at the Maximum setting—726KB.

File ➢ Save for Web Options

To create a JPEG by using the Save for Web plug-in, choose File ➢ Save for Web, or click the Save for Web button ( ) in the shortcuts bar. When you do this, the Save for Web box shown in Figure 11.6 appears. You'll notice that the Save for Web plug-in loads and then starts to optimize your image by using either the default or the last saved settings. If you want to stop this sometimes time-consuming process, wait until the image has loaded (as indicated by the status bar at the bottom of the work area) and then, when the image starts to be optimized (as indicated again by the status bar at the bottom of the work area), type Esc/(Command+period).

Figure 11.6: The Save for Web work area and options.

Now you are faced with several options. I suggest you do the following:

- If it's not already, select the JPEG format from the pop-up window.
- Select the Optimized check box and make sure that the Progressive check box is not selected. As I said before, *Progressive* creates a JPEG that downloads in increments but isn't read by all browsers. *Optimized* creates a better and smaller JPEG file.
- Unless you've made a strong commitment toward color management, be sure that the ICC Profile box is deselected. If it is selected, you will be adding data of dubious value and increasing your file size. This will be an option only if your Photoshop Elements color preferences are set to include ICC color profiling, which I recommended against earlier in the book (↪ "Setting Preferences" in Chapter 1).

With two views of your image, one showing the original image, and the other showing the effects of the compression, it's easy to compare them and choose the optimal setting. As I mentioned in the preceding section, start with the Medium setting and experiment.

You may notice that both the Save for Web and Save As options include Low,

Medium, High, and Maximum settings. However, the Save for Web numerical values are different, ranging from 1–100 rather than 1–12. Unfortunately these numbers do not have that much in common. A Save for Web 50, for example, doesn't create a similar sized JPEG as a Save As 6. However, the process of starting at a Medium setting and experimenting until you get the optimal setting is the same for both methods.

If your image is larger than the image window, you can use the Hand tool (🖑) in the Save For Web dialog box to navigate around various parts of your image, or you can hold down the spacebar and drag in the view area to pan over the image. To zoom in with the Hand tool selected, hold down Ctrl/Command and click in a view, or choose the Zoom tool (🔍) and click in a view. To zoom out with the Hand tool selected, hold down Alt/Option and click in a view, or choose the Zoom tool and click in a view. You can also select a magnification level—or type one in—in the Zoom box.

If you hold down the Alt/Option key, the OK and Cancel buttons change to Remember and Reset. If you choose the Remember button, the next time you open the Save for Web plug-in it will open with the current settings.

The Save for Web dialog box has two other relevant options: Preview Menu, which offers a variety of monitor compensations and modem download rates found by clicking the little arrow at the top right of the image window, and Preview In, which gives you a choice of which web browser to use for previewing your work.

When you are finished, click OK and save your JPEG.

Optimizing a Digital Image for JPEG Compression

Some digital images compress more efficiently than others. If you understand why this is true, you'll understand why it is possible to optimize any digital image so it JPEGs more efficiently.

Look at Figure 11.7. It's 1000 × 1000 pixels, and uncompressed it's 2.87MB. I saved it by using the Save for Web Medium 50 JPEG setting, and the file size shrunk to 98.14KB.

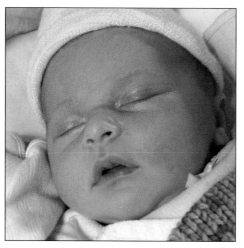 

Figure 11.7: This image compresses better because it contains smooth, gradual tonal variations.
Figure 11.8: This image doesn't compress as well because it contains lots of high-frequency data.

Now look at Figure 11.8. It has exactly the same dimensions as Figure 11.7, and uncompressed it's also 2.87MB. I applied the same JPEG settings to it and got a file size of 207.6KB, a whooping 110KB bigger than Figure 11.7! Why?

The first image (Figure 11.7) is smooth, with gradual tonal variations. This kind of data is easier for the JPEG algorithms to handle, hence the smaller file size. The second image (Figure 11.8) contains lots of high-frequency data in the form of thin strands of hair. It takes a lot more work to compress this kind of data, therefore the higher file size.

Now let's take this knowledge and apply it to other digital images.

Global Blurring

As you've seen, JPEG compression works more efficiently on images that contain fewer details. It follows, then, that if you slightly blur an otherwise sharp image, you'll get a JPEG with a smaller file size. The more blurring, the smaller the file size. Fortunately, this is a realistic option because for many digital images a small amount of blurring won't effect the perceived quality of the image.

Let's apply a small amount of blurring to the image in Figure 11.9, which is 1800 × 1800 pixels for a 9.28MB file. Before blurring, I compressed the image by using a Save for Web JPEG Medium 50 setting and got a file size of 530.7KB. After globally applying a Gaussian blur of 0.7 pixels with a Radius of 0, the same image weighed in at only 374.6KB. See, even slight blurring will suppress some of the higher spatial frequencies enough to reduce the JPEG file by 156KB. If you look at Figure 11.10, you'll see that the slight blurring didn't noticeably affect the image quality. If I apply more blurring, I'll get even more reduction in file size.

 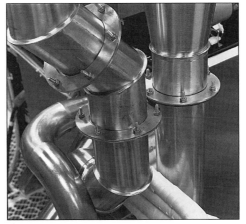

Figure 11.9: Before applying a Gaussian blur, this image compressed to 530.7KB. (Photo by Maurice Martell.) Figure 11.10: After applying a slight Gaussian blur, it compressed to 374.6KB.

Granted, the results you get will depend on the type of image you are working with and the size of the original file. Sometimes this method saves you only a few kilobytes, but even that can make a difference if you are hindered with a slow modem or are optimizing images for the Web.

Selective Blurring

Let's take this blurring thing further. What if parts of your image really need to remain sharp, and other parts could be blurred with little or no consequence? In this case, you can apply a Gaussian blur selectively only to the parts that aren't critical.

Figure 11.11 shows an image with a large expanse of background area (sky and clouds) and details in the foreground (the human artichoke). The original Photoshop file is 1200×1802 pixels, for a file size of 6.19MB. Saved by using a Save for Web Medium 50 setting, it comes down to 398.5KB.

Figure 11.11: Saved with no optimizing, this image compressed to 398.5KB.

Next I selectively blurred the image before compressing it. I selected only the background and then blurred it by choosing Filter ➤ Blur ➤ Gaussian Blur and setting the Radius to 3.6 pixels. When I compressed the image by using the same Save for Web setting, the file size reduced to 354.6KB, a savings of 44KB with no loss of important details (see Figure 11.12).

Figure 11.12: By applying a strong Gaussian blur to the areas where detail isn't so important, this image JPEGed down to 354.6KB.

To push the benefits of blurring a little further, I applied a Gaussian blur of 0.5 to the entire image—in addition to the 3.6 Gaussian blur applied to the sky. This resulted in a file size of 295.1KB, a savings of nearly 100KB. This final image is shown in Figure 11.13.

Figure 11.13: After selectively and globally applying a Gaussian blur, this image now compresses to 295.1KB.

Resize to Optimize

Earlier in this book, I warned you about the consequences of resizing a digital image too radically in one step (☞ "Resizing" in Chapter 2). I showed that if you didn't resize incrementally, you'd end up with a soft, mushy looking image. Well, I am going to contradict myself. There are times when resizing radically can work in your favor.

What did I say about blurring an image to optimize for JPEG compression? The more blurring, the more efficient the compression, right? OK, let's resize an image and see what happens when you apply the JPEG compression.

Figure 11.14 shows an image taken with a digital camera. It is 2240 × 1680 pixels, and uncompressed it takes up 10.8MB. Figure 11.15 shows the same image reduced to 300 × 225 pixels. I've resized as I suggest in Chapter 1, no more than 50 percent at a time, applying an Unsharp Mask between each step. After applying a Save for Web Medium 50 JPEG setting, it weighed in at 15KB.

Figure 11.16 shows the same figure resized in one swoop with no Unsharp Mask applied. With the same JPEG settings, it's 11KB. So, 4KB may not sound like much, but when it comes to optimizing an image for the Web, every kilobyte counts.

Figure 11.14: The original image is 2240 × 1680 pixels. Figure 11.15: Resizing down to 300 × 225 pixels incrementally and then applying a Medium JPEG setting created a 15KB file.

Figure 11.16: Resizing in one swoop to 300 × 225 and then applying a Medium JPEG setting created an 11KB file.

The neat thing about this method is how quick it is. There is no need to apply a Gaussian blur or make a selection. Still, this technique isn't for every image. Some images suffer too much in quality when you resize them radically. Also, this method works only if you have a large enough image to begin with and need a much smaller image.

In any case, now you know three ways to use Photoshop Elements to optimize a JPEG: global blurring, selective blurring, and resizing. You can choose the technique, or combination of techniques, that works best for your image.

Converting GIFs to JPEGs

Sometimes, for the sake of file size or compatibility, you'll want to turn a GIF into a JPEG. You can do it, but do it smartly.

In the process of reducing and indexing colors, a GIF image often becomes choppy or coarse because fewer colors are available to create smooth transitions. Dithering, while fooling the eye into believing that the image has more colors, actually introduces even more noise at a subpixel level.

Because the JPEG file format doesn't handle high spatial frequency noise well, the result can be a larger file size than you started with, as well as a lousy-looking image.

If you must turn an indexed file such as a GIF into a JPEG, first convert your file to RGB and then apply a Gaussian blur to soften the image as much as possible without noticeable visual degradation. When JPEG compression is applied, there will be less noise to interfere with the compression process.

Note: Avoid JPEGing a JPEG. Every time you open, manipulate, and save an image in the JPEG format, you lose data and increase the risk of creating a larger file size. Those distinct blocks of pixels that you saw in Figure 11.1, the ones that resulted from applying high JPEG compression to an image, add high spatial frequency to the image. The more high spatial frequency information in an image, the less efficient the JPEG compression. Save your original in the Photoshop format (or other 24-bit format) and save subsequent JPEG files from the original.

12

What's the good *of having all your hard work on a digital image if you can't make a print and pass it around among friends and colleagues? This chapter focuses on ways to use Photoshop Elements to get the most out of your desktop printer or to access an online photo service. It also shows you ways to automatically create picture packages of single pages containing various sizes of the same image and to process folders full of several images to the same file format, size, and resolution.*

From Hard Copy to Many Copies: Sharing and Processing Images

Using Desktop Printers
Using Online Photography Services
Using Picture Package
Using Batch Processing

From Hard Copy to Many Copies: Sharing and Processing Images

Using Desktop Printers

Nowadays, ink-jet desktop printers that produce photo-quality prints are common and inexpensive. Sure, printer companies make most of their money on the ink and paper, but the overall cost of a print is still reasonable when compared to the cost of a commercial print. When it comes to larger size prints, such as 5×7 and 8×10 inch, the ink-jet prints are really a bargain.

Still, it's not a plug-and-print world. You can't just select File ➤ Print from the Photoshop Elements menu or click the Print icon (🖨) in the shortcuts bar and get a faithful rendering of your digital masterpiece. At the very least, you'll need to do the following:

- Choose a resolution and print dimension
- Choose a paper size and image orientation
- Choose a quality setting and paper type

I'm going to suggest you go even further and spend a little time experimenting with different print settings. Printers vary in the way they handle Photoshop Elements files, and the trial-and-error method is the best way of establishing a standard that you can subsequently use on all your digital images. Later in this section I'll show you how to make a *test strip* so you won't waste a lot of expensive photo paper and ink in the process.

Selecting Resolution and Print Dimensions

You can select the dimensions of your print in three ways: through the Image Size dialog box (Image ➤ Resize ➤ Image Size), through the Print Preview dialog box (File ➤ Print Preview), or by clicking the Print Preview icon (🖺) in the shortcuts bar. Some printer software also gives you the capability to set the dimensions of your image. You can set actual image resolution only through the Image Size dialog box.

The Image Size dialog box is shown in Figure 12.1. Just type the dimensions of your desired print in the Document Size fields. You can use the pop-up menus to select different measurement systems, ranging from inches to centimeters. If you are printing to 8.5×11 inch paper, don't make your image the same size. Allow for at least a 0.25 inch border because most desktop printers aren't capable of printing, or *bleeding* an image to the edge of the paper. If your print dimensions are bigger than the paper size as determined by the printer or Photoshop Elements' Page Setup settings (↝ "Selecting a Paper Size and Orientation," next) you'll get a Photoshop Elements warning message saying, "The image is larger than the paper's printable area; some clipping will occur." If you get this message, either change the print dimensions in the Image Size dialog box or change the paper specifications in the Page Setup dialog box. You can also go into Print Preview and select Scale to Fit Media; I'll tell you more about that later in this section.

Note: What does the Auto option in the Image Size dialog box do? It's a professional printer's option that automatically adjusts your document resolution based on the line screen value of your printer. Unless you are working in the high-end prepress world, I suggest you pass on this option.

Figure 12.1: Set your print dimensions and resolution in the Image Size dialog box.

You'll also need to set the resolution of your image in the Image Size dialog box. How much resolution is enough? Don't be mislead by the specifications of your printer. For most desktop ink-jet printers, 150–200dpi is enough, and anything over 200dpi is a waste. Your print quality won't suffer, nor will it improve with the higher settings. You'll just create a huge file that will take forever to print. Later, when you make a test strip, you can confirm this fact by trying different resolution settings and seeing what works best.

Keep in mind that the quality of your image is ultimately determined by how much data is contained in your original file. If you look at the top of the Image Size dialog box next to *Pixel Dimensions*, you'll see two numbers; one is in parentheses. The first number displays the amount of data as determined by your new document size settings, and the second number displays the original amount of data in your digital image. If the first number is larger than the second, it means that you are pushing your luck. To create the larger size, Photoshop Elements must resample the image or add data based on a sophisticated algorithm. Sometimes, depending on the content of the image, you won't notice the difference. However, for images that contain a lot of detail, interpolation or resampling decreases the clarity. You can improve the resampled image slightly by using an Unsharp Mask filter (↷ "Resizing" in Chapter 2) but it'll never be as good as the original. In Figure 12.1, you can see that my original image contained 10.8MB of data. This represents an image taken with my 4.0 megapixel digital camera. If I try to print a 10 × 7.5 inch image at 175dpi, I'll have plenty of data left over. In fact, I can easily go up to 11 × 14 inches and still get a great looking print.

The Print Preview window is shown in Figure 12.2. Here you can set the image dimensions manually, have Photoshop Elements do it for you based on the size of your paper, or print from the dimensions you established in the Image Size dialog box. In the example shown, I've selected the Scale to Fit to Media check box. As you can see in the preview window, my image is automatically resized to fit an 8.5 × 11 inch paper. You can also see in the Scale box that it did so by enlarging the image 160 percent. If my original image were larger than the specified paper, it would have reduced the percentage. With Scale to Fit Media deselected, you can also type in dimensions. Or if you select the Show Bounding Box check box, you can drag a bounding box handle in the preview area to scale the image. Whatever you do, Photoshop Elements won't override the border settings set by your printer.

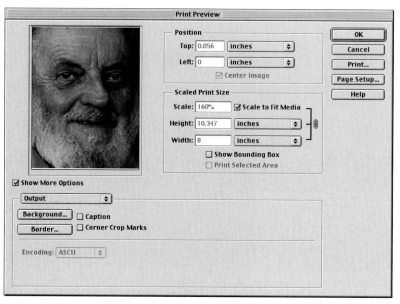

File 12.2: The Print Preview dialog box.

You can't set the resolution of your image in the Print Preview dialog box. It defaults to the setting in the Image Size dialog box. If your image is enlarged in the Print Preview dialog box, either by using the Scale to Fit to Media setting or by you manually, the resolution will be automatically reduced proportionally. If you reduce the size of your image, the resolution will automatically increase proportionally. The bottom line is, if you resize by using the Print Preview dialog box, you don't change the overall number of pixels or affect the original image file in any way.

Other options in the Print Preview dialog box include:

- Adding a black border of your specified width.
- Printing any caption text typed in the File Info dialog box in 9 point Helvetica, centered just below the image. You have no control over the size, type, or placement.
- Adding corner crop marks to show where a page is to be trimmed.
- Selecting a background color, such as black or red, to fill the non-image areas of your print.

You can also use the Print Preview dialog box to reposition an image on the paper. In the Position section at the top of the dialog box, either click the Center Image check box to center the image in the printable area, or type values in the Top and Left fields to position the image numerically. You can also select the Show Bounding Box check box and drag the image in the preview area.

Selecting a Paper Size and Orientation

You can select paper size or image orientation through Photoshop Elements' Page Setup dialog box (File ➢ Page Setup), shown in Figure 12.3. You can also access this dialog box from within the Print Preview dialog box. Many times you can get more options by using the printer software that comes with your printer, in which case this command might not be very useful.

If the image size you selected in the Image Size dialog box doesn't match the size of the paper set in the Page Setup dialog box (or within your printer software), you'll get the warning message described earlier.

Make sure the orientation of your image matches the orientation of your page. For example, if you try to print an image set to 10 × 8 inches on an 8 × 10 page, you'll get clipping. Either rotate your image in Photoshop Elements (Image ➢ Rotate) or change the orientation of your page in the Page Setup dialog box or from within your printer software.

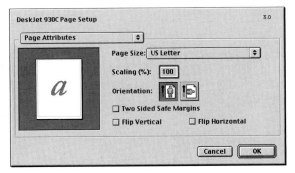

Figure 12.3: The Page Setup dialog box will look different depending on the type of printer you are using.

Choosing Quality Settings and Paper

You'll need to set your quality settings and paper type via the software that comes with your printer. Just be sure you match the quality with the characteristics of the paper. It's a waste to use an expensive, photo-quality paper and set your quality to Low. It's also a waste if you use plain paper and set your quality to High.

> **Note:** To print a selection made with the Rectangular Marquee selection tool (⬚) and exclude everything else in the image, select Print Selected Area in the Print Preview dialog box and click Print.

Creating a Test Strip

If you are using Photoshop Elements and your printer together for the first time, or if you are not satisfied with the quality of print you are getting, consider creating a test strip by using various print options.

Here is what I do:

1. Create a new document, 8 × 10 at 175dpi (File ➢ New). Later, if you wish, you can create another document at a higher or lower dpi setting and see what works best. When I create this new document, in the New dialog box, under Contents, I select Transparent. I name this **Test Strip** and date it.

2. Open a digital image. I choose one that is shot with my digital camera and optimized by using the methods I described earlier in the book (↩ Chapter 2). It helps if the image you choose has a range of colors and tones. I also resize the image (Image ➢ Resize) to match the resolution to my test strip document: 8 × 10 at 175dpi.

3. Use the Rectangular Marquee selection tool (⬚) to make a 2.5 × 10 inch selection that contains a good representation of my image (see Figure 12.4).

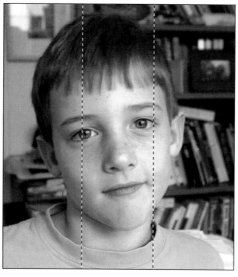

Figure 12.4: Select a representative image and then make a 2.5 × 10 inch selection of an area containing a variety of colors and tone.

4. Copy this selection and paste it three times onto the new document (see Figure 12.5). I then use the Move tool (▶⊕) to position the three pasted images adjacent to each other. If you want to test more print options, make your initial selection narrower and paste it more than three times. You can also make a horizontal selection if that orientation picks up more variety of color and tone.

5. Name each layer, as you can see in Figure 12.6.

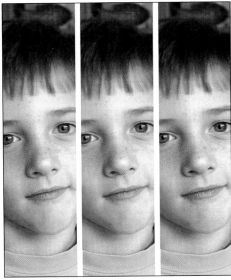

Figure 12.5: Copy a selection three times onto a test strip document. Figure 12.6: The Layers palette of my test strip.

6. Turn off the visibility of all the layers except for the one named **Default**.

> **Note:** By default, Photoshop Elements prints a composite of all visible layers. To print an individual layer, make it the only visible layer in the Layers palette before choosing the Print command.

7. Select Print Preview from the File menu or from the Print Preview icon (📷) found in the shortcuts bar.

8. Select Show More Options from the bottom left of the Print Preview dialog box and then in the first pop-up menu, select Output. Then I select Print and from my printer software I select the highest quality and Premium Paper settings. You'll need to select what is appropriate for you, taking into consideration the specifications of your printer and the type of media you are using.

9. After the first strip has printed, I go back to my **Test Strip** document and turn off the layer that was just printed and turn on the next one, called **Printer/Brightness**. This time I just select Print and bypass the Print Preview options, which remain the same as in the first test. Instead, in my printer software, I increase the brightness values by about 20 percent. Why do I do this? I've noticed that with my particular printer, an HP 932C, the prints are consistently darker than what I see on my monitor. My monitor is well calibrated, so I'd rather try adjusting the printer than mess with my digital files.

10. I place the same page of paper back into my printer and print by using the new settings.

11. When the second strip is finished printing, I select the third layer, called **Full Color Management**. This time *before* I choose Print Preview, I choose Edit ➢ Color Settings and select Full Color Management—Optimized for Print. I know,

I wrote earlier in the book to avoid using this option (☞ "Setting Preferences" in Chapter 1). However, at times—depending on the specifications of your printer and print software—this setting actually helps. In any case, it doesn't hurt to try. Just be sure to reset your Color Settings to No Color Management if you determine that it doesn't do any good.

12. In the Print Preview dialog box, I select the following options: Color Management (instead of Output), Profile: Working RGB-Generic RGB Profile, Intent: Perceptual. I then select Print, which brings up my printer software. At this point, I set my printer to Image: Color Sync. The way you do this with your printer software will vary. Then I replace the sheet of photo paper in the printer and print the last test strip.

At this point, I make a visual examination and compare the results. First I look for the obvious. Is one strip too dark, too light? Is one more saturated with color than the other?

It's important to consider the light that you view your test strip under. Prints will reflect the ambient light. It's best to avoid florescent lights, which produce a green cast. Sunlight coming in through a window is fine as long as it doesn't pick up reflections from a colored wall.

Some variations in the strips will be subtle. Look in the shadow and highlight areas for color casts, which are more visible in those areas. Are the highlights completely blown away? Are the shadows completely dark? Some of these factors depend on the original digital file, but compare and see whether any of the settings produce better results than others.

Sometimes you'll notice results that have nothing to do with the print settings. Streaking is often caused by a dirty printer head or a printer that is low on ink. If the colors bleed into one another, that is a sign that you might have selected the wrong paper quality setting. If the image is heavily pixilated, you just don't have enough resolution.

I also hold the print up to the monitor and compare it to the digital image. This is useful in determining what print setting to use but it also can help determine whether something should be done to the digital file itself. For example, I might determine that my prints are consistently 20 percent darker than the image on the screen. Keep in mind that a digital image on a monitor will always display colors slightly differently than a print. This is because monitors create colors by combining red, green, and blue light, whereas ink-jet printers create colors by combining cyan, magenta, yellow, and black ink.

In the preceding example, I used three settings that produced subtle variations. I ended up preferring the results of the second strip, the one for which I boosted the brightness values by using the printer software. You can choose your own set of parameters. For example, you might try making a test strip with different resolutions. Or adjust the saturation and brightness/contrast controls within Photoshop Elements. If it's any consolation, remember that even great photography masters such as Ansel Adams routinely made test strips whenever they mixed new chemicals, used new photographic papers, or printed from a negative for the first time. The good thing is once you get something that works, you can apply it to all your other digital files—that is, until you buy a new printer and have to start all over again...

Using Online Photography Services

Online photo services can be easier and cheaper to use than making your own print: you simply upload your work to their website and order prints produced with real photographic paper and delivered to your doorstep overnight or in a few days. After you place your images online, anyone you designate, anywhere in the world, can go online, view your digital image, and with a single click of the mouse and a few keystrokes order their own prints in a variety of sizes. Now when people ask you for a print, you can point them toward the online service and have them order their own. What a great invention!

When you choose File ➢ Online Services, you select an online service from the Online Services Wizard. At the time of this writing, Shutterfly is the default, and you might see only this one service listed. After you select a service, click Next. You'll be prompted to provide login information, and if this is your first time using the online service you might need to sign up before proceeding; a Sign-Up button is provided. Keep in mind that the Shutterfly service is available only in the United States. Other online photo services are available by simply going online. For example, **www.ofoto.com** is an especially popular online service. To find other services, go to my web site, **www.shooting-digital.com** and look under the section titled "Create and Share Your Own Photo Albums Online."

Using Picture Package

Picture Package is a way to automatically create a variety of layouts with your images that otherwise would be extremely time-consuming. Figure 12.7 shows the Picture Package dialog box with the settings used to create the package on the right. Figure 12.8 shows the Picture Package dialog box with the settings used to create another package.

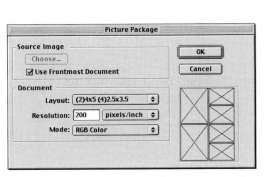

Figure 12.7: The settings in this Picture Package dialog box (left) create the package shown on the right.

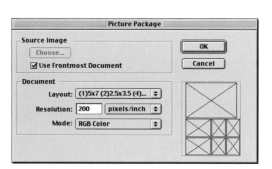

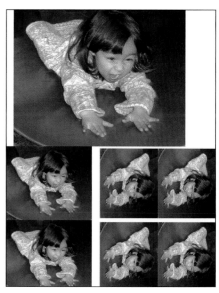

Figure 12.8: Changing the settings in the Picture Package dialog box (left) creates a new package (right).

I created the first one by following these steps:

1. I selected File ➤ Automate ➤ Picture Package.
2. I selected the image I wanted to use. Because my image was open in a Photoshop Elements window, I selected the Use Frontmost Document check box. I also could have clicked the Choose button and specified a saved image file as the source.
3. I chose (2) 4 × 5 (4) 2.5 × 3.5 from the Layout options. A preview of my choice appeared in the dialog box.
4. I typed 200dpi as my resolution for the package layout.
5. I left the color mode set to RGB and clicked OK. Picture Package did the rest.

To create the package shown in Figure 12.8, I followed these same steps but chose a different package.

Scanning Digital: What is the Correct Scanner Resolution?

Even if you know your image is destined for the Web, there is some logic in setting your scanner resolution to its highest-quality setting. That way, you create a file that can be used later if, say, you want to make a print. However, if you are scanning an image that you have easy and constant access to, consider this: you'll get much better results if you scan at exactly the needed size and resolution. Most scanning software nowadays provides simple methods for calculating the proper scan settings depending on the desired output. Follow these guidelines and don't get greedy. You'll get better results.

Note: If you are feeling ambitious and none of the several preset Picture Package packages work for you, you can make your own custom layouts. You'll need to use a text-editing application, such as MS Word, and follow the instructions provided with the online Help. After you are finished, your text file goes into the **Layouts** folder located inside the **Presets** folder. The next time you open the dialog box, your custom settings will be available to you. Because most of the presets are set with 8 × 10 inch paper in mind, this customizing feature is especially handy for those with printers capable of printing larger prints.

Using Batch Processing

If you have a folder of digital images that you want to print at the same size and resolution, or that you want to convert to a similar file format, you can use the batch processing command to automatically do all the work for you. Here's how:

1. Choose File ≻ Automate ≻ Batch. You get the dialog box shown in Figure 12.9.

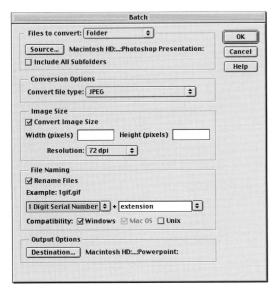

Figure 12.9: The Batch dialog box with options.

2. Choose which files you want to process. You can process files on your computer or, if you have the correct import plug-ins installed, import images directly from a digital camera. You can also use batch processing on all open files.

3. Under Conversion Options, you can choose a variety of file formats.

4. If you select the Convert Image Size check box, you can specify a resolution for all the images. You can also specify the width and height of the processed images. However, this is almost useless unless all your images have the same aspect ratio and you choose new values that are proportional. In other words, if your folder contains both vertical and horizontal images and you type in the values 640 × 480, the horizontal images might look OK, but the vertical images will be distorted.

5. In the File Naming section, you can choose different filenames by selecting the Rename Files check box and you can add different file extensions protocols.

6. Choose a destination folder. Click OK and Photoshop Elements does the rest.

Zooming In

A Reference to the Tools and Features of Photoshop Elements

Up to this point, *this book has focused on giving you straightforward solutions to common problems associated with digital images. This appendix is more reference oriented, zooming in on the details of some of Photoshop Elements' tools and features. This is by no means a definitive guide. For that, it's best to refer to Adobe's excellent online help, where you'll find a massive hyperlinked and searchable document with tons of information not found even in the Adobe Photoshop Elements User Guide.*

A Reference to the Tools and Features of Photoshop Elements

All about Layers

Effects

Selection Tools

Viewing & Navigation Tools

Painting Tools

Filters

Liquify Filter

A Reference to the Tools and Features of Photoshop Elements

All about Layers

Following most of the examples in this book requires an understanding of layers and the Layers palette. For example, in one chapter, multiple layers were required to give a soft focus effect (☞ "Making People Glow" in Chapter 3). In another, layers were used to create many special effects, including a way to imitate sunset light (☞ "Changing the Time of Day" in Chapter 4). Layers are one of the most powerful features in Photoshop Elements, and once you use them, you will never understand how you managed without. Some people use layers as a filing cabinet, where they keep various versions of their work as well as commonly used templates. One such template is a screen shot of a web browser window that is used for previewing web graphics and type. Many users make changes on a duplicate layer while always keeping an original version of their work handy on a separate layer for comparison.

Let's start with some basics. When you first open a digital image, Photoshop Elements places the image on a layer that is by default called the **Background** layer. Many Photoshop Elements users may never have a need to go beyond this point. As you saw earlier in the book, you can resize, crop, or apply simple color and tonal corrections to a digital image, without going beyond one layer (☞ Chapter 2). However, even if you never consciously create a new layer, layers will creep into your document. For example, a new layer is added automatically when you cut and paste a selection.

The minute you have more than one layer, the relationship between different layers is controlled by the Mode and Opacity settings in the Layers palette. For example, if the Mode is set to Normal and the Opacity set to 100 percent, pixels in the top layer replace pixels in the layer underneath. This relationship changes when you select another Mode or you lower the Opacity. Several ways of using different Mode settings for effects have been shown throughout the book.

Figure ZI.1 shows a Layers palette with a number of layers. Note the various states of the layers. Some have their visibility turned on, as indicated by the eye icon in the leftmost side. Others are turned off, as indicated by the absence of the eye icon. Only a single layer can be selected at a time, as indicated by the blue shading. One of the most common mistakes people make is not selecting the layer that they want to work on. The result is that a command, such as a blur filter, doesn't affect the desired image at all, but in fact affects the content of another layer instead.

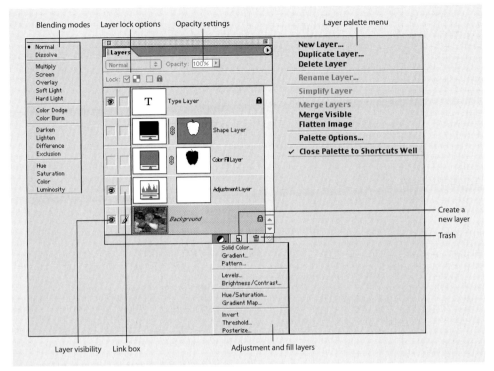

Figure ZI.1: The Layers palette revealed.

Most of the time, when you add a layer, you are increasing the file size of your image. How much size depends on the contents of the layer. Adjustment and fill layers, which are discussed later, don't add any appreciable file size. Also remember that you'll need to save your work in the PSD or advanced TIFF file formats in order to keep layers intact. The JPEG file format, for example, doesn't allow you to save layers, and if you save your file as an animated GIF, layers are retained but not in the same state as they were saved.

Here are some of the other things you need to know to create and otherwise work with and manage multiple layers. Notice that Photoshop Elements offers many ways to accomplish the same tasks:

- Turn the visibility of layers on and off by toggling the eye icon in the leftmost side of the Layers palette.

- Select layers in the Layers palette by clicking the layer thumbnail or name. Blue highlighting and the paintbrush icon ( ) indicate the layer is active. Selecting the Move tool ( ) from the toolbar and clicking on an image in the image window will select the layer containing that image. With the Move tool selected, right-clicking (PC) or Ctrl+clicking (Mac) will bring up a pop-up menu listing the names of the various layers and indicating which layer is active.

- Link layers by clicking in the link box. A link icon ( ) appears, indicating these layers are treated as one.

- Group layers by holding down Alt/Option and positioning the pointer over the line dividing two layers in the Layers palette. Click when the pointer changes to two overlapping circles ( ). When layers are grouped together, the bottom-most layer, called a *base layer*, becomes dominant and defines the subsequent layers. Imagine a base layer consisting of type grouped with a another layer containing texture. The type would define the shape of the texture. You can also choose Layer ➢ Group with Previous (Ctrl/Command+G) after selecting a layer. To ungroup layers, choose Layer ➢ Ungroup or hold down the Alt/Option key, position the pointer over the line dividing the layers, and click.

- Lock the properties of a layer in the Layers palette by selecting a layer and clicking the Lock All check box (🔒). Note the appearance of a solid black lock icon to the right of the layer name, indicating the layer is protected from any changes.

- Lock layer transparency in the Layers palette by selecting a layer and clicking the Lock transparent pixels check box, just to the left of the checked square icon. Note the hollow lock icon in the layer bar, which indicates that changes will be made on this layer only on existing pixels. This is useful for modifying an image while maintaining its exact shape and size.

- Move layers by selecting a layer in the Layers palette and dragging and dropping it into a new position. A background layer cannot be moved from its background position without first changing its name. You can also reorder layers by choosing Layer ➢ Arrange.

- Add layers in the Layers palette by clicking the top right triangle and choosing New Layer from the pop-up menu or by clicking the Create a New Layer icon (🗋) at the bottom, just to the left of the trash icon (also called the Delete Layer button). Some actions, such as cut and paste, automatically create a new layer. You can also choose Layer ➢ New ➢ Layer or press Shift+(Ctrl/Command)+N.

- Duplicate a layer in the Layers palette by clicking the top right triangle and choosing Duplicate Layer from the pop-up window. Or in the Layers palette, select the layer you wish to duplicate and drag it to the Create a New Layer icon (🗋) at the bottom of the Layers palette. Or choose Layer ➢ Duplicate Layer.

- Delete a layer in the Layers palette by dragging a selected layer to the trash icon (🗑) at the bottom-right corner, or select a layer and click the trash icon. You can also choose Layer ➢ Delete Layer.

- Rename a layer in the Layers palette by double-clicking the layer name or clicking the top right triangle and choosing Rename Layer from the pop-up window. Or choose Layer ➢ Rename Layer.

- Flatten linked layers into one layer in the Layers palette by clicking the top right triangle and choosing Merge Linked from the pop-up window. Or choose Layer ➢ Merge Linked (Ctrl/Command+E).

- Flatten visible layers in the Layers palette by clicking the top right triangle and choosing Merge Visible from the pop-up window. Or choose Layer ➢ Merge Visible or press Shift+(Ctrl/Command)+E.

- Flatten all layers in the Layers palette by clicking the top right triangle and choosing Flatten image from the new pop-up window. All layers will become one. All layer information will be lost after the image is flattened. You can also choose Layer ➢ Flatten Image.

Adjustment & Fill Layers

When Adobe first added layers to Photoshop many years ago, I was thrilled. When they came up with adjustment and fill layers, I was amazed. What a concept. As you've seen throughout the book, adjustment layers enable you to affect a single layer or group of layers while making it possible to remove the effect any time later without changing the rest of the image or greatly increasing your file size. Adjustment and fill layers retain the same opacity, blending, and grouping properties. Pretty amazing.

Access adjustment and fill layers by clicking the black-and-white circle at the bottom of the Layers palette (◐) or via Layer ➤ New Adjustment Layer, or Layer ➤ New Fill Layer.

You can choose the following kinds of adjustment layers:

- Levels
- Brightness/Contrast
- Hue/Saturation
- Gradient Map
- Invert
- Threshold
- Posterize

In the book, I've referred mostly to using the Levels, Brightness/Contrast, and Hue/Saturation adjustment layers. However, I encourage you to try the others. *Gradient Map*, for example, is a great way to create special color effects by mapping the equivalent grayscale range of your image to a colorful gradient fill. *Invert* makes your image look like a negative. *Threshold* converts images into high-contrast, black-and-white images that look like lithographs. *Posterize* gives you control over the number of tonal levels for each color channel; choosing lower numbers radically changes the look and feel of your image.

Fill layers include fills based on the following:

- Solid color
- Gradient
- Pattern

I've used fill layers throughout the book, especially when manipulating product shots (&∽ Chapter 5).

To change an adjustment or fill layer, double-click the thumbnail in the Layers palette or choose Layer ➤ Layer Content Options. To delete an adjustment or fill layer, drag it to the trash icon located at the bottom of the Layers palette, or with the adjustment layer selected, choose Layer ➤ Delete Layer.

Layer Styles

Another amazing feature is layer styles. You likely have no idea how long it used to take to create a simple drop shadow before Photoshop introduced layer styles. Now you can do it with a click of the mouse.

Layer styles provide a way to apply a predetermined look and feel to a layer itself. These are removable and nondestructive. You can choose the way layer styles are displayed—list or thumbnails—via the two icons at the bottom of the Layer Styles palette. Thumbnails are the most useful in previewing a style's effect.

To apply a layer style, drag and drop a style from the Layer Styles palette onto an image or onto a layer in the Layers palette. You can also double-click a style to apply it to the active layer. Be careful: clicking more than one style will apply all your choices additively. This is great if this is what you want, but if not, make liberal use of the Undo or History commands.

The Layer Styles palette offers eight categories of styles as starting points. However, with the power to customize style settings, the possibilities are endless. You can manipulate layer styles in the following ways:

- **Customize a layer style** by double-clicking the *f* symbol in the Layers palette, which brings up a dialog box where you can specify the exact thickness, angles, and other characteristics of the style you desire. Or choose Layer ➢ Layer Style ➢ Style Settings from the menu.
- **Repeat a custom layer style** on other layers by simply copying and pasting styles from one layer to another. Choose Layer ➢ Layer Style ➢ Copy Layer Style and then choose Layer ➢ Layer Style ➢ Paste Layer Style.
- **Clear a layer style** by choosing Layer ➢ Layer Style ➢ Clear Layer Style or by clicking the Default Style (None) box found in the Layer Styles palette.

Note: Don't forget, you can find information about any tool in the toolbox by positioning the pointer over it. The name of the tool appears below the pointer. If you open the Hints palette, you'll find more information about a tool. Clicking the More Help button in the Hints palette and selecting Help ➢ Help Contents from the menu bar opens a hyperlinked document in your web browser with even more information and a searchable database. Be sure to check out the recipes found in the palette well. They are step-by-step instructions for many common image-editing tasks. Adobe is constantly adding more recipes, so periodically select Download New Recipes from the Recipes pop-up menu.

Effects

Effects are like automatic cameras. They make you look good even if you don't know what you are doing. Built into most effects are a complex series of filters, layer styles, and/or program functions. If you open the History palette and watch as an effect is applied, you'll see what I mean.

To apply an effect, click Apply from the Effects palette or drag an effect from the Effects palette onto an image. Remember that you don't have to apply an effect to an entire image. If you make a selection, the effect will apply only to that selection.

It may seem that effects are similar to layer styles, but there are some huge differences: effects are not changeable in the same way that layer styles are, and they often require you to simplify a type layer before you apply an effect to it. Reverting an effect isn't as simple as taking one step backward with the Undo command. You'll need to use the History palette to go back several states and select the state that existed before you applied the effect.

Figure ZI.2 shows all the effects in the Effects palette window.

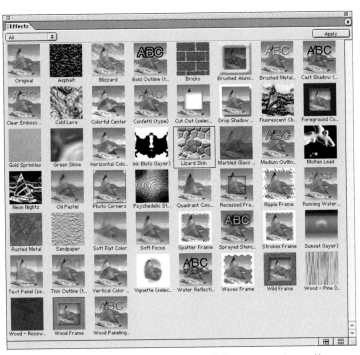

Figure ZI.2: Thumbnails provide a useful preview of an effect.

Selection Tools

Much of the power of Photoshop Elements lies in its capability to manipulate both entire images and discrete portions of images. Selection tools enable you to target which pixels to operate upon. As you've seen throughout the book, knowing which selection tool to use when makes a big difference. Some selection tools, such as the Rectangular Marquee, are straightforward to use; others, such as the Magic Wand and the Magnetic Lasso, are more complex and require a little more skill to use. Each selection tool has multiple options for its use, which are accessed via the options bar found below the shortcuts bar.

Marquee Tools

The Marquee tools include the Rectangular ([:]) and Elliptical (○) selection tools. They share the same spot on the toolbar.

Press M at any time (except when you are in text edit mode) to select a Marquee tool. Click and hold on one Marquee tool to access the other, or right-click (PC) or hold the Shift key while pressing M (Mac) to toggle back and forth between tools.

These tools are most appropriate for making selections in the general area of what you want. Holding down the Shift key forces a Marquee tool into a uniform circle or square shape. You can also use either Marquee tool as a cropping tool. Just make your selection and then choose Image ≻ Crop. If you are using the Elliptical Marquee tool, the crop will go to the outermost points of the ellipse but still be rectangular.

Lasso Tools

Lasso tools include the Lasso, Magnetic Lasso, and Polygonal Lasso. All three tools are at the same spot on the toolbar. Press L at any time to select the Lasso tool. To toggle back and forth between the Lasso, Magnetic Lasso, and Polygonal Lasso tools, right-click (PC) or hold the Shift key while pressing L (Mac).

The Lasso tool (♀) is great for tracing areas with jagged edges. Hold down the mouse button and freehand trace the desired selection shape. When you release the mouse, Photoshop Elements will close the shape if you haven't already done so. To get maximum accuracy, magnify the image to see border details.

The Magnetic Lasso tool (♔) is an enhanced version of the Lasso tool that snaps to pixels of similar colors. Width, edge-contrast, and frequency parameters let you specify the range of pixel similarity to which the lasso is attracted. Double-click to finish making your selection. Again, Photoshop Elements will close the shape if you haven't already done so. I explain the Magnetic Lasso in great detail elsewhere in the book (☞ "Separating a Product from Its Background" and "Adding Motion Blur" in Chapter 5).

The Polygonal Lasso tool (♔) lets you specify the points of a multi-sided shape you wish to select. This is useful for selections with straight edges.

In the process of using either the Magnetic Lasso or Polygonal Lasso selection tools, you can start over by hitting Esc.

Magic Wand

The Magic Wand tool (✎), located in its own spot in the toolbar, magically chooses pixels of the same color within the specified tolerance limits throughout your image. Use this tool for irregularly shaped areas of the same color. I explain the Magic Wand in great detail elsewhere in the book (☞ "Separating a Product from Its Background" in Chapter 5).

Selection Tool Options

Generally, selection toolbar options include the following:

- Adding, subtracting, or merging selection shapes. You can add to (Shift), subtract from (Alt/Option) or cut multiple selections (Ctrl/Command) by holding down these additional keys while making selections. You can also click the respective icons in the options bar.
- Moving, copying, or pasting selections and layers. After you make a selection shape, you can move the outline of the defined area with the Move tool or you can more precisely position it with the arrow keys.
- Softening edges of a selection. You can blur edges of selections by typing a specific number of pixels in the Feather field or by choosing Select ➤ Feather (Alt+Ctrl+D for the PC, or Option+Command+D for the Mac).
- Anti-aliasing a selection. By default, the anti-aliasing option is checked. This controls the smoothness of selected shapes' edges by including transition pixels.

Controlling Selections

There are several ways to control the shape and size of a selection.

- You can specify the exact dimensions or proportions of a Marquee selection in the options bar Style pop-up menu.
- You can reverse any selection and choose nonselected pixels by choosing Select ➤ Inverse or pressing Shift+(Ctrl/Command)+I.

There are several ways you can modify a selection as well:

- **Select ➤ Modify ➤ Border** selects a border of pixels the specified number of pixels above and below the current selection.
- **Select ➤ Modify ➤ Smooth** excludes pixels outside the specified range from the current selection. This is especially useful when you use the Magic Wand and get small selections all over the image. The Smooth option unifies the many selections into one.
- **Select ➤ Modify ➤ Expand** makes the current selection larger by the specified number of pixels.
- **Select ➤ Modify ➤ Contract** makes the current selection smaller by the specified number of pixels.
- **Select ➤ Grow** incorporates pixels into the current selection that are similar and in a contiguous area.
- **Select ➤ Similar** incorporates pixels into the current selection that are similar anywhere within the image.

At any time, you can cancel a selection by pressing Ctrl/Command+D. The trusty Undo command (Ctrl/Command+Z, or whatever keystroke equivalent you set in your preferences) will get it back for you. You can also click the New Selection icon (▪) in the floating toolbar. Or choose Select ➤ Deselect (Ctrl/Command+D), Select ➤ Reselect (Shift+Ctrl/Command+D), or Undo (Ctrl/Command+Z).

Note: You can turn a selection into a colored outline by using the Stroke command. Make a selection with any of the selection tools and select Edit ➤ Stroke. In the Stroke dialog box, specify a line width and color as well as the location of where the pixels fall in relationship to the selection outline: inside, center, or outside. You can also select a blending mode and opacity.

Viewing & Navigation Tools

For precise work, it is essential to be able to zoom in and out of an image, and to navigate around the window if the image is large. Several tools and commands are available to help you.

Zoom Tool

Click with the plus Zoom tool (🔍) to increase image detail. The negative Zoom tool (🔍) achieves the opposite effect. Press Z to get the Zoom tool. The Alt key toggles the Zoom tool between zooming in and out. Double-clicking the Zoom tool icon (🔍) in the toolbox returns the image to 100 percent.

The percent magnification and dimensions appear in the lower-left corner of the work area. You can type a desired percent magnification in this box. You can also choose View ➤ Zoom In, or View ➤ Zoom Out.

With the Zoom tool selected, you can fill the screen with a particular area of the image by clicking and dragging the mouse until the bounding box surrounds the area of interest. Let go of the mouse, and zoom!

Note: In the Zoom tool options bar, if Resize Windows to Fit is selected, the Photoshop Elements window is resized as necessary to display the image. When the option is deselected, the window remains the same size regardless of any magnification.

View Commands

Several view commands are found in the main menu bar. These include the following:

- **View ➤ New View** creates multiple views of the same image. Any changes made will apply to all views. As you close individual views, you will be asked to confirm that any changes should be committed to the final image.
- **View ➤ Fit on Screen** fills the entire window with the entire image.
- **View ➤ Actual Pixels** displays an image at 100 percent while taking into account the height and width of the image as well as the resolution of the monitor. Two images can have the same height and width and different resolutions and yet appear the same size on the monitor.
- **View ➤ Print Size** displays an image at 100 percent while taking into account the resolution of the image as well as the resolution of the monitor. Two images can have the same height and width, and if the resolution is different they will appear as different sizes on the monitor.

Navigator Palette

The Navigator palette is located in the palette well. The red box in this palette helps orient your current position in the image. This is useful when an image gets too large to display onscreen. The slider at the bottom of this palette offers yet another option to increase or decrease the percent magnification of the image. The Navigator palette is shown in Figure ZI.3.

Figure ZI.3: The Navigator palette.

Hand Tool

The Hand tool (🖐), located in the toolbar, is used to move the image around in the work area when the image is magnified outside the boundaries of the work area. The Navigator palette provides a thumbnail view to orient your position relative to the entire image. The hand in the Navigator palette also enables you to move to targeted areas within the image. Areas not visible in the work area remain intact but are simply off screen. You can access the Hand tool at any time by pressing the spacebar or the H key.

Painting Tools

Painting tools include the Paintbrush (B), Pencil (N), Airbrush (J), Red Eye Brush (Y), and the Impressionistic Brush (A) tools. Although in the book I use these tools in only a limited way, they can be a lot of fun. They mimic their counterparts in the analog world and therefore should feel very familiar. This section outlines some of the more important things to keep in mind when using the painting tools. The Blur, Sharpen, Sponge, Smudge, Dodge, Burn, Clone Stamp, Pattern Stamp, and the eraser tools all use a brush, so you can apply much of what I write to these tools as well.

Custom Brushes

You can customize the shape, size, and nature of the area affected by these tools by clicking the brush-shaped icon in the options bar, found next to the word *Brush*. The arrow to the right of this icon pops up a window of numerous preset brush shape choices. Click the triangle in the top right of this dialog box and you'll get a list of brushes organized by shape categories. You can also save and retrieve your own custom brush sets for endless possibilities. See Figure ZI.4.

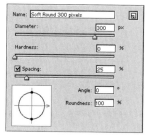

Figure ZI.4: Create custom-sized and -shaped brushes in this options bar palette.

Blending Modes

Blending modes apply to the way pixels relate to each other. By default, in the Normal mode, new pixels are superimposed on the old. If you select Soft Light from the Mode pop-up menu, however, a new brush stroke will blend "softly" with the old pixels. Furthermore, you can control how much blending occurs through the Opacity settings also found in the options bar. Photoshop Elements provides 16 blending options to help you achieve the effect you want. Each mode uses a different method to relate the pixels on one level to the pixels on another. It's difficult to predetermine exactly what effect each blending option will produce, so you'll just have to experiment.

Pressure

When using a pressure-sensitive tablet, Photoshop Elements translates the feel of your touch to the painting and editing tools. For example, if you are using a Wacom tablet or similar device, click the Brush Dynamics icon (✐) in the options bar and choose Stylus from the Size pop-up menu. By selecting a higher numerical value, you will create a broader brush stroke when more pressure is applied to the stylus. You can also control the Opacity and Color settings in the Brush Dynamics dialog box.

Wet Edges

As in the real world, Photoshop Elements simulates the build-up of paint near the edges of your virtual brush. This creates a watercolor-like effect.

Brush Dynamics

This option lets you specify how quickly brush size, opacity, and color diminish over the length of each brushstroke.

Opacity

Like layers, the opacity of your work can be adjusted from 0 to 100 percent, determining how strongly the new pixels are imposed over the old.

Use All Layers

When using the editing tools, you can specify whether Photoshop Elements should make changes based exclusively on the active layer or use all layers in your image.

> **Note:** If your brush stroke is on a transparent layer, you can modify the brush stroke by choosing Edit ➤ Stroke. Use this command to add an outline around the brush stroke in the color of your choice. You can also determine where the pixels fall in relationship to the brush stroke and select a blending mode and opacity.

Impressionist Brush

I don't use the Impressionist Brush in this book. It's one of the complex tools, and you can spend countless hours just trying to figure out what it does and then realize that you've only scratched the surface. Through different texture and color settings, you can simulate various painting styles—think Van Gogh and Cezanne. Play with different Styles, Fidelity, Area, and Spacing settings. Then when you've figured those out, change the Mode and Opacity settings and see what else you can come up with. The possibilities are limitless. Enjoy!

Filters

Photoshop Elements includes a large number of filters. I use many of them throughout the book. Filters can be applied through the Filter menu selection or via the Filters palette. Like effects, filters can be applied to a selection. Figure ZI.5 shows most of the filters at a glance.

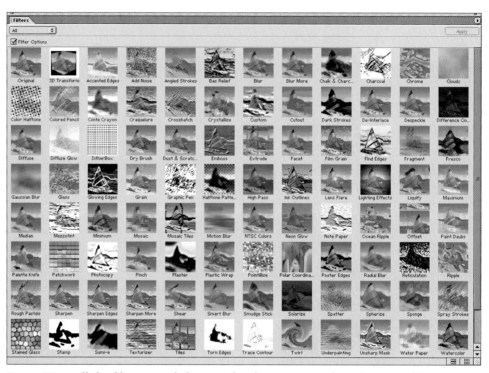

Figure ZI.5: All the filters revealed except for the Wave, Wind, and ZigZag filters.

Liquify Filter

It seems inappropriate to refer to the Liquify filter as a mere filter in the same way that the Unsharp Mask is a filter. The Liquify filter is more of an experience. When you select the Liquify filter, you enter a world where the image becomes totally fluid, as if it were molten pixels that you can move and shove around much like fingerpaint. In many ways, it's like an application within an application.

In the book, I use the Liquify filter for several purposes—for example, straightening a crooked nose, fixing a broken tooth, and altering type. But I encourage you to just play around with all the Liquify filter's tools and options. You'll find yourself spending hours and hours getting to know the filter and exploring its creative capabilities.

A couple of points to keep in mind when using the filter:

- There are no Liquify filter magnification tools, so make a selection of the area you want to liquify before you open the filter.
- To revert an image to its original form, click Revert in the Liquify work area.

- To reset the Liquify filter tools to their previous settings *and* to revert an image, hold Alt/Option and when Cancel changes to Reset, click.
- Use the Reconstruct tool () to restore specific areas of your image. Just brush over the areas you want to reconstruct.

Figure ZI.6 shows the Liquify filter work area and tools. Figure Z1.7 is an enlargement of the toolbar.

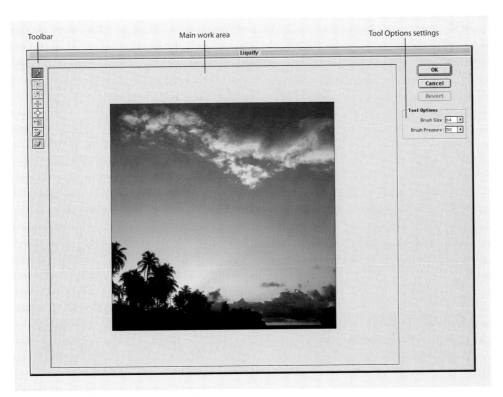

Figure ZI.6: The Liquify filter tools.

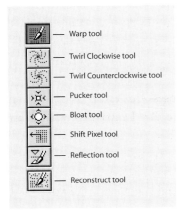

Figure ZI.7: The Liquify filter toolbar.

About the Team

The Author

Mikkel Aaland is a photographer, writer, web producer, and the author of seven books including *Photoshop for the Web* (O'Reilly, 2000), *Digital Photography* (Random House, 1992), and *Still Images in Multimedia* (Hayden, 1996). Aaland's documentary photographs have been exhibited in major institutions around the world, including the Bibliothèque Nationale de France in Paris and the former Lenin Museum in Prague. He has contributed both text and/or photography to *Wired*, *Outside*, *Digital Creativity*, *American Photo*, *The Washington Post*, and *Newsweek*, as well as several European publications. Aaland is also the co-founder of Tor Productions, a multimedia and web production company founded in 1989 and based in San Francisco.

The author has led public workshops on the effective use of digital images and graphics in new media at institutions and conferences such as the University of California, Berkeley; Stanford University; Drexel University; Photo Expo in New York City; and CNET's builder.com. He has held private consultations with new media companies such as Corbis, Washington Post.com, and Newsweek Interactive. He can be reached at **mikkel@cyberbohemia.com**.

Design

TonBo designs is a full-service design studio in Sausalito, California established in 1989 by Lori Barra. TonBo provides complete art direction, design, and production services for books, magazines, marketing collateral, web design, promotional materials, packaging and corporate identity. TonBo manages and executes all aspects of communications projects, from concept through delivery of the final product. Their client list includes Adobe Systems, Apple Computer, Chronicle Books, Revo Sunglasses, Isabel Allende, Newsweek, HarperCollins, Macworld, Global Village, Infoseek, and Stanford Business School. **www.tonbo.com**

Production

Command Z is a design production studio established in 1988 by Jan Martí. Based in Palo Alto, California, Command Z provides graphic production and desktop publishing services to a wide range of clients in Silicon Valley and the San Francisco Bay Area. Jan can be reached at **comz@comz.com**.

Contributors

Michael Angelo is a man of many talents. He has worked as a video producer and editor, and special-effects wizard. He splits his time between Hollywood and North Beach. Be sure to check out his web site, www.michaelangelo.com.

Marcia Briggs is a freelance product designer who uses Photoshop to create color stories for her design presentations. Her clients include L.L. Bean and Discovery Toys, and she is currently working on a line of garden accessories. Marcia can be reached at mbriggs590@aol.com.

Maggie Hallahan is an award-winning editorial and advertising photographer based in San Francisco. Her clients include CBS, Hewlett-Packard, Eastman Kodak Company, Martha Stewart, and the American Red Cross. She founded Network Images, a stock photo agency, in 1985. Her work can be viewed at www.networkimages.com.

Scott Highton is one of the most experienced virtual reality (VR) photographers in the world, and is known for his high-quality, innovative QuickTime VR and iPIX work. Currently he is writing the definitive book on virtual reality photography. His website is www.highton.com.

Laura Laverdiere is an R & D scientist with Syngenta Crop Protection who uses a digital camera extensively for her work. Her background is in horticulture and plant pathology.

Monica Lee is an award-winning San Francisco–based freelance photographer specializing in corporate and editorial photography since 1982. Her e-mail address is mleephoto@earthlink.net.

Maurice Martell is a San Francisco–based photographer specializing in industrial and corporate photography.

David Mlodzik is an architect versed in both design and high-end digital imaging. He provides design visualization and graphics services to fellow architects and the construction community. He can be reached at dmlodzik@pacbell.net.

Tom Mogensen is an artist in San Francisco whose clients include Oracle, Macy's, and the San Francisco Giants. He has been using a computer as a design tool and medium in art for seven years. His work can be viewed at www.fotom.com.

Bretton Newsom is a graphic designer and Photoshop expert who works for PJA advertising agency in San Francisco. He can be reached at bnewsom@agencypja.com.

Sean Parker is a partner in the Washington, D.C. design and production studio, ParkerGrove. He is always buried under code but he has time to talk and can be reached at spike@parkergrove.com.

Valerie Robbins is a designer based in Annapolis, Maryland. She designed the author's sites, www.cyberbohemia.com and www.shooting-digital.com. She is also the former senior designer at nationalgeographic.com and is now the principal of her own studio, Buttercup Studios. She can be reached at valerie@buttercupstudios.com.

Sally Rogers is a San Francisco real estate and leasing broker who uses a digital camera extensively to showcase her properties.

William Rutledge is a professional photographer and manager of QVC Inc.'s in-house photo studio. He can be reached at william_c_rutledge@qvc.com.

Mark Ulriksen works as both an artist and an illustrator in San Francisco. His work appears in *The Atlantic Monthly, Newsweek, Rolling Stone,* and *The Washington Post.* He is a regular contributor to *The New Yorker* magazine, where he has contributed 16 covers. Mark's paintings have been exhibited all over the world. View his work at www.markulriksen.com.

Michelle Vignes has documented diverse cultures and socio-historical events in California for the past 30 years. She has been exhibited and published internationally. Her work can be viewed at www.yourwall.com.

Index

C

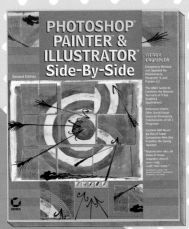
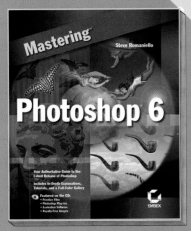
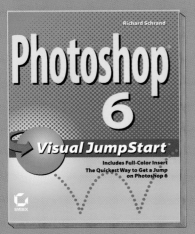
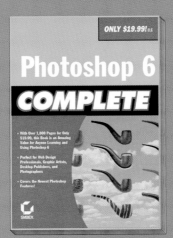
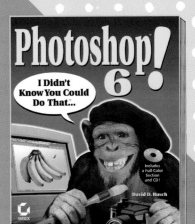

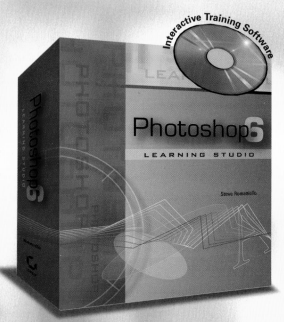
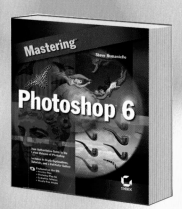

Software License Agreement: Terms and Conditions

The media and/or any online materials accompanying this book that are available now or in the future contain programs and/or text files (the "Software") to be used in connection with the book. SYBEX hereby grants to you a license to use the Software, subject to the terms that follow. Your purchase, acceptance, or use of the Software will constitute your acceptance of such terms.

The Software compilation is the property of SYBEX unless otherwise indicated and is protected by copyright to SYBEX or other copyright owner(s) as indicated in the media files (the "Owner(s)"). You are hereby granted a single-user license to use the Software for your personal, noncommercial use only. You may not reproduce, sell, distribute, publish, circulate, or commercially exploit the Software, or any portion thereof, without the written consent of SYBEX and the specific copyright owner(s) of any component software included on this media.

In the event that the Software or components include specific license requirements or end-user agreements, statements of condition, disclaimers, limitations or warranties ("End-User License"), those End-User Licenses supersede the terms and conditions herein as to that particular Software component. Your purchase, acceptance, or use of the Software will constitute your acceptance of such End-User Licenses.

By purchase, use or acceptance of the Software you further agree to comply with all export laws and regulations of the United States as such laws and regulations may exist from time to time.

Software Support

Components of the supplemental Software and any offers associated with them may be supported by the specific Owner(s) of that material, but they are not supported by SYBEX. Information regarding any available support may be obtained from the Owner(s) using the information provided in the appropriate read.me files or listed elsewhere on the media.

Should the manufacturer(s) or other Owner(s) cease to offer support or decline to honor any offer, SYBEX bears no responsibility. This notice concerning support for the Software is provided for your information only. SYBEX is not the agent or principal of the Owner(s), and SYBEX is in no way responsible for providing any support for the Software, nor is it liable or responsible for any support provided, or not provided, by the Owner(s).

Warranty

SYBEX warrants the enclosed media to be free of physical defects for a period of ninety (90) days after purchase. The Software is not available from SYBEX in any other form or media than that enclosed herein or posted to www.sybex.com. If you discover a defect in the media during this warranty period, you may obtain a replacement of identical format at no charge by sending the defective media, postage prepaid, with proof of purchase to:

SYBEX Inc.
Product Support Department
1151 Marina Village Parkway
Alameda, CA 94501
Website: http://www.sybex.com

After the 90-day period, you can obtain replacement media of identical format by sending us the defective disk, proof of purchase, and a check or money order for $10, payable to SYBEX.

Disclaimer

SYBEX makes no warranty or representation, either expressed or implied, with respect to the Software or its contents, quality, performance, merchantability, or fitness for a particular purpose. In no event will SYBEX, its distributors, or dealers be liable to you or any other party for direct, indirect, special, incidental, consequential, or other damages arising out of the use of or inability to use the Software or its contents even if advised of the possibility of such damage. In the event that the Software includes an online update feature, SYBEX further disclaims any obligation to provide this feature for any specific duration other than the initial posting.

The exclusion of implied warranties is not permitted by some states. Therefore, the above exclusion may not apply to you. This warranty provides you with specific legal rights; there may be other rights that you may have that vary from state to state. The pricing of the book with the Software by SYBEX reflects the allocation of risk and limitations on liability contained in this agreement of Terms and Conditions.

Shareware Distribution

This Software may contain various programs that are distributed as shareware. Copyright laws apply to both shareware and ordinary commercial software, and the copyright Owner(s) retains all rights. If you try a shareware program and continue using it, you are expected to register it. Individual programs differ on details of trial periods, registration, and payment. Please observe the requirements stated in appropriate files.

Copy Protection

The Software in whole or in part may or may not be copy-protected or encrypted. However, in all cases, reselling or redistributing these files without authorization is expressly forbidden except as specifically provided for by the Owner(s) therein.

What's on the CD-ROM

Adobe Photoshop Elements

Photoshop Elements is a stand-alone product designed specifically for photographers, hobbyists, and business users who want an easy-to-use yet powerful digital imaging solution. With Photoshop Elements you can

- import photos from digital cameras and scanners
- learn to use sophisticated Photoshop editing tools
- prepare images for e-mail, print, or posting on the Web and much more!

The tryout software on the CD-ROM will be fully functional for 30 calendar days after installation. At any time during or after the tryout period, you can purchase Photoshop Elements by simply clicking the Buy button and following the on-screen instructions. Click the Information button for installation instructions and special offers.

Sample Images

On the CD you'll also find sample images, which you can use to follow along with the solutions given in the book. When you see the CD icon in the caption for a figure, go to that chapter's folder on the CD to find the image. All images are in Photoshop format (.psd), with the exception of the .gif animation file from Chapter 10.

The images on the CD-ROM are for personal use only. Image copyright is retained by the original copyright holder. Copying or redistribution in any manner for personal or corporate gain is not permitted. Any public or commercial use of these images without prior written permission is a violation of federal copyright law.